# BEING SCOTTISH

# BEING SCOTTISH

Personal Reflections on Scottish Identity Today

*Edited by Tom Devine and Paddy Logue*

POLYGON
AT EDINBURGH

© Individual contributors and Polygon at Edinburgh, 2002

Polygon at Edinburgh
An imprint of Edinburgh University Press Ltd
22 George Square, Edinburgh

Typeset in Minion by
Koinonia, Manchester, and
printed and bound in Great Britain by
Biddles Ltd, Guildford, Surrey

A CIP Record for this book is available from the British Library

ISBN 1 902930 36 3 (paperback)

# Contents

Introduction by Tom Devine and Paddy Logue ..................................................... ix

Leila Aboulela ............................................................................................. 1

Ginnie Atkinson .......................................................................................... 4

Alan L. Bain ............................................................................................... 7

Euan Baird ............................................................................................... 10

Anne Bardsley .......................................................................................... 13

Mary Beith .............................................................................................. 15

Margaret Bennett ..................................................................................... 18

Alan Bissett ............................................................................................. 21

Ronald Black ............................................................................................ 23

Sheena Blackhall ...................................................................................... 26

Vivian Bone ............................................................................................. 29

Alison Bowden ......................................................................................... 32

Sheila Brock ............................................................................................ 33

Craig Brown ............................................................................................ 36

Steve Bruce ............................................................................................. 40

Duke of Buccleuch .................................................................................... 43

Angus Calder ........................................................................................... 46

Owen Campbell ........................................................................................ 50

Eddie Clark ............................................................................................. 53

Robert Crawford ............................................................... 55

Tam Dalyell .................................................................... 57

Fauzia Davidson ............................................................... 59

Isla Dewar ..................................................................... 62

Owen Dudley Edwards ........................................................ 65

Kevin Dunion .................................................................. 68

Donald Findlay ................................................................ 71

John H. Fitzsimmons .......................................................... 74

Douglas Fraser ................................................................ 77

Simon Frith ................................................................... 80

Sandy Grant Gordon .......................................................... 83

David Greig ................................................................... 85

Robin Harper .................................................................. 87

Christopher Harvie ............................................................ 90

Gerry Hassan .................................................................. 94

Joy Hendry .................................................................... 97

Richard Holloway ............................................................. 100

Hamish Horsburgh ............................................................ 103

Tom Hunter ................................................................... 106

Craig Hutchison ............................................................... 108

Billy Kay ...................................................................... 111

Charles Kennedy .............................................................. 114

Mark Kennedy ................................................................. 117

John Laird .................................................................... 121

Phyllida Law .................................................................. 124

Helen Liddell ................................................................. 127

Baroness Linklater ............................................................ 130

Jacqui Low .................................................................... 133

Bashir Maan ........................................................ 136

E. Mairi MacArthur ........................................... 139

Bridget McConnell ............................................. 142

Jack McConnell .................................................. 146

John McCormick ................................................ 149

Neil MacCormick ............................................... 152

Mukami McCrum ............................................... 155

Finlay Macdonald .............................................. 159

Margo MacDonald ............................................. 162

John McGurk ...................................................... 165

Ian Mackenzie ................................................... 168

Sheila McLean ................................................... 171

David McLetchie ................................................ 174

Duncan Macmillan ............................................ 177

Douglas McNaughton ........................................ 180

Kevin MacNeil ................................................... 183

Susie Maguire .................................................... 187

Martin Mansergh .............................................. 191

Alex Massie ....................................................... 194

Donald E. Meek ................................................ 197

Steven Osborne .................................................. 200

Anna Paterson ................................................... 202

Don Paterson ..................................................... 205

Lindsay Paterson ............................................... 208

Norman Pender .................................................. 211

Hugh Pennington .............................................. 214

Robina Qureshi ................................................. 217

Selma Rahman ................................................... 220

Harry Reid ........................................................................ 222

Susan Rice ...................................................................... 225

Kat Roberts ..................................................................... 228

Kenneth Roy ................................................................... 230

Trevor Royle ................................................................... 233

Michael Russell ............................................................... 236

Suhayl Saadi ................................................................... 239

Alex Salmond ................................................................. 242

T. C. Smout.................................................................... 245

Bill Speirs ...................................................................... 248

David Steel .................................................................... 251

Stewart Sutherland .......................................................... 254

John Swinney .................................................................. 257

Alan Taylor .................................................................... 259

Brian Taylor................................................................... 261

Gregor Townsend ............................................................. 264

Kirsty Walker .................................................................. 268

Jim Wallace .................................................................... 271

Charles Warren ............................................................... 274

Mike Watson .................................................................. 277

Irvine Welsh ................................................................... 282

Kevin Williamson ............................................................ 284

Ruth Wishart.................................................................. 287

Kenyon Wright ............................................................... 290

Mel Young ..................................................................... 293

Postscript: *Being Irish* and *Being Scottish* by Tom Devine ................................. 296

# *Introduction*

A shared interest in identity nurtured this collection into book form.

For one of the co-editors it was part of an on-going search for the core constituents of Scottish identity and their standing in the modern world. His *The Scottish Nation, 1700–2000* (Allen Lane, The Penguin Press, 1999) has helped to prepare the ground for this examination. Two key themes emerged in that volume that are of relevance to this book. The first was the robust survival after the Union of the strong sense of Scottish identity within the overall context of Britishness despite the close economic, political and cultural partnership with England and the fears of some Scottish intellectuals that Scotland would simply become another region within the United Kingdom as assimilation intensified. After 1707 Scotland was a stateless nation but a nation nonetheless with an enduring emotional appeal.

Second, Scottishness itself meant different things at different periods. Identity was subject to change and reinvention and the process undoubtedly continues apace in the early years of a new millennium. *Being Scottish* therefore offers an opportunity to penetrate behind the statistical surveys and explore the rich complexity of changing identity from a varied range of opinion. The question, 'Who are we?' continues to perplex many Scots today. The essays in this book help to expand the debate and provide at least some of the answers.

For the other co-editor it was a continuation of a reflection on the nature of identity, on the ways that identity can be commonly shared, made individually manifest, put on like a costume, enforced, transformed and/or reconstructed, on the way that identity not only changes for a whole people in different times and circumstances but also how the understanding and expression of identity changes in the lives of individuals.

His involvement in the European Union Irish Peace Programme led him to the conclusion that peace would not have become a possibility in Ireland if a sea-change in the ways identity is understood, re-evaluated, realigned, made inclusive, given a new sense of direction had not taken place. Catholic Ireland and Protestant Ulster are dead and gone and the pall-bearers were Ireland's involvement in the European Union, the Celtic Tiger economy, the Good Friday Agreement and the crisis in religion. His sister collection *Being Irish* (Oaktree Press, Dublin, 2000) benchmarked these dramatic changes.

## Context

Contemporary events and developments in the British Isles and the world provide the general political and social context of this collection:

- The state of the Union.
- Devolution (a symptom of confident strength or of decline and fall?) in Wales and Northern Ireland as well as in Scotland, and tensions in all three countries between unionists/devolutionists and nationalists.
- The rise of English nationalism: the seeking of a devolved national assembly in London and regional assemblies, and the implications of all this for Scotland.
- The debate about the distribution of public spending in different parts of the UK and the future of the Barnett formula.
- Britain's membership of the European Union and the debate about future British political and economic sovereignty and its relevance to Scotland.
- The steamroller advance of USA-led global capitalism with important economic decisions, which have implications for Scotland, often being taken elsewhere.
- The lingering after-effects of the loss of Empire with its resultant crisis of identity for Scotland, a nation which played a key role in the imperial project.
- The new global world order based on the USA-declared war against terrorism in the aftermath of the events of 11 September 2001.

The situation in Scotland brings this context into sharper focus: how is devolution perceived in Scotland? Is it working? Have the Scots embraced their new parliament, and has this created a stronger sense of identity? Is devolution seen as an end in itself or an irreversible step on the road to independence? Has it created a stronger sense of nationalism? Do contemporary Scots define themselves more or less against the English or the British? Or do they place their identity within a European context? Does possible future 'independence' for Scotland have any real meaning given the extent of Europeanisation and globalisation? Has devolution been relevant at all to the sense of what it is to be Scottish?

## Scottishness

These key questions make this an appropriate time to publish a series of personal reflections on what it means to be Scottish. A historic shift seems to be underway in the nature of national identity. For most of the last three centuries, the majority of Scots were comfortable with a dual identity in which the sense of Scottish distinctiveness could complement and indeed reinforce the broader emotional loyalty to Britishness. This duality was at its most potent in the era of Empire, global economic dominance and during the two world wars of the twentieth century.

The husk of that identity has not yet been broken in more recent times, despite the relative decline of such traditional symbols and supports of Britishness as the monarchy and the Protestant religion. The latest information, published in 2002 in the Scottish Social Attitudes Survey, suggests that three out of five Scots still feel some sense of being British. On the other hand, Scottishness seems to have soared to unprecedented levels. According to the Survey, over three-quarters of those asked classified themselves as more Scottish than British. Seven out of ten respondents were proud of the Saltire, much more so than of the Union flag. In addition, the proportion who actually denied a British identity almost doubled over the last decade from one in five to nearly two in five. Remarkably, the survey also reveals that people rank the importance of being Scottish second only to being a mother and father and ahead of issues of employment and class.

The evidence also suggests that these changes in attitude were already underway before the devolution referenda and the establishment of the first Scottish Parliament since 1707. Indeed, this historical constitutional change was probably more the effect than cause of the new sense of Scottishness. Self-evidently, however, this heightened identity must affect Scottish politics in other ways. Some have blamed the electoral catastrophe that overwhelmed the Conservatives in 1997 *inter alia* on the perception that their policies and ethos were seen to be stridently 'anti-Scottish'. On the other hand, thus far at least, being more Scottish has not yet unleashed a great popular demand for independence. Cultural nationalism still seems able to co-exist with political unionism. How long this will continue remains one of the most intriguing questions in post-devolution Scotland.

## Method

The method we chose for this examination was to invite a balanced cross-section of Scots to contribute a short, personal article of around 800 words on what being Scottish means to them at this time in their own lives and in the history of the Scottish people. The invitations were sent to the famous and not-so-famous, to people at the centre of things and to people at the margins, to men and women, to nationalists, unionists and devolutionists, to those who live in Scotland and those who live abroad. We also sought several 'views from the side', from people who are not Scottish but who have an obvious interest or connection. We asked them to identify and give expression to that special something that is (more or less) instantly recognisable as Scottish, to detect and describe changes in it, and to record for the present and future generations the rich tapestry that is Scottish identity today, highlighting the new and the traditional, the universal and the particular, the conventional and the unconventional, the good and the not-so-good.

We did not aim to produce a self-congratulatory volume of smug opinion as we believe there is no contradiction between national pride and honest self-criticism. The editorial aim was to create a debate about Scottish identity, to ack-nowledge difference and to encourage tolerance. The method of commissioning a set of short articles would make the book accessible to many Scots who would not take the time to read a 'big' book about identity. We are not claiming, and the contributors certainly don't claim, that this collection of essayists constitutes a group truly and scientifically representative of contemporary Scottish identity. Nor did it turn out as balanced a group as we, on the basis of the wide cast of our net, had hoped it to be. Inevitably, not all requests to contribute were answered in the affirmative. What we do claim is that this group is one cross-section of

Scottish people who have taken the time to reflect on their identity and have had the courage to publish their reflections in order to stimulate debate among a wide readership on what it means to be Scottish today. It is one snapshot of Scottish identity. Other editors would no doubt have produced a different one.

The contributors succeed in going beyond the social and political context outlined above and exploring above all what it means personally to be Scottish. Some of the contributors, as well as the reader, will be surprised at the insights contained in this book. Some delve into their personal histories or their sense of place to give meaning to their identities. Others deal in political and cultural realities, while others rely on storytelling, humour and lyricism to approach a tentative sense of identity upwind. Honesty, courage and humour are not lacking in these stories.

We don't intend to summarise or highlight all the points made by the contributors. They speak for themselves. However, some conclusions are inescapable:

- The palpable reality of Scottish identity, its persistence and integrity, rises from these pages.
- It is remarkable how many contributors refer to the importance of place, landscape and belonging.
- Remarkable also is the number who refer to the English, or as it is sometimes put, 'the southern neighbours', in delineating the sense of identity. The impression is given of an older stepbrother who is at best patronising, most of the time indifferent, and at worst a bully.
- But it's not all England's fault. Some contributors detail their own disappointment at being Scottish on a batch of issues which include racism, indifference to the poor, self-importance and inadequate economic performance. Taken as a whole, the collection is far from being self-congratulatory.
- There are signs of an alternative form of identity, more in keeping with the homogeneity of global lifestyles, emerging around the idea of choice, of a deliberate commitment to being Scottish in the best possible way.
- The overall impression is of a serious, thoughtful group of people whose critical and sceptical analysis of the past and present is balanced for some

by an excitement about the future, an expectancy that a new explosion of Scottish achievement, excellence and performance is just around the corner.

In a short postscript, one of the editors looks again at these and other issues, by briefly comparing the Scottish perspectives on identity that are revealed in this book with those of the Irish, the subject of a previous publication. This, however, should be read last, after the reader has had the chance to reflect personally on the remarkable variety of views which came through in the individual essays, and which are all part and parcel of being Scottish today.

Tom Devine
Paddy Logue
*August 2002*

# Leila Aboulela

*Leila Aboulela grew up in Sudan and moved to Scotland in her mid-twenties. Her first novel* The Translator *(Polygon, 1999) was long-listed for the Orange Prize, and serialised on BBC Radio 4. In 2000, she won the inaugural Caine Prize for African Writing for her story 'The Museum', included in the recent collection* Coloured Lights *(Polygon, 2001).*

## Barbie in the Mosque

I grew up in Khartoum, where there were no Barbie dolls. Now in my house in Aberdeen there is Action Man and Biker Mice for my sons, no doll with long hair for me to comb. So when I see Barbie in the mosque I pick her up and hold her on my lap, rest my back on the wall, and smooth her hair. It's the month of Ramadan, it's a Saturday. Everyone in the mosque has finished the sunset prayer and we are waiting for the night ones. The doll belongs to Aisha's daughter, who is playing with my son and the other children. They run around in the free space of the prayer hall, no furniture to bump into, nothing in the way except us women sitting on the floor.

Aisha puts the tea tray near me. The cups tinkle when the tray hits the carpet. Then she is off to yell at a child or change another or mop up the kitchen floor. She is always marching around doing things or making sure that things get done. The men in this mosque are afraid of her. 'Brother ...', she would start her complaint and in alarm they would stare down at the ground, subdued under her voice. I look at Barbie's face, her cheekbones, the way her hair sticks up from her scalp and then falls. Her body is too hard; I remember my dolls being soft, I remember pushing a stomach, yanking out an arm and tucking it back in.

I hear the children and the tinkling blur of Turkish; one woman is breast-feeding a huge baby, the other has a mole on her cheek. They are louder than the

Bengali woman and her sister. I can understand neither Turkish nor Bengali, and this soothes me. It is as if I am a child, too young to understand what my mother is saying to her friends. I want to braid Barbie's hair, I split it into three parts.

'You haven't given anyone tea,' Aisha glares down at me, hands on her hips. Her denim dress reaches her ankles. She is wearing a scarf with blue and red flowers. It covers her hair which is blonde and straight, down to her waist, like Barbie's.

I put Barbie away and start to lay the tea cups in a straight line. Aisha sits on her heels and pours the delayed tea. 'Laid-back Leila,' she sighs.

'Serene,' I say, 'not laid-back, serene.'

She rolls her blue eyes up to the ceiling. She is not fooled; I can't hide my faults in this place. The light is too bright and we are pared down, without our shoes, without chairs to lift us off the ground.

Outside is a city that knows nothing about us. Outside is a Europe uneasy with our presence. Outside they speak in a different way. Enter a newsagent, pick up a paper, pick up *The Times* and read: *It is ironic that most British converts to Islam are women, given the widespread view in the West that Islam treats women poorly.*

I try and imagine Aisha before she became a Muslim. Long hair swaying under the disco lights of Glasgow. She was a Catholic then. Things she said to me: she was closer to her stepmother than to her real mother; she had a boyfriend, a mechanic, who once came in angry from work and wiped his hands on her pink mini-skirt – black grease marks that made her cry. Her name, the one she had before she converted and changed it to Aisha.

Yesterday, Aisha and I took our children and their friends to the park. Flowers on her daughter's dress, a Barbie umbrella. I sat on a bench and watched Aisha and the children play ball. Aisha running, black headscarf, long coat, and me mesmerised by the children: Sudanese, Lebanese and half-Bengali, speaking in the Scottish accent of Froghall and Tillydrone. 'It's his turn now,' Aisha shouted, her smile that needed no lipstick. She has never been outside Britain, not once, yet she is closer to the world than those who go abroad On Holiday every year.

We've passed the tea, I've finished braiding Barbie's hair and now Aisha sits next to me. I talk about her. 'You must have been even lovelier when you were young,' I say.

She frowns. 'I was banned from a baby competition, I kept winning every time.'

I laugh at her solemn voice. I laugh because she makes beauty sound like a burden.

'But when you were a teenager,' I say, 'when you were older, it must have been nice. You must have got loads of attention.'

'No,' she says, guarding some pain, guarding stories she will not tell me. 'No, it wasn't nice.'

# Ginnie Atkinson

*Ginnie Atkinson is Managing Director of the Edinburgh International Film Festival, prior to which she ran a commercials production company. A graduate of Edinburgh College of Art, she worked in education in London before returning to Scotland to run a theatre in education project and then jumped the tracks into the broadcast and film community in the 1980s. She is also currently co-producer on a film version of the Scottish classic* Sunset Song.

## On Being Scottish

Working, as I do, in the film industry, the questions of nationality and cultural identity are brought into sharp focus every so often when we grapple with the wider issues such as 'defining characteristics' or the universality of that language, which is a passion shared.

Being Scottish for me means being born and bred – knowing no other, only slipping for a time into the metropolis, where it was handy to wear as a hat. It allows a certain individuality to surface faster than those whose identity is not easily defined by virtue of their hailing from Surrey; I will milk to death the social potential that being Scottish offers, with its reputation of hospitality, irascibility, meanness, dry wit or strength of feeling.

## On Heritage

As I've never been one for celebrating routs, the litany of battles for just causes and freedom from repression have never defined, for me, being Scottish. For me, being Scottish is an unenviable mixture of conditioning and characteristics set in motion eras ago and influenced by the variables of the weather, the diet, Celtic chromosomes and who made it to the shores from other gene pools to cheer us up or make us fiercer, taller, bluer eyed, better engineers, more artistic, more soulful. This is because we were these things before and we will continue to be so, despite our territorial concerns.

## On Being Careful

It's about having to learn about hedonism and knowing I'll never get the hang of it entirely, although I'll give it a good try. It's about finding the joy of a car stereo at the ridiculously late age of thirty-two. It's about swimming naked off a Caribbean beach, in spite of it. It's about not looking for ways to have a good time but about being worthy instead, which brings me to rebellion. The psychology of being Scottish is, for me, to be industrious and well behaved and then to do something outré just to prove I'm not hodden doon by oney wan. Wha dare meddle wi me? I'll show you!

## On Relentlessness

We're good at relentlessness. All that fighting in the land of old, year in year out, to deliver our daily bread – it leaves its mark generations down the line; on some who can't let up from the commitment to deliver, never to shirk a duty or a deadline; to live a miserable life rather than change it and to have defined yourself as a bastion of the relentless life – such arrogance and such a legacy; embodying those sins of the father. And as if getting drunk actually made you happy, in compensation.

## On Intensity

Being Scottish is about identifying myself as intense; intense about life, about the things I love, intense about 'doin' whit a say a'll do'. It's about darkened rooms with the flickering light and trying to convert others to my causes.

## On Humour

Being Scottish is knowing why every syllable Billy Connolly speaks is funny; it's meeting Sean Connery in the midst of a bunch of luvvies and recognising him as Scottish just from a wee aside. It's about adopting any form of Scottish accent or persona to advantage in a sticky social situation. It's about having your granny's generation's rituals to laugh about and imitate in wondrous playacting. It's about a family humour where references go further back than just your granny.

**On Cities**

Being Scottish is about ancestors from the glittering granite city of Aberdeen, laughing at the difference between east and west, liking vinegar on your chips outside your city wall. It's about cities being the place of education. It's about castles in the middle of the town, about seeing Edinburgh anew after two years away and being gobsmacked at what spectacle is in our front garden. It's about a wee lassie behind the bar in a Glasgow bistro asked for a coffee, then saying, 'Aye, the kettle's just on.'

**On Hills and Vales**

It's about having the best countryside, the best land in the world; about reflecting on that as you fly over a turquoise sea where there are hills and valleys under the water and you can see every runnel on a sunny day, on the way to Islay. It's about a primeval landscape where history can be imagined in an instant. It's about getting to it from the cities, very quickly. It's about a scale of vista that allows you to feel you are part of it, not dwarfed by it. It's about feeling you belong to it. It's home.

# Alan L. Bain

*Alan L. Bain, an English barrister and New York State qualified attorney, is founder and Chief Executive Officer of World-Wide Business Centres, Inc., a pioneering office business centre operator with licencees throughout Europe. Mr Bain was elected President of the American-Scottish Foundation in 1993 and in 1995 received the Ellis Island Medal of Honor in recognition of his work on behalf of the American-Scottish community.*

S ince becoming President of the American-Scottish Foundation ten years ago and, in particular, since taking a leadership role in the development of National Tartan Day over the past five years in New York City and Washington, DC, I have had many opportunities to reflect on the question of what 'Being Scottish' means, both to me and to others.

In my own case, why did the arrival of a letter announcing the need to 'Save our Foundation' – the American-Scottish Foundation, a cultural organisation of which I had only been a peripheral member – so offend me? After all, I had been born and educated in England and had served in an English military regiment. I had married an American and I lived in New York City at the time. To the extent that I acknowledged my heritage at all, I had thought that Scotland had little claim on me. My English public school education taught me little of Scottish history. My connection with Scotland and its culture, modest though it seemed, resulted from benign parental influence happily reinforced by relatives who imported Scottish culture into my English household and village. I also enjoyed frequent trips to Scotland, when I learned of Scotland's history, and was exposed to the grandeur of its scenery and the appeal of its cuisine.

So I was surprised to notice how the prospect of the imminent demise of the Foundation had such an immediate and profound impact on me. It awakened and brought into sharp focus my pride in my Scottishness. How could a *Scottish* organisation fail, I asked myself incredulously? Inspired by the thought of those many Scots that were near and dear to me, I wrote offering whatever assistance I could.

I liked and admired my Scottish parents, their brothers and sisters, excellent role models all. But, it was only since my experiences working with the Foundation that a real sense of belonging developed. I now look forward to my return 'home', as I have come to think of Scotland. As salmon are drawn by instinct to spawn in a particular river, so Scotland draws back its own, I have discovered. The bond that I feel both with the land and its people is almost mystical in nature, not rationally explainable, perhaps, but palpable nevertheless. This feeling of 'home' and 'belonging' was dramatically revealed on a flight into Edinburgh airport. I was sitting in a window seat looking downward when I experienced a sharp 'tug', as if a magnetic force, seemingly emanating from the ground below, was pulling at me, conveying in the most indelible of ways the sensation that my true home beckoned.

My romanticised view of the land and its people frequently bumps up against reality in my work for the Foundation, however. This may be unfair. I realise I expect more of Scots than I do others. For example, I quickly discovered that the very name 'Tartan Day', so happily adopted by those outside Scotland as a day on which American, Australian, Canadian and New Zealand Scots choose to celebrate with pride their Scottish heritage, arouses intense antipathy in Scotland. 'Tartan' seems not only irrelevant to many, but, worse, it is felt to make a mockery of their past and distort their present. Yet, I, like countless others, am proud to wear my family's tartan as a symbol of my heritage and of my attachment to it. The pride demonstrated in this fashion stems from my appreciation of the country's very real contemporary as well as historic achievements. For me, Tartan Day is simply a vehicle for bringing to the attention of my adopted country the accomplishments of my ancestral home.

When I work on Foundation business in Scotland issues arise that are in stark contrast to my expectations. While noting with approval a number of worthy initiatives directed to capitalising on the Scottish diaspora, as an outsider, I wonder why there does not appear to be more of a desire on the part of Scotland's business, political, tourism, cultural and academic institutions to work 'collectively' on developing a unified strategy benefiting all and to collaborate whenever practical. In the Scottish press, as elsewhere, I detect more cynicism than is healthy. Failure there often seems to be more welcomed than success and positive efforts are frequently debunked. Although not absent in my work with my fellow American-Scots, I find these tendencies particularly distressing since Scotland is a small country with limited resources that it can ill afford to squander.

I wonder, too, why Scots, who have and continue to be so extraordinarily successful outside of Scotland, do not appear to fare so well at home. Does Scottish society impose a 'ceiling' on achievement there or is it just a practical matter of the difference in market size, opportunity and available capital? Is it simply a reluctance to 'toot its own horn'?

# Euan Baird

*Euan Baird was born and brought up in Aberdeen, Scotland. At the age of seventeen he left home and country for a world adventure which has lasted forty years. He now lives with his Danish wife, who is the writer of the family, between New York and Paris. He is the Chief Executive Officer of Schlumberger.*

It is impossible for me to dissociate my Scottish experience from that of my parents, who gave me a very distinctive childhood in Aberdeen in addition to my genetic code. They were born at the turn of the century near Glasgow so that our combined Scottish experience covers the whole of the twentieth century.

And what a varied experience the last century proved to be. The first fourteen years were a continuation of the Scottish economic miracle of the nineteenth century. During this period the population of Scotland tripled despite extensive emigration to the four corners of the world and our engineering products became the envy of the world. Twelve million people attended the Kelvin Grove Exhibition held in 1901 in Glasgow. To match this performance the Dome would have had to have attracted more than a 100 million visitors. The outbreak of war in 1914 heralded in a period during which two world wars and a prolonged global recession seriously weakened the fabric of Scotland's society. In 1945 Scotland, full of hope and idealism, turned to socialism and a centrally planned economy. Sluggish growth, a decaying and uncompetitive industrial base and a society increasingly dependent on the state replaced initial successes. Scotland's economy had become a sad shadow of its vibrant nineteenth-century self. The inevitable but painful restructuring of our industrial base during the 1980s paved the way for an economic and cultural revival in the final years of the century.

My consciousness starts as the Second World War ended and the great socialist experiment was about to begin. For my parents, who had been young doctors in Glasgow in the 1920s, the promises of social justice and shared human values without recourse to restrictive religious traditions were enormously appealing. They became active participants in the Labour movement, one as a pillar of the National Health Service and the other as a Labour politician. The socialist convictions of my parents, driven by their keen desire for social equality, justice and close kinship with the underdog, are emotions that I associate closely with being Scottish. Robert Burns may have articulated these sentiments for our nation; my parents lived them.

Their passion for this socialist experiment was not at odds with the fact that they themselves came from very comfortable backgrounds. Convictions, not conventions, were what were important to them, even if that meant being different. I have always felt that being Scottish involves a capacity and, indeed, a willingness to be different.

However, for a teenager, the force and certainty of my parents' convictions and the narrowness of Aberdeen society became suffocating. Being Scottish can be a joyless exercise where fantasy and dreaming seem to have no part. Unable to breathe, I fled not only the strictures of Aberdeen but also the values of collective dependence and responsibility, which had been a large part of my upbringing.

My escape ended with a company called Schlumberger and a Dane called Angelica. Two French brothers who had never asked any government for support had founded the company with some financial help from their father. My wife came from a Danish fairy tale and had trouble understanding the dourness and lack of emotion which can be part of the Scottish character. Both gave me new perspectives about being Scottish.

The Schlumberger brothers were immensely proud of their independence and conscious of the responsibilities that went with it. I discovered a world in which values and morality were self-imposed. I met people who were convinced that their main contribution to society was to make the best economic use of the available resources. In other words, their role was to make money. I found this unassuming honesty of purpose and their respect for the individual instantly appealing to my concept of being Scottish. It awakened me to what was missing from my parents' socialist vision and why the traditional socialist system could never succeed in Scotland. Our burning desire to be independent and to make our own way in the world is at odds with a state-imposed system of values and social obligations. I do not know if this desire for independence is more marked among Scots due to the size of our country compared to our imposing big brother to the south or to the rugged, broken nature of our terrain, but it remains an important element in being Scottish.

On the other hand, my wife's Danish culture made me aware of the emotional poverty of being Scottish. The inability to express emotions and enjoy unself-consciously the simple love of the people who are part of one's daily life are traits that I now associate with being Scottish. Today, I feel like someone who has escaped the force of emotionless gravity but would be easily sucked back if I were ever to return to live in Scotland. It is a measure of our national character that being Scottish and not living in Scotland is something many Scots have learnt to do quite well. Indeed, the Scottish diaspora can be helpful in reviving aspects of our culture in Scotland, such as our independent spirit when it is temporarily suppressed by mistaken social policies. But can we ever shake off our Scottish dourness and capture part of the continental warmth? I have my doubts!

# Anne Bardsley

*Anne Bardsley is forty-two years old, writes poetry, looks after her mother and enjoys learning ceilidh dancing.*

## What's it Like to be Scottish?

Let's start by getting the myths out of the way even for today's world. I don't have one leg shorter than the other so that I can chase haggis round hills. I'm not mean or tight-fisted. Phew! Right, now that we have got the silly bits out of the way let's just find out what it means to me to be Scottish.

I am proud to be Scottish, though not to the extent that I am a radical nationalist who believes that Scotland should be an independent nation. Being Scottish for me is being proud of our heritage, our landscape, our friendliness – which is second to none – our traditions, music and language, although I personally know not one word of Gaelic, and our dancing, which at the grand old age of forty-two I am learning for the second time, the first being at school as a much embarrassed eleven-year-old.

The sound of the pipes and drums stirs national pride like no other musical instrument that I know. Can you really imagine singing 'Flower of Scotland' to the piano or the guitar? It just does not have the same ring to it.

When it comes to sporting achievements for Scotland this is a bit of a mixed bag. But my real bug-bear is athletics. Any Scottish win is a win for Britain. Any English win is a win for England. Double standards or what? Come on all you sporting commentators, at least acknowledge the achievement is by a Scot. The latest case in hand is the gold curling medal and bronze ski medal at the Winter Olympics in Salt Lake City. The other side of this particular coin came pointedly to mind when Alain Baxter was found to have traces of a banned substance in his urine sample – he is suddenly 'the Scottish skier'. I rest my case.

One of the most important points to me of being Scottish is my sense of humour. It has carried me through the rough times in life and sees me being positive even when I don't want to be.

What does make me angry about being Scottish is the way this devolved Scottish Parliament has wasted so much money on a building which always seems to need more money, and the budget has already gone through the roof. I would have been much happier if all this £200 million had been used to provide the Scottish people with better services. Especially since there are plenty of buildings in both Edinburgh and Glasgow that would have been more than adequate for the needs of MSPs. This building, when it is finally finished, will be Scotland's Millennium Dome. Too expensive to run and nobody wanting to buy it afterwards.

However, being Scottish is my very essence and I am proud to be so.

# Mary Beith

*Mary Beith is a writer, lecturer and journalist. She lives in Sutherland.*

How fitting for the kaleidoscope to be a Scottish invention. Notions circling the mind in search of a 'Scottish identity', as any identity, are only too often captives in an arrangement of mirrors, a constantly shifting pattern of a few well-trapped components. The resulting views: a matter of perception and variation, reality and illusion, definition and fragmentation, certainty and uncertainty; a hall of mirrors, reflections, changing lights and angles. Some may seek remedies for the ambivalence in hidebound bias but that, too, can swither – all on the one spot, getting nowhere – around sentimentality or cynicism. 'Identity' can mean two opposites, both sameness and individuality, and maybe that's appropriate to Scottishness, too.

Is it enough, in the opening years of this century, simply to play variations of light and movement on the same old bits and pieces? Or must we carefully break open the instrument of identity, remove some of the old fragments and replace them with new bits and pieces? To misquote Byron (born in England, Aberdeenshire mother, partly brought up in Scotland, died of rheumatic fever while involved in struggle for Greek independence): 'There is a tide in the affairs of *nations*, which, taken at the flood, leads – God knows where.' And we live in an age of riptides and whirlpools.

Defining identities would appear to be a popular planetary activity for our times, and Scotland is not top of the league in winding its collective mind around a sense of national selfhood. A quick spin in cyberspace reveals (at the time of writing)

89,200 sites with articles based on or containing references to the keyword query 'Scottish+identity'. But weighed against humanity+identity (1,320,000 sites), England (1,040,000) has more angst than Scotland, I'm telling you. The Gaels (4,120) barely show signs of a serious syndrome when compared with the Scots as a whole, perhaps as good an argument as any for holding to a distinctive language and culture. Although it must always be remembered that for the tree to flourish there must be fresh shoots and judicious pruning as well as a good rootstock. (On the subject of kaleidoscopes it is permissible to tumble the metaphors.)

However statistically suspect, the brief internet search is muttering something pertinent, but in the interests of sanity it seems safer to go where the kaleidoscope takes us. Its inventor, Sir David Brewster, devised it in 1816 for scientific purposes although it quickly became a popular toy and its magic endures. Brewster was born and bred in Jedburgh, a bare ten miles north of the border. The town's distinctive game of Jethart Hand-ba' allegedly began with a little jolly tossing around of the decapitated heads of English soldiers. Such extreme forms of identity assertion will, it is hoped, have no place in the twenty-first century when the game will continue in its present more benign form.

The brilliant mathematician, and first woman member of the Royal Society, Mary Somerville, after whom the Oxford college was named, was born in Jedburgh in 1780, although she was brought up in Burntisland, Fife. In her childhood home, Somerville lay in bed and gazed at a ceiling decorated with the stars and planets of the universe. Brewster helped to promote the early use of Fresnel lenses in Scotland's lighthouses, providing beacons of hitherto unparalleled brilliance for seafarers. It's the Brewsters and Somervilles we now need to celebrate, rather than the gore, mayhem and struggles so beloved of late twentieth-century theme centres.

My own identity prompted the thoughts of the kaleidoscope. Apart from my two half-brothers, who have more Irish in them than I, the only person I know of with the same mix of Scots, Irish and Bohemian Czech as myself is the late Patrick Campbell, humorist to trade and notable stutterer by affliction. What else could the poor soul do but take a wry look at the world and become a man of d-d-droll l-l-letters and amiable b-b-blether. In addition, I was born in London and educated for several years at an American school in Jamaica. There are distant memories from the 1940s onwards of Wicklow and Somerset as well as the High-lands. There's more, but to go further into the background would overload the prism.

I sit on the north coast of Sutherland and write of the notables of faraway Jedburgh, but am also mindful of distinguished Gaels who contributed much to national and international life and who will continue to do so in the future. I look out at rocks sticking though the browning deer grass like the bones of a mangy old lion, yet (without resort to giddy substances – what need?) imagine Scotland as the girl in the Lennon/McCartney song: 'Picture yourself in a boat on a river with tangerine trees and marmalade skies. / Somebody calls you, you answer quite slowly, a girl with kaleidoscope eyes.'

Such Scottishness as mine will doubtless become more common in years to come. Answers to identity will need to come more slowly, more thoughtfully. With or without the hint of a stutter.

# Margaret Bennett

*Margaret Bennett grew up in the Hebrides. She is a folklorist, singer, university lecturer and broadcaster and has written prize-winning books on emigration, Scottish customs and traditional lore.*

Being Scottish I'm rooted in this Land of the Mountain and the Flood, Old Red Sandstone, Grey Granite and *Trainspotting*. The land of my birth evokes a disparity of responses reflecting the place I happen to be, at home or abroad. There's awe at Edinburgh's skyline, a smile at Glasgow's Loby Dosser (in dreichest rain or traffic), rankle at Sutherland's stoney duke, tranquillity at the Quirang, a sense of wonder at Soutra Aisle, and curiosity at the smells of linoleum factories or breweries. Callanish and Jarlshof amaze me, but so do my compatriots who'd swap them for a football match. Being Scottish, however, we raise a glass together:

> Scotland thy mountains,
> Thy valleys and fountains
> The home of the poet,
> The birthplace of song!

And here's to porridge, penicillin, bicycles, bagpipes, steam engines, tartan, tar macadam, thistles, whisky and Dolly the sheep. Oh, flower of Scotland …

Sometimes I wonder if I belong to a country of the imagination. Outside it, I'm expected to explain, dismantle stereotypes, or justify my claim to being Scottish.

'You have an accent,' and they don't.

'You don't sound Scottish! Where's your rrrrrrrrroamin in the gloamin? What part of Ireland are you from?'

These folk make me explain my species of Scottishness. A Hebridean, Gaelic-speaking mother and Lowland, Scots-speaking father, who both spoke English. One sang Gaelic songs, the other hee-durram-haw-durram'd and played the bagpipes. One leaned far to the left, the other did not. They raised four children between two cultures, three languages, surrounded by a wealth of domestic, social, religious, cultural and political paradoxes.

Apprenticeship in philosophy begins at birth, and, in Scotland, cradle of the paradox, lasts a lifetime. Being Scottish, I'm proud of David Hume and his ilk but grapple with the inconsistencies, absurdities, and impossibilities of our homeland. Faith of our fathers, yet not my father's faith. The fear of the Lord is the beginning of wisdom – don't be afraid to speak your mind. Children should be seen and not heard – mind, you've a guid Scots tongue. Cleanliness is next to Godliness. The clartier the cosier. Here's to pure air, pure water, pure filth – pure dead brilliant.

Dichotomy aside, this same cradle nurtured culture – literature, song, music, dance, cinema, art, photography, theology, engineering, science, law, sport, education and medical knowledge. Being Scottish, I glow with pride at world acclaim for our famous medical schools – I reflect on the centuries of clan physicians that predated them. What was that about the worst health record? Excuse me, we're talking about achievements.

Being Scottish I love tartan, even badly worn, but not worn badly. I'm proud of the tartan armies (those of tanks, trenches, prison camps and freedom), despise tartan terror, and wish Scotland could harness enthusiasm like the Tartan Army. Such whole-heartedness would do wonders for Scotland's languages, education, health, industry – the stuff of dreams, what could be, should be, and, my daily hope, it yet can be.

Perhaps this world of contradictions may make more sense if I look through Scottish eyes at how we live. Rowans planted to keep away witches – you'll see them in Edinburgh gardens on the way to church. A bridegroom stripped naked and blackened before his wedding – indecent and cruel any other night but that one. A lassie on a busy road jumping over a chantie filled with salt – her pals stop double-decker buses and a local bobby kisses her. Men carrying a huge barrel of blazing tar on their shoulders through packed streets ignoring peril. People climbing Arthur's Seat in the middle of the night to watch the sunrise and wash in the dew. Families tying rags on trees to wish away disease. Horse riders galloping at breakneck speed through their town, risking life and limb to remember centuries past. Others on foot, stampeding across anything and over anyone to capture a wee ball covered in ribbons. That's what real Scots do because they know what it means to be Scottish. 'It's priceless, incomparable, unique,' say thousands of foreigners flocking to Princes Street and George Square on a freezing night – they've paid for a taste of being Scottish. (Give me the Flambeaux, the Tron or the fireside.)

An undefined sense of Scottishness follows unbidden wherever I go. Ordinary at home, but celebrated abroad, grand style. 'We'll offer you better prospects,' some say. 'You can earn your living here just by Being Scottish. You'll never want to leave.' But, like the love-struck partner in a bad marriage, back home I go, not driven by homesickness or mindless duty – just unprecedented devotion. There's nothing like a bit of temptation or a wee fling, though, to keep the Scottish passion alive:

> The rose of all the world is not for me.
> I want for my part
> Only the little white rose of Scotland
> That smells sharp and sweet – and breaks the heart.

# Alan Bissett

*Alan Bissett was born in Falkirk in 1975. He has edited the collection* Damage Land: New Scottish Gothic Fiction *(Polygon, 2001), been shortlisted for the Macallan/Scotland on Sunday Short Story Competition, and in 2001 his first novel* boyracers *(Polygon) was published.*

When I was growing up, I didn't even realise I lived in Scotland. At the age of four, I asked my dad if he would take me and my brother on holiday there. He blinked.

'You're in Scotland,' he said.

'Yes,' I replied, 'I know. But I want to go to the real one.'

So it was true what my dad had heard them say. The Bissetts had brought an idiot-child into the world.

'Alan, what are you talking about?'

I wasn't quite sure. I fumbled about with the words to explain it to him. What I arrived at was: 'I want to go to the Scotland where the Loch Ness Monster lives and people wear kilts.' I was certain the housing scheme we lived in could not possibly be the real Scotland. What a disappointment if it was. What would people coming to see the Loch Ness Monster think when they found this!

After reading my first novel *boyracers*, a few people have repeated back to me a phrase I'd considered fairly throwaway. It's a line that says, 'We can do anything, go anywhere, see anyone, be anyone in this little Scotland-or-something country.' I've been asked often enough what I mean by 'Scotland-or-something' that I'm going to have to make some attempt to come up with an answer. So bear with me, because I don't have much of a clue (generally, but especially about this). I just thought it seemed like a cool phrase at the time. Most writers, yanked along by the big dog of their intuition, don't have time to consider what any of it means. Think about it too hard and you'll write the type of stories I did at university. One of them was called 'Attack of the Cultural Signifiers'. Nuff said.

If you're forcing my nose to the page, though, I can probably trace the roots of 'Scotland-or-something' for you. I was raised in a typical working-class house-hold in the 1980s; that is, one trying to gather and clutch to its bosom the trinkets of the middle-classes. This country might have rejected Thatcherism at the polls, but we couldn't prevent it erupting in our midst. The sight from the window of the house I grew up in is an oasis of satellite-dishes, patio-doors, double-glazing, garden-extensions, and other nice things with hyphens in them, all barricaded off from each other by seven-foot-high fences. In 1975, when my parents moved in, those fences were a foot high.

Like most people under thirty-five, I grew up saturated with American popular culture. Scottishness was something dusted off and brought out from the cupboard for football matches or Hogmanay. Neighbours and relatives piling round, the Corries and bagpipe music playing, everyone singing about 1314. I loved it. It was the 'real' Scotland I'd asked my dad to take me to as a kid. There was a community and a pride in everyone sharing in it, everyone being on the same side. The Scotland we shouted at to just kick the bloody ball or listened to on scratchy vinyl was obviously not the Scotland we were living in, though, because come New Year's Day everyone was back to their positions, rats behind seven-foot-high starting-gates.

New millennium. Devolution. Et cetera. But I think that for many people of my generation, Scotland barely exists now. It's just a name we give to the place where we live. Scotland or something. Our high streets look exactly the same as those anywhere else in the West – sanitised, pedestrianised retail dreams, flanked sleekly by Virgin, McDonald's and Gap. We amble through it, selecting lifestyles off the peg, listening to Robbie Williams, ignoring our spiralling debt and the guy selling *The Big Issue.*

That land of tartan and Nessie I wanted to visit might not have been the real Scotland, but I'm still pretty sure this isn't it either.

# Ronald Black

*Ronald Black (Raghnall MacilleDhuibh), writer and journalist, was born in Glasgow in 1946. He is Gaelic editor of* The Scotsman *and* Am Paipear; *a* West Highland Free Press *columnist; and editor of the poetry anthologies* An Tuil, An Lasair. *He was formerly Lecturer in Celtic Studies at the University of Edinburgh.*

## Yearning for Normality

'Shaoileadh daoine gum bu chòir dhaibh a bhith anabarrach toilichte le'n staid; oir cha robh a bheag de thrioblaidean cumanta na beatha seo a' cur dragh orra.

'Bha àiteachan còmhnaidh tioram, seasgair, blàth aca; cha robh éis bìdh no aodaich orra; bha iomadh seòrsa toil-inntinn aca; cha robh iad riamh air an sàrachadh le obair thruim; cha robh màl no cìs aca ri phàigheadh; cha chuireadh maor no bàillidh no uachdaran dragh no tuairgneadh orra aig àm sam bith; a dh'aon fhacal, cha robh creutair beò air an talamh a bha cho saor o dhraghannan 's o thrioblaidean 's o àmhghairean 's o chùraman na beatha seo riutha. Ach ged a bha 'chùis mar seo, bha farmad gu leòr aca ris na daoine bu bhochdainne crannachur a bh' air an talamh gu léir.

'Car son a bha seo mar seo? Bha, do bhrìgh gun robh iad ag amharc orra fhéin mar phrìosanaich aig nach robh dòchas sam bith gum faigheadh iad an saorsa gu bràth.'

One interesting thing about Scotland in 2002 is that more people buy Gaelic poetry (with translations) than English poetry. Gaelic is understood by only 1.4 per cent of the population (a big drop from equilibrium, 50 per cent, in the sixteenth century), so presumably 98.6 per cent of Scots think they can find their soul that way.

Why didn't I start with poetry then? Well, prose is more *normal.*

The quotation is from the Rev. John MacRury, a Benbecula man writing in 1898. He's saying: 'You would have expected them to be very content; for they were beset by few of the everyday worries of this life.

'They had dry, comfortable, warm dwelling-places, suffered no lack of food or clothing, enjoyed a variety of pleasures, had never been oppressed by hard work, paid no rent or tax, were at all times undisturbed and unharried by ground-officer or factor or landlord; in a word, no living creature on earth was as free as they were of this life's trials and troubles and anxieties. But for all that, they deeply envied those whose fate was the most wretched of all on earth.

'Why so? Because they saw themselves as prisoners who had no hope of ever obtaining their freedom.'

He's explaining beliefs about fairies, but it serves well as a metaphor. To me, Scottish identity is about freedoms won and freedoms denied. About communities. And about how we speak as well as what we want to say. It's *not* about what a Portobello youngster once memorably called 'moont'ns an' wa'er'.

Scotland's a big country, full of competing identities, sharing only a willingness to be Scottish. 'Scot' itself is an Irish term for a Gaelic speaker thought to derive from a root *scuit* meaning 'wander'. The word 'British' is interesting too: Strathclyde, my native place, was a British (i.e. Welsh-speaking) kingdom, nowadays the term means UKish. 'Gael' means a Gaelic speaker, now there are 'new Gaels' as well as old ones. 'New Gaels' can turn out to have an American, Canadian, German or English accent when they speak English; sometimes I've known them for years before I hear them do that, and it comes as a nice surprise.

'Celt' is the simplest – 'a speaker of a Celtic language or a descendant of a speaker of a Celtic language'. That's why Scotland is a Celtic country. Its people are over 50 per cent Celtic.

Languages are important. In a media-conscious age, they are media. They convey messages and symbols, not always welcome ones. Governments destroy languages by 'education' in the same way that the Taliban destroyed Buddhas with bombs. Scottish education is the worst in the world, because it destroyed Gaelic. (Nowadays it's trying to destroy itself with things like 40 per cent passes in our universities, instead of improving itself with 60 per cent ones.)

Last year I was invited by the Scottish Parliament to take part in discussions with the visiting President of Catalonia. I asked him what action he would have taken if Catalan speakers had declined to 1.4 per cent of the population. He replied by telling me about a language in the Pyrenees spoken by so few people that I hadn't even heard of it. 'We made it an official language of Catalonia. Why? Because it was the right thing to do.'

That's a European attitude. We could do with it here. First, we need to declare Gaelic and English as national languages. They're both ready for it. Then we must legislate for community languages: Scots, Urdu, Punjabi, Cantonese, Gaelic and so on. With hard work, Scots could become a third national language. The aim is for all Scottish children to study four languages during their school years, normally including both national languages, a community one and foreign one.

Then the language at the top of this piece will be *normal*, and Scotland will be a *normal* European country. I yearn for that.

# Sheena Blackhall

*Sheena Blackhall is currently Creative Writer in Scots at Aberdeen University's Elphinstone Institute. She has published many books of poetry and short stories, mainly in Scots, and is also a traditional folk singer. She exhibits artwork under the name of Sìne Nicthèarlaich, and publishes academic work under the name of Sheena Middleton.*

## On Being Scottish: A Touch of the Tar Brush

I am the family face
Flesh perishes, I live on
Projecting trait and trace
Through time, to time anon.

Thomas Hardy

The first time I met a certain north-east poet (I will refrain from naming and shaming him) he asked where I came from. I replied rather smugly, that my ancestors had farmed in the north-east since 1623. 'Mm ...' he observed, 'but I'm sure there's a touch of the tar brush there as well.' Recently, a visiting lecturer asked the same question. 'You do surprise me,' she said. 'I was sure I detected a hint of Sephardic Jew!'

Let me state here and now, I'm 100 per cent north-east Scots. I have the language and the pedigree to prove it. The purer the breed, the higher the incidence of inbreeding, and, yes, my parents were related to each other. I believe the Pharaohs in ancient Egypt also kept it in the family ... it saves on wedding invitations. Father's family were descended from Norman Scots, De Midletons, who settled in Cromar in 1623, supposedly linked to John, 1st Earl of Middleton (1604–74), the Covenanting general turned Royalist who led a revolt in the Highlands for Charles II in 1653. The general has a bit part in Sir Walter Scott's 'Wandering

Willie's Tale' as 'Bloody Middleton' seated at Auld Horny's right hand. 'I wouldn't tell anybody I was related to him, dear,' an old lady told me after I crowed about the connection at Fettercairn, the general's home ground. 'He was a bit of a drunken beast. And he shot people.' (Generals generally do.)

There are Flemish genes on both sides of the family. The first mention of them appears in the Records of Aboyne (1230–1681: 309). Johan Crab was a pirate who so incensed the Count of Flanders that he threatened to break him on the wheel if he ever caught up with him. When Crab wasn't plundering shipping he was a military engineer who designed a war machine which devastated the English troops during the siege of Berwick. After this, he is recorded disputing the rights to lands in Cromar, where the Crabs/Craibs eventually farmed. Interestingly, at the height of the oil boom there was an area in Aberdeen known as 'Little Holland', and the Aberdonian word 'loon' is of Dutch origin, as is the diminutive '*ie*' as in cuppie, mannie, wifie.

Mother's family were descended from Booths and Philips. Patrick Morgan in the north-east annals of Woodside and Newhills (1886) refers to a 'worthy and well-known family of the name of Booth, farmers in the estate of Auchmill for nearly 200 years'. The name may have originated in Yorkshire or Lancashire. Stinch, kirk-gyaun farmers. The Philips though, were quite exciting. Legend has it that the first north-east Philip was Juan Phillipe a Spanish seaman who swam ashore from the *Santa Catalina*, a galleon of the Spanish Armada, which sank off Collieston in 1588 in the bay of St Catherine's Dub. Apparently, neighbours in Aberdeen, who had never heard my mother in full Doric flight, were convinced we were a family of Spaniards. Velasquez is one of my favourite artists, and my brother was very fond of oranges … George Philip, my maternal great-grandfather was born in 1857 near Balmoral castle in Crathie, brought up by his grandmother there till he was nine, in a core Gaelic-speaking area (Horsbroch, 1997), George was alleged to be an illegitimate son of Edward VII (1841–1910). His second claim to fame lies in being the paternal great-grandfather of David Ogston, the Doric poet and novelist.

With the very first BBC cheque I received for a short story, I bought my lair in the parish of Coull in the Howe of Cromar. Book early and avoid disappointment. When I buried my father there, the gravedigger introduced himself as an Anderson (a Viking name), a second cousin of mine. 'He winna be lonely lang,' he said, shovelling in the turf. 'His cousin frae ower the back o the knowe's nae in a gweed wye. We're expeckin tae beery her aroon Christmas.'

North-east Scots could never be accused of verbal overdrive. We have mastered the minimal. We aren't big on hugs. Our silences say as much (and often more) than our speech. But if asked to tick a box on ethnic origin, I'd choose the Celt category, because like most north-east Scots, I'm a kirn of European races. I'm a Celt because place matters to me, and every word of the Celtic poet Amheirgin resonates with me at the deepest level:

> I am a stag o seeven tines
> I am a spate alang a lea
> I am a win ower lochan deep
> A tear, the sun lats doondrap, free.

That's almost Buddhist in its universality. Read it, Calvin, and weep!

# Vivian Bone

*Vivian Bone was/is a Londoner, and permanently resides in Bow of Fife. The appropriate degree at the University of Sussex led to a post of Maths and Physics Editor at Oxford University Press and marriage to a Scot-at-Balliol, followed by a transfer to Edinburgh University Press as Editor for Everything (especially Scottish Studies and Islamic Studies). This metamorphosed into Managing Director of Edinburgh University Press as a financially independent company, then into Consultant Editor (especially for journals and institutional histories) and itinerant university principal's wife.*

## Being Other

Moving from England to Scotland over twenty years ago, and being married to a Scot for ten years more than that, left 'Scottish' or 'British Other than Scottish' as equally inaccurate alternatives on the last Census, so I went for 'Other' and wrote in British (English and Scottish).

The Scottish part comes mainly from the simple fact that my home is in Scotland. The house that I love in every detail, the garden, the village, the Fife countryside, Cupar, St Andrews, Perth, the slightly more distant Edinburgh – they just *are* where I have had the centre of my being for the last twenty years and more. I was away during the events of 11 September 2001 and the terrible fear of worse arising from the inevitable retaliation – and experienced that internal cry to get home.

I thought this fundamental feeling would make this piece easy to write, but in practice the rest proves quite problematic. I bristle when 'English' is wrongly used instead of 'British', but overall my involvement in publishing and the academic world tends to make me see similarities rather than differences.

Publishing is of its essence international, as is, to a certain extent, the academic world, which does not make a big distinction between jobs in England or Scotland despite the differences in secondary schooling. I see professional similarities out-weighing national or regional differences, linking Edinburgh academics to Oxford academics more than to Edinburgh non-academics. The same seems true with Czech academic friends, and Americans …

Professional life or middle-class life or affluence (all guilt-provoking words) are in general unifying factors. Different aspects of this upset different people: I am not fond of identikit-architecture spreading across the land, but I quite like the fact that Armani jackets are available as easily in Glasgow as in London, or that a fair selection of wines can be found in the Orkneys and across Britain.

I have been very lucky: I have had the honour of working for two cultural institutions, and an initially somewhat reluctant move from Oxford University Press to Edinburgh University Press provided not only a rapid education in Islamic Studies and Scottish Studies, especially history and social issues, but also a much more hands-on knowledge of production and marketing (not to mention hands-on furniture-removing and other little jobs that had been done by others in the OUP empire), leading to a whole new universe of management in a re-thought EUP.

Many of my interests outside publishing are not Scottish: historical interiors, things French, music – thank God my love of sailing depends strongly on the haunting beauty of the Western Isles. The music is Austrian/German in the main – I am entirely happy with a European identity, but not with a decreasing national one. I prefer the widening of horizons.

The fine White Paper 'Scotland's Parliament', which I bought and totally agreed with, degenerated, I felt, into a campaign where football loyalties were thought relevant and produced a result from such a low turnout that the per-centage of the total electorate was not much different from the percentage that had been rejected previously. The Census question formed a sad sequel.

I have been honest, perhaps too honest, so I feel a need to point out – perhaps just a further revelation of middle-class angst – that EUP is Scotland's only academic publisher and so anyone with previous experience is going to come from outside and by-and-large from England. I can see this is a subset of 'the English coming in to all the top posts' (an epiphenomenon of the professional classes being more geographically mobile than the non-professional classes, and a flow that goes in both directions). I can hear every word I say being interpretable as English arrogance or complacency, but it would be more arrogant of me to dissemble. There are inevitable problems of cultural hegemony if you divide into a bigger and a smaller nation next to each other. These problems feature both on the larger scale all round the world from the huge like US/Canada to the perhaps most relevant Sweden/Norway, and, on the smaller, many English people hated Mrs Thatcher as much as most Scots did, and Yorkshire or Cornwall can feel as alienated from the prosperous south-east as Scotland can. If my cosmopolitan husband has been called an ambassador for Scotland, then perhaps in a minor way I can be an ambassadress for it. Wells' dictum remains alarmingly true: 'Human history becomes more and more a race between education and catastrophe,' and I would like to think that my work as well as this book contribute their pennyworth to the side of education, understanding, and hence of love.

# Alison Bowden

*Alison Bowden is a Commissioning Editor for Polygon, and Rights Co-ordinator for Edinburgh University Press.*

Okay, I confess. I'm a mock-Scot. I live in Scotland, I work in Scotland, I even grew-up in Scotland. But I'm not Scottish.

Technically I'm Irish, in that I was born in Ireland, and lived there until my family moved to Scotland when I was eight. I've lived in Scotland for twenty years now and I know more about Scotland, the land, its people, its politics and its culture than I will ever know about Ireland. On the few occasions I've been back to Ireland, I've been a stranger to it. I think my family, though, have rumbled me on this. If I had to sit a test to get into my family I'd probably fail. When they talk about Ireland, about living there, they'll name a street or a person and there will be nodding, people chipping into the story. Recognition. Me, I glaze over and nod convincingly in order to fit in. What memories I have of Ireland have become distorted, embellished, and as I get older they mesh together with bits of Scotland and our family's Scottish history.

But the bottom line is that I was born in Ireland and brought up in an Irish family, with an Irish sense of humour, Irish sensibilities. So in the big ebb and flow, locality loses and the bloodline wins, I'm Irish. At least on paper.

It seems strange, though, to lay claim to a country I know so little about, to which I don't connect when it is Scotland that is my home, and Scotland which has influenced me and continues to do so. When people ask me (the acid test), '*Are you Scottish?*', I swither. It's tempting.

# Sheila Brock

*Sheila Brock was formerly Head of Public Affairs, National Museums of Scotland (1983–94); Museum of Scotland Campaign Director (1994–9); and is currently a fund-raising consultant, a member of various committees, and a church warden, gardener and grandmother.*

Being Scottish? I don't think that I was especially aware of being Scottish until I went to Oxford as a student. Born just before the Second World War, there was no time in my young life for nationalist niceties. The maps in my atlas showed confident tracts of red across the world. What mattered was being British and my only concern was that the Germans might plant a bomb under my bed. In common with most children, the sense of place came first. I wrote myself into my street, my city, my country, the World, the Universe, but awareness of difference depended on whether or not I was in Edinburgh, my mother's birthplace, or in Aberdeen, where my father came from. His sisters, a unique conglomeration of feisty, humorous women, made me want, more than anything else, to be an Aberdonian. My father had been taken prisoner at the Somme but spent the rest of his life as a schoolmaster teaching French, German and Russian and communicating his affection and respect for the language and culture of others. Scots, he reckoned, had an advantage: it was easier to speak good French and German unhindered by an Oxford accent! Perhaps being Scottish is in the genes.

Growing up at a time when hitchhiking was safe, I travelled the country and indulged in serial love affairs with mountains and lochs, villages and youth hostels, from the Borders to north-west Sutherland. The smell of pine trees on Deeside and the hush of a heron's wings in the fading light near Dervaig, crossing the Minch in a gale or sunbathing on the sands near Findhorn left an indelible imprint like poetry learned by heart. With these went the music, the sentimental and scurrilous songs, the unique sound of the metrical psalms, the words of great preachers in Edinburgh or Iona, the noisy, laughing, painful sense of being one of a group. Perhaps being Scottish is nurture not nature.

Oxford taught me, although it did not persuade me, that I might be an alien, not one of them, but one of 'them'. It was at first the humour that made the difference. We are, by turns, self-deprecating and bombastic, proud to a fault and yet 'all fur coat and nae knickers'. Brought up with the throwaway line, the wisecrack and the play on words, the silly side of English humour seemed to me deeply unfunny. Scots may not be silent – I certainly was not that – but we are more reticent, inclined to speak when we have something valid to contribute. Still, as it happened, coming from Scotland (coupled, it must be said, with reading theology and playing cricket) had the overwhelming advantage of providing a distinct identity. Perhaps being Scottish is simply not being English.

The nineteenth-century Scottish missionaries who were the subject of my research did not seem to be especially concerned about their Scottishness. Like David Livingstone, they would readily have described themselves as English men and women. Their Scottishness was their mindset – dourness, practicality, radicalism, equality in the eyes of God, compassion, inflexibility, the 'old Scottish causticity' and what some Africans called 'the disputativeness' of the Scot – at best love of argument, at worst self-justification leading to religious and social schism. My mother's version of this frequently applied to me was 'argumentative teeny', for I was inclined to be thrawn and a right scunner as she never failed to remind me when she was at her most perjink. Perhaps being Scottish is an attitude of mind, pronounced – like Patterson – with two t's?

The last years of my career in the National Museums were spent as Campaign Director for the new Museum of Scotland, raising money, promoting the cause at home and abroad. I met Scots of all tartans and none, not a few of whom professed kinship with a country which had more in common with historical fiction than historical fact. Transplanted Scottishness produced some strange hybrids. At the same time, 'the settled will of the Scottish people' was being defined and modern Scotland was seeking to reposition itself in the United Kingdom and in Europe. The new Museum offered to illuminate this process, providing real evidence of the past, demonstrating the strengths and weaknesses of a wee country and a peculiar people. It's all there: power and loss of power, religious in-fighting and religious imagination, financial success and failure, poverty and plenty, inventiveness and creativity, exile and exploration, influence and insignificance. But perhaps being Scottish is having a dangerous preference for the *Braveheart* version of our past.

Being Scottish is more a way of thinking, an acquired culture rather than a genetic imprint, a vocabulary, an attitude bent and humoured by cold winds and midgies. It is a positive, mature characteristic not simply a defiant reaction to an Auld Enemy. In the twenty-first century, it could be the hallmark of a small country looking outwards or it could be the stamp of a close-knit family bent of fighting age-old quarrels. Being Scottish? It makes life interesting.

# Craig Brown

*Craig Brown is Director of Football Development at the Scottish Football Association. He was in charge of the Scottish National Team on seventy occasions between 1993 and 2001, and has an outstanding record, having lost only nine competitive matches.*

Having had the privilege of working for sixteen years with the Scottish International Football Team, eight years as Assistant and eight in charge, I have an acute perception of what it is to be Scottish. Such is the sharp focus in which the national sport is seen in this country, all aspects of football are examined, dissected and evaluated. No informed observer could dispute my contention that there are two overriding factors when discussing the job of International Team Manager. The first is that, invariably, there is a tremendous response from the players, many of whom are millionaires but all, in my experience, are extremely patriotic. Equally, there is the terrific support of the famous Tartan Army, which, at times, is almost tangible.

The privilege of travelling worldwide with the Squad, and in a position to influence the eventual outcome of matches, was never taken for granted. At times I had to remind myself that to be *Scottish* and to be in charge of such a high-profile group of national heroes was such a privilege. It was a job never to be taken for granted and always to be appreciated.

One of the principal attractions of football, whether with the National Team or not, is the humour which abounds in the game. Clearly it is essential to be able to accept a joke and never to take oneself too seriously. With the quick-witted one-liners of the players and supporters the recipient would be devastated if he were not able to smile readily and see the fun in most situations. To be able to take a joke and, better still, to tell one against oneself are essential parts of Being Scottish.

Any notion of self-aggrandisement was quickly dispelled from me when, in a match playing for Dundee against Celtic in the early 1960s, I was berated throughout the first half by a gentleman in 'The Jungle' bedecked with a huge green scarf. He concluded his abuse of me by saying, 'Anyway, this is the worst game I ever saw!' We were a goal ahead and, thinking smartly (or so I thought), I replied, 'You're the mug, you paid to get in!' Without hesitation or apparent time to think he replied, 'Aye, but you'll be paying next season!' The fact that the gentleman was a prophet, or almost a prophet, made the remark even more poignant.

The famous Manager of Dundee FC at the time, Bob Shankly, when arranging the team group photograph at the start of every season, would carefully position his star international players in the centre of the photo and, eventually, place inferior performers like Craig Brown at the end of the row with the remark 'a pair of scissors will get rid of you!' It is pretty obvious, then, that Being Scottish in the world of professional football means that you are required to accept the massive amount of humour which exists among players, officials and fans.

Eventually, when I became Manager, the 'advice' continued! After seven years as Manager of Clyde FC I was asked to become a Director of the Club. This received moderate publicity in the press, just enough for a Clyde fan the following Saturday to shout, 'Haw, Broon, now that you are a Director, how's about getting us a decent Manager!'

As a Manager I always insisted on the players giving 100 per cent effort and this sometimes, mistakenly, led to some of my charges becoming 'over enthusiastic'. One such responsive player was Joe Filippi, whom I signed from Celtic for a modest fee. Joe was extremely conscientious in carrying out instructions and when advised to deal with an imposing player from his home-team town, Ayr United, he committed a rather horrendous foul. The referee waved him over and said, 'You were a bit late there number three.' Joe politely replied, 'I got there as early as I could, ref!' The match official produced his notebook and, in the process of taking the particulars, asked for the offender's name. At this point I thought that some further co-operation with the referee would be helpful, so I shouted from the Technical Area, 'Joe, spell it! Spell your name!' Joe very politely said to the official, 'Mr Syme, it's Filippi with two p's!' The referee smiled even more politely, brought out his red card and said, 'Mr Filippi with 2 p's, for you it's off with 2 f's!'

Being Scottish and enjoying the humour in football are not the sole prerogatives of men. There is an increasing number of women in the game, both participating and spectating. One of my fondest memories is when I was Manager of Clyde FC and we had a lady, Sadie, from Bridgeton, who did everything around the ground including distributing the Bovril and pies at half-time. When our Scottish Cup match was postponed one Saturday it was rescheduled for the following Wednesday. Sadie sought advice from me and, thereafter, put the Saturday pies in the fridge ready for distribution on Wednesday. The first guy in the queue asked for 'The usual, Sadie. A Valium Bovril and a pie.' Sadie duly produced the necessary but, being from Bridgeton, he did not take the pie at face value. There are three tests prior to eating a pie in Bridgeton. The first is visual, the second tactile and the third is smell. Having administered these tests, and still harbouring a little suspicion, the gentleman allowed the pie to drop on the table. It landed with a thud, whereupon he pointed an accusatory finger at Sadie and said, 'Hey, Sadie, this is Saturday's pie!' Quick as a flash, Sadie replied, 'What the hell are ye wantin'? This is Saturday's gemme!'

In the world of football, arguably the personality who exemplified Being Scottish more than anyone was the late, great Jock Stein. In the mid-1970s I was Assistant Manager at Motherwell FC and I recall Jock, who knew everyone in the game, arriving at Fir Park with his famous Celtic team. He immediately called our groundsman by name and said, 'Andy, what's your park like tonight?' Andy's response, 'Good enough for what's going on to it!' did not in any way please the famous Manager, but again exemplified typical Scottish humour.

During my spell with the National Team there was never a dull, humourless moment. With guys like Ally McCoist, Ian Durrant, Tosh McKinlay and Archie Knox around, this was not possible. But maybe the finest example of Being Scottish was the famous Celtic masseur for half a century, Jimmy Steel. Jimmy regaled the lads with story upon story and, typically Scottish, his famous quote was, 'Listen lads, my funeral will be all ticket … and there will be no complimentaries!' Never did a man speak a truer word because his funeral was, in football terms, a 'sell out' and the other famous footballing Scot, Sir Alex Ferguson, gave a eulogy which had smiles on the faces of those in attendance at Daldowie Crematorium. Only in Scotland could I imagine humour being universally accepted at a funeral.

Being Scottish makes me very proud.

Proud of the country, proud of the culture, proud of the people and proud of the humour.

# Steve Bruce

*Since 1991 Steve Bruce has been Professor of Sociology at the University of Aberdeen. He was educated at the Queen Victoria School, Dunblane, and then the University of Stirling and was formerly Professor of Sociology at the Queen's University, Belfast. He is the author of sixteen books on religion and politics including* Fundamentalism *(Polity, 2001) and* God is Dead: Secularization in the West *(Blackwell, 2002).*

## But No Accordions

Nineteen-sixty-eight. A house in Lincoln. We had stayed in the English city after my father retired from his last army posting. My mother hated the accordion. She especially hated Jimmy Shand. Once every few months, when she went off for a day's shopping, my father would get out his old Beltona brand 78s and play them loudly. He sang and hummed along to 'The Muckin o'Geordie's Byre', 'My Big Kilmarnock Bonnet', and 'The Duke of Perth'. I was much too intent on being precociously cool to be bothered with that old nonsense. I listened to Chicago blues and be-bop jazz. But I shared her dislike of the accordion. It makes too much noise. It has too many notes. It does too much.

The year 2000. The Beaton Hall in Methlick. Third tune in a four-tune reel set. My hand moves up the guitar neck from A minor to D and the band swings into 'Geordie's Byre'. The key change lifts the dancers. Then the grand finale of 'Calliope House'. The dancers stop and applaud. The ladies of the 'Rural' go off to serve the stovies and the band sits down in the backstage changing room. 'Bet this place has not been painted since the 1930s,' says our piper, looking at the chipped scumble varnish. 'My dad played here a lot in the thirties,' I say. 'He lived just up the brae. He was an accordianist.'

And so the circle closes. Twenty years away and I end up where my father started. He's back too. He died in Lincoln but I bought him a lair in the Methlick cemetery, just opposite the croft where he grew up. He left for work. I returned for the same reason. He saw a tractor and realised faster than many what implications that would have for farm loons. He joined the army and started his military career in that wasteland that is all too familiar now from the television: Afghanistan. We had an empire then and our relatives emigrated to it: Canada, Australia, South Africa.

We have lost our empire and with it one of the reasons for the Union. Scotland and England are drifting apart, and I cannot say I mind. I have sometimes resented the Union but I have never felt positively Scottish. I am comfortable in familiar surroundings and know I belong here. If I was in the phone book my name would be buried in two pages of Bruces. I am comfortable with devolution and if outright independence comes, fair do's. But I cannot feel any romantic attachment to a Scottish *nation*. What spirit unites the citizens of Lewis and Glasgow and does not more closely unite the former with north Wales or the latter with Newcastle? What do the Catholic descendants of Irish immigrants in Coatbridge have in common with Gaelic-speaking Wee Frees in Shawbost and Anglophone bankers in Edinburgh or Doric farmers and oilmen?

Scotland makes sense as an administrative unit. The argument from efficiency gives a good reason to shorten the line from Brussels to London to Edinburgh by knocking out the second station. However, I cannot feel an ethnic unity. On my way home, I pass the monument to the Battle of Harlaw, at which invading Highlanders were driven back west and north by Lowland Scots. When I was a child the only people from these parts who wore kilts were soldiers. Now kilts are common in Gordon and Buchan, which shows at least the surface appearance of unity. The decline of religion has weakened the identities that divided the Irish, the Highlanders and the Lowlanders. Improved communication has brought the disparate parts of Scotland closer together, but it has also brought us all into a global American culture, an international politics, and a worldwide trade system. My farming neighbours are from England; my friends work for US oil companies. I cannot conceive of these people as an ethnic group or suppose that the world would be improved if we tried to create a homogenous ethnicity by driving out the incomers and the traitors.

I might be unusually unsentimental but when I hear the opening line of that semi-ironic self-aggrandising toast, 'Here's tae us! Wha's like us?', I privately mutter the only honest reply: 'Most people actually'.

For all that romantic nationalism leaves me cold, I do want the local culture to survive and I want my children to feel a sense of belonging to this part of Scotland, whatever its political regime. My eldest daughter plays the fiddle. Her rebellious cool is the vicious lyrics of smacked-up ghetto blacks but she will grow out of that and nothing would cheer my old age more than to see her gigging at the Beaton Hall. Just so long as there are no accordions.

# Duke of Buccleuch

*The Duke of Buccleuch and Queensberry was born in 1923 and was raised in the Scottish Borders. He served with the Royal Navy between 1942 and 1946 – Ord. Seaman to Lt. Cdr. to Hon. Captain RNR. He married Jane in 1953; they have three sons and one daughter. He was MP (Conservative) for Edinburgh North as Earl of Dalkeith from 1960 to 1973. He succeeded to the double Dukedom in 1973, was Lord-Lieutenant and Chairman Lrd-Lts. Assn. (1974–98), and was made Knight of the Thistle (KT) in 1978. He is President and Chairman of numerous charities and trusts.*

M y family name is SCOTT. Scotland is my home. I was reared in Scotland. My super wife of fifty years, come 10 January 2003, is a west Highlander. I am registered Chief of Clan Scott. I am thankful to be a citizen of Great Britain.

By accident of birth, I eventually found myself responsible for managing large areas of southern Scotland: 96 per cent of its beautiful, windswept hills. Much of the land was acquired, honourably, in the interests of collective security. This was during the periods of conflict in the fifteenth and sixteenth centuries. Several clan chiefs throughout the Borders did the same; some of our estates survive, albeit greatly reduced. Most of us who do survive are very conscious that we are not so much owners of the land but its custodians and stewards. Very few of our mainly urban population can begin to understand what incredibly long-term policy decisions are needed for the successful management of the countryside.

So much of our lovely landscape, which everyone wants to preserve, has been due to the way in which our forebears have integrated woodlands with farmland. They achieved superb results over huge swathes of countryside. The Almighty provided the valleys and the hills, but far-sighted humankind has clothed them. To their credit, and to our benefit today, our ancestors planned for five generations or more ahead. Today's estate managers, such as myself, try to follow their good example. It is a big risk, but the thought that one's great-, great-grandchildren may benefit is a big incentive. Today there are politicians who want to break up the traditional estates that created what we now prize. They seem wholly unaware of the tragic consequences. Short-termism is a depressing feature of this third millennium. The determination of the surviving estate owners to carry on with such activities as planting and replanting broadleaved as well as coniferous woodlands is crucially important. The chain of continuity has held for 500 years and no present steward of the land wants to be the weak link that snaps under the pressure of urban politicians who just do not understand what is at stake.

A rural estate today is in effect a community within a community – a working partnership or co-operative. The landlord/tenant system of farming now accounts for about 30 per cent of all farm holdings; eighty years ago it was 80 per cent. Nevertheless it still covers a large part of the total area of Scotland. This is quite simply because much of the least productive and most unprofitable areas are in estate ownership. This is the sort of land that requires up to 10,000 acres to support one shepherd's wage. It has little appeal to owner-occupier farmers seeking their living off the land.

The hills in southern Scotland can mainly support one ewe to three acres. These areas are of great significance to British agriculture as a whole. The Blackface and Cheviot lambs born to healthy, hardy parents have pedigrees spanning hundreds of years. These are the mainstays of innumerable flocks on farms throughout the UK, fattening top-quality lamb for the table. Likewise cattle from these areas, and further north, provide the world's best beef, thanks largely to Galloway and Aberdeen Angus bloodlines. The most important aspect of this incomparable enterprise is the men who rear them – the shepherds and stocksmen. Sadly, the profitability of such farming is at present almost zero and diversification is being forced upon us all.

Fortunately the sporting potential of these wide-open spaces, with stags, grouse and fishing, does appeal to a limited number of people who can afford the maintenance of heather, associated woodlands, and particularly local jobs which could otherwise become a considerable burden on public funds. While tourism related to Scotland's unique sporting opportunities could be invaluable for remote communities, it will almost certainly take time and money to achieve this. The big question is, who will have the confidence to proceed?

Everyone applauds the National Trust for Scotland, and with good reason. It has rescued so many of the country's historic features from oblivion. Buildings and landscapes are being saved, but what a pity that they need to be. As often as not, it was because their creative owners were driven out by a century of penal taxation and huge maintenance costs. Inheritance tax and wealth tax are one and the same thing; several generations of owners were crushed by it. It is doubtful whether the fiscal benefits the Trust enjoys can compensate for family commitment that treasures the atmosphere as well as the fabric.

To me, Being Scottish means being wedded to the soil, with the exciting challenge of passing my part of it, and all upon it, on to the next generation in a better state than when I received responsibility for it.

# Angus Calder

*Angus Calder, poet and historian, was for many years Staff Tutor in Arts with the Open University in Scotland. He now lives (in Edinburgh) as a freelance writer.*

It seems to me that I am required to explain why if I heard bagpipes from afar up country in Africa or in the streets of Bangladesh – anywhere outside Scotland – I would quite certainly break into tears.

I went 'up' to Cambridge University in 1960. King's College farmed its first-year students of English Literature out to a great scholar, Helena Mennie Shire, from Aberdeen. One day Helena announced a treat. Jeannie Robertson was coming to sing to the local chapter of the Saltire Society. She would give a special performance for us, her King's students, in Helena's living room. This occurred. Afterwards Helena took us to the local pub, where we sat outside and Jeannie kept on singing, prefacing yet another ballad with such a remark as 'A long time ago – well, not so long ago – when King James V roamed the roads as a gaberlunzie man, they sang this about him …' I think she believed that every word she sang was true. I reckon that was the moment when I decided I had to be Scottish, though it has taken me four decades to clarify what is now my settled view – that it is, precisely, through our songs and the language of them that we are Scottish.

Mv devoutly Scottish parents had raised five children in England. I had the option of being English. My only visit to Scotland before I met Jeannie had been a dampener. Auntie Bella, the baker, with whom we stayed in Forfar, seemed as dour as the relentless grey weather. (She can't have been all that grim – I was told, as a dire warning, that my cousin had lost all his teeth by his twenties because of the sweet cakes she let him eat.) My positive memories were of the wonders of

Scottish High Street baking – then truly distinctive – of the cricket pavilion that J. M. Barrie donated to Kirriemuir, and of watching Ed Murrow destroy Joe McCarthy on TV, which rich Bella had and we didn't.

But actually, my first girlfriend, pre-Jeannie, was the daughter of Scots exiles. (Her mother is still alive in Lochaber.) My first wife was likewise an 'Anglo-Scot' and the first book which either of us published was a joint effort on Walter Scott. When I got to teach in Africa, the locals, despite my RP accent, had no trouble at all understanding that I wasn't English and some may have tended to see me, I am embarrassed now to think, as a representative of an oppressed race victimised by imperialism like their own people.

Scotland's population is falling, and ageing into the bargain. We could do with lots of immigrants, illegal if necessary. If I survive till 2020 I hope to see black and brown Scots in every street. They will be Scottish – as Jews and Italians and Poles have become Scottish – by virtue of adapting to our language and our music, both of which they will in turn influence. Burns in this context is more clearly than ever our most important historical personage. My friend Joy Hendry once came upon someone singing 'My Love is Like a Red, Red Rose' in a Chittagong street. He said firmly that it was by Tagore. The great Bengali poet, who indeed translated Burns, probably did not know that Rabbie specifically disclaimed writing that song and said he took it down from a rustic singer. He made it his business to preserve, repair and extend that living tradition of song, which Jeannie carried into our own times. Some of the results proved 'universal'.

My next book, due out from Luath, will be called *Scotlands of the Mind*. I insist on the plural. I am very queasy about any attempt to integrate all the different Scotlands of history and the present into some bogus essential Scottishness. Nevertheless, I think I identify common continuities in the cultures occupying these expanses of territory which have retained the same borderline since the fifteenth century.

First, olden Scotland as a sparsely populated, largely pastoral country had more affinities with democratical Scandinavia and Gaelic Ireland than with England. Distances paradoxically make for closeness. People stand out separately, look like men and women not mass. Serfdom simply doesn't feature as a factor in Scottish history. Ballads, tying wee folk in with great, do. In the Middle Ages, Froissart noticed the uncanny lack of deference towards their lairds shown by Scottish agriculturalists. 'I am Little Jock Elliott – wha daurs meddle wi *me*?' is proverbial in the Borders. The Highlands were different, but the notion that the chief was head of a family, not an alien superior, clearly did prevail. John Brown's self-assertive relationship with his Scotophile queen sums it all up. The sense of close-ness across 'classes' which persists to this day, I believe, in many contexts, can be seen in the evolution of Scottish Presbyterianism, in the practical, sociable character of our Enlightenment – I cherish the image of Hume and Smith carousing in an Old Town howff as they discuss Free Trade – and in the roles of Scots working together in the Empire. It can be discerned in Johnny Buchan's Toryism as clearly as in Jimmy Maxton's socialism.

Why am I so sure it's persisted? Music and language tell me this. An Anglo-Scottish toff James Kennaway, serving in Highland regiments after the war, identified the significance of musical tradition in that great novel, *Tunes of Glory*. The 51st Highlanders *were* the tradition, shared among all ranks. I would say that the significance of Burns and Scott in this tradition is more important than any role assigned to them as vastly influential innovators in Scottish, English and European literature, or as precursors of socialism and conservatism respectively. They were prouder of collecting songs than of anything else. And closeness to 'folk', or as we currently say 'popular culture', all the way from Henryson to now, marks almost every major Scottish writer, one way or another. (Miss Jean *Brodie*, for instance, from urban myth.)

Now language – what immigrants learn from us to say. May no one ever seek to impose on immigrant Afghans and economically-attracted Africans some dire 'standard Scots'. Our 'speak' remains distinctive enough. The process I have in mind is exemplified by David Daiches' recollection, in his memoir of an Edin-burgh childhood as the son of the rabbi, *Two Worlds*, of the Eastern European Jew who always greeted him, 'Vell, Davie, howyer keepin?'

I am fascinated by the Scottish diminutive. When Morningside Person refers to someone as a 'keelie' or a 'schemie' the diminutive expresses at the same time contempt and a kind of – what? – not affection, but incorporation in a common humanity. My elder sister, who lives in York, is harrying me at the moment over the word 'wifie'. Our mother reared us in outer London suburbia, instructing us to speak proper, because she'd trained as an elocution teacher. Her own background was professional Kelvinside. Nevertheless, Fiona claims that in childhood Mother called her a 'real wee wifie'. I guess this was because F was fussing maternally over younger children. Harassment on this matter arose because I was speculating to F about when a lassie becomes a wifie, which latter is not a term confined to married women. Anyway – same point. Concise *SND* unperceptively marks 'wifie' as usually pejorative. It seems to me that it has a spectrum of connotations, in different contexts, some affectionate. There are no southern English equivalents that I know of to 'schemie' or 'wifie'. Immigrants, who have given us curry pies and many Premier League footballers, will no doubt influence our lexicon also. But I think our habits of speaking, adapted, will survive.

# Owen Campbell

*Owen Campbell (32) works in Marketing and Public Relations for Paisley Partnership, Scotland's most dynamic and innovative organisation in the Social Inclusion field. A graduate of both the Universities of Ulster and Stirling, he hails from Hamilton.*

I did most of my growing up in the seventies when we had real heroes. Archie Gemmill, Alan Rough, Ally McLeod. Your name didn't have to start with an A, but it helped. Heroes of the seventies – A-List and top notch in every way. Your duty was to collect World Cup wall charts, filled in after every match; button badges; key rings; Pannini sticker albums; and skinned knees from playing football in the streets.

Your team was the one in the dark-blue jersey with the huge yellow and red badge on the left breast. The white diamonds down the sleeves that peeled off with one pull of the dangling thread. At family parties you dueted with your sister to 'Mull of Kintyre' but only after slaps and threats followed by crying and screaming (unfortunately that was me, not my sister). Your aunts dutifully lined up to take photos or cine footage that you know will one day come back to haunt you.

In case you haven't guessed yet, I am a boy, oh, and Scottish. A species of an era forever scarred by learning to be Scottish the hard way. The promise of greatness, the hope, the expectation, the belief, then the despair, the misery, a brief flicker of hope once more, then crushing disappointment. Choosing misery over joy, obscurity over legend, infamy over exhaltation, grasping gut-wrenching defeat from the gaping jaws of a long-cherished dream of victory. Scotland the brave, my arse. This is us. This is who we are. This is our choice.

In the words of Ewan McGregor, Mark Renton (or was it Irvine Welsh?): 'It's shite being Scottish.' I am not yet old enough to use phrases like 'it wasn't like that in my day', but it wasn't. Where did it all go wrong, or did it? We used to be Saturday night superstars, legends in our own drinking time. The tunes could be in Maryhill or Nitshill but they echoed Memphis and Nashville. We could be Frank or Patsy or The King, timeless and enduring. Now we settle for Popstars and False Idols. Gareth or Whatshisname.

In today's Scotland, nothing is real anymore. We don't build anything, we don't create anything. We answer phones. People invest here because we have nice accents. They take our subsidies and shaft us. And we let them, again and again and again. An MSP lives on benefits for Lent as an experiment and finds out it's crap being poor. A week later we glory in finding out who's up and who's down in a list of the country's 1,000 richest people. What do we get? A puppet parliament for the puppet people, the only issue being 'Who pulls the strings?' You would laugh if this wasn't so fucking real.

Don't give me the sentimentalists, traditionalists, nationalists and political apologists with their 'who's like us', the ninety-minute patriots, the lovable drunken Scots, welcomed wherever we go, routine. People all around the world love us because we are crap and we just can't see it. Second rate, second best, second fiddle, at least that what we've been told. No threat to anyone and definitely NOT ENGLISH! Is that all we aim to be? Do we have such low expectations? Apparently so!

Failure is not the killer; we are used to that. It's the hope that gets you every time. But you can never stop hoping. Without hope you will die and I put that second best to not dying, every time.

Truth is, we are strong, proud and resilient. We have brains, skills and character. We have a history of creativity, invention and resourcefulness. We have a cultural and historical legacy that stands comparison with any nation on earth, despite being a tiny off-shoot of England's dying Empire.

At the start of this new century, it is time to grow up, move out and find a place of our own. We must stop defining ourselves as what we are not and start looking more closely at who we are or who we want to be. In short, it is time to take responsibility.

Apathy is no longer an option. John F. Kennedy famously said: 'Ask not what your country can do for you, ask what you can do for your country.' Everyone has a contribution to make and our infant parliament must take the lead. We must relearn the true meaning of words like community, democracy, tolerance and responsibility, create a society where wealth is divided more evenly and everyone has opportunities to be what they want and do what they want to do.

We must build a society comfortable with being multifaith, multirace, where actions speak louder than words and politicians remove their snouts from the trough long enough to serve the people who employ them. I think this used to be known as socialism – small 's'. Call me naive in believing in and espousing some kind of idealistic vision, but you must believe in some kind of 'vision thing' or society doesn't work. In the words of the great Memphis philosopher, 'I just can't help believin'.'

# Eddie Clark

*A decade's worth of retail bookselling took Eddie Clark from Aberdeen to Glasgow to Stirling, among other places, but he now edits books with an academic publisher in Edinburgh. A founder-member of Desperado Theatre Company, he is also secretary of Murrayfield–DAFS Cricket Club; however, being married with a young daughter, too, he hasn't much play-time to himself these days.*

You'll sometimes hear me saying 'aye', but not 'och aye the noo',
And maybe now and then 'forbye' – and even 'gardyloo!' –
I've not a braid Scots tongue, though. I am really quite RP.
You'd likely classify me more E. Nesbit than Rab C.
Yet once a lady told me I possessed a lovely lilt
That spoke to her of heather and the waggle of the kilt,
Of Edinburgh Castle and a plate of steaming porridge.
(This happened when I worked in books at Watterstane's in Norwich –
The lady, let me say, was old enough to be my grannie.)
And yet I would have uttered 'can't' in preference to 'cannae'.
  Ah d'a ken if ye'd cry that bein' Scottish.

My people have been Scottish folk through countless generations,
From Caithness and from Fife – my cousin Hamish had the patience
To do a family tree once. Well! the bodies he uncovered:
Those nobles from Barnbougle and that Provost of the Burgh
Of Stirling. One granddad I had, a man of letters, he
Commissioned theologians via his imprint, T&T.
The other one (Edina-trained, a student medic star
Who later left for Canada) helped build the CPR.

And then there's unassuming me, a not-bad job held down,
Commuting every morning from my humble seaside town.
     Ah d'a ken if ye'd cry that bein' Scottish.

But listen! It's in London I was born – you should be told.
I didn't breathe in Scottish air until some two months old,
And in my youth attended one of London's nicest schools.
In truth my background hints at my suspension twixt twa stools.
In birth and education I could play for England's team,
But who can ever justly try denying men their dreams?
Flash back – a history master says, 'You stupid Jocky shit!'
I'd just been celebrating Bannockburn, so asked for it,
No doubt, in the back row; but nonetheless I feel at class
That day I suffered something for the country of my past.
     Ah d'a ken if ye'd cry that bein' Scottish.

And now dear Scotia is my present. She's my future too.
The truth, of course, is not so black and white or white and blue.
The Scottish blood is mixed with English, Welsh, and let's be fair:
The Picts, though non-existent now, were my sincere forebears.
I've flown the flag at Murrayfield, worn the Braveheart face;
'O Flower of Scotland' I can sing; but see the *Selkirk Grace*? –
That's not a thing I'm often quoting. But when I hae meat,
No matter if it's haggis, bridie, deep-fried, I shall eat!
Some days, I love the Union: it's the way that we should be.
On other days I yearn to see our country breaking free . . .
     Ah d'a ken if ye'd cry that bein' Scottish.

# Robert Crawford

*Robert Crawford's most recent collection of poems is* Spirit Machines *(Cape, 1999). With Mick Imlah, he edited* The New Penguin Book of Scottish Verse *(2000).*

## Wund

The wind blows hard down the Royal Mile, blethers round Mallaig and the toty ballerinas of Unst. The Scottish A-wind from Atlantic and Arctic, heading for Belgium, then changing into the dowie wund of France. The wind blaws hard – inspires you and takes away your breath.

I like how our new parliament was sketched out using twigs and leaves. How it grew from old boats and photographs of puddles. How Enric Miralles' surname flutters in English, flapping like a flag between 'miracle' and 'mirage'. I wish I had met him, but the snell wind has blown him away.

The wind blew down Donald Dewar, standing-stone thin, our parliament's First Millionaire. It ruffled the pages of every rare book in his carelessly loved, *Trainspotting*-free library.

The wind took Henry McLeish, a minor footballer. At the building site of the new parliament a dozy easterly soughs and danders, then spins in hail off the Forth.

When I was wee I hardly noticed the wind. I never registered how it captured Hamilton, then blew over to Brussels that woman called Madame Ecosse. The wind strips tenement roofs, capsizes dinghies off Harris, scours away Stalin's granny and William Wallace, but the newness of it blows in new breath.

I like best the wee cyclones of the larynx, the ones that come out as a playground yell or a poem: deft breezes of Mairi Nighean, Alasdair Ruaidh, a Force Ten called Robert Burns.

In the champagned, douce public relations offices of The New Scotland, all double-glazed and chamoised with a snobby dash of royalty, the poet is the traitor who lets in the sly north wind. On terraces and in discos where deals are done, where hard men and hard women chant their mantras, the traitor-poet, un-noticed, gusts away their clothes, leaving them in the open, cold, nervous hands cupped over shrivelled tits and willies.

The wind blew Muriel Spark to Umbria, Big Tam to Hollywood, J. K. Rowling to Auld Reekie. The wind blows here, but it is not Scottish. Policy advisors think they can bag it and sell it.

The wind blew all the Dollies from the fields, blasted the Cold War back to Scotland, cutting off the East from the West. The gusts blow the cities one way and the countryside in the opposite direction. Though Max has whistled its farewell to Stromness, Kathleen Jamie spoken it, and Douglas Gordon examined it frame by frame, no one yet has sequenced the genome of the West Sands wind.

Let gales blow Glasgow down to Kirkcudbright, Croftfoot to Barra Head. Give us then a storm so gentle it feels like big, five-year-old Chandra blowing a grouse feather softly off the back of her hand.

Set barometers on top of the White and Brown Caterthuns. Hoist an anemo-meter high over East Kilbride. Think of all the wind that has blown round Bishop Elphinstone's outside tomb, hauled long ago from Italy, all carved, finely worked and glorious; just too big to get through the chapel door. Double all those blashes. Add on the tradewinds Hercules Linton summoned, blowing his *Cutty Sark* to Oz and back in double quick time. Add the result to a Leuchars jet's slipstream. That should do for the moment, this moment. That should be enough inspiration.

# Tam Dalyell

*Tam Dalyell, MP for West Lothian, 1962–83; for Linlithgow, 1983–present; Father of the House of Commons, 2001–.*

The late John Strachey, who was Member of Parliament for Dundee until his death in 1963, wrote a seminal book called *The End of Empire*. He examined what Trotsky called 'the Belgianisation of Britain'. Strachey eloquently pointed out, with numerous examples, how we had begun to look in on ourselves and take far less interest in the world around us than the previous four or five generations.

The Scots had played a major part in the process of Britain going out into the world – mostly as engineers and builders rather than Pro-Consular rulers. This was the real Scottish diaspora. When I go abroad, I feel part of the Scottish diaspora myself for family reasons and, curiously, feel more of a Scot in Latin America or Arabia than in Scotland itself – not an unusual phenomena.

One incident brought home to me how the British had changed, and not for the better. My bride, Kathleen and I, in January 1964 were on honeymoon in Egypt. When we were in bed, during our last night in Cairo, there was a knock on the door and an Egyptian asked me to get dressed because the President would like to see me – albeit I had not asked for a meeting with him or any government minister. I was driven out to President Nasser's house in Heliopolis and taken into a big room. Two minutes later, Gamal Abdul Nasser swept in and opened what turned out to be a most friendly conversation with the words, 'We know about you, that your mother and father both spoke Arabic – why don't you?' I stammered a promise that I would try! The Scots of a previous generation were wonderfully well-travelled, and more 'sympathique', as the French would say, than the more aloof English. I am proud to think of myself as a legatee of the Scottish diaspora.

# Fauzia Davidson

*Fauzia Davidson is British by nationality, Scottish by culture, Bangladeshi by ethnicity. She lives in Edinburgh and works in science research and education.*

I arrived in Scotland on 4 November in the swinging 1960s era, an infant transported from a poor, tropical, Muslim country, then at war. It was cold and foggy and I still remember the shock and puzzlement of my first bonfire night on an East Kilbride housing estate. We later moved to Newton Mearns, where, perhaps inevitably, my best friends were Jewish. We were together in our exclusion from school church services. Of course, everyone joined in together for the non-religious traditional activities like school concerts.

My memories of this time are very happy. There were long summer holidays playing with all the neighbourhood children, roaming in the woods, cycling on country roads, weeks of freedom when the only contact with adults seemed to have been at mealtimes. Hallowe'en was knocking on every door in the area and returning home with large quantities of nuts and fruits. I found later that this was a real west of Scotland experience.

My secondary school education was in Edinburgh, where my school friends were a mix of Scottish, English, part-French and returned ex-pat from Africa. The whole school experience, for me, was excellent. The teachers were young and enthusiastic; the schools were well run and supported. It was still the pre-Thatcher era.

This was also a time when the Scottish education system was considered among the best in the world. I feel privileged to have had that experience. This is one of the best aspects of my life and something to which I still aspire to live up to.

It became a constant source of mutual surprise to discover how much broader my education experience was than that of my contemporaries from south of the border.

It was when I went to live in Surrey, during Margaret Thatcher's second parliament, that I first became conscious of my Scottish culture. (Although I had previously travelled across Europe by inter-rail and visited the USA.) My first impression about going to live in England was, unfortunately, their backward home-buying system. If there is one thing the Scots can feel unquestionably superior about, it is the Scottish legal system, from my own admittedly limited experience.

While in the heartland of Thatcherism, I saw the 'poll' tax being implemented north of the border. I witnessed then that it was only when it was brought to their own homes south of the border that 'they' realised how iniquitous the policy was.

In the six years of living and working in Surrey, I never lost that feeling of defending 'Scottishness' from the ignorance and demeaning attitude of people so close to the influence of the Westminister Parliament. This generated an impression that our largest partner in the Union often fails to acknowledge when a smaller partner makes a disproportionately large contribution.

Viewing life in Scotland from both sides of the border seems to have opened my mind to the treasures of culture and heritage, as well as to flaws and deterioration. Certainly, devolution in Scotland was well earned. Thank you, Mrs Thatcher and English Conservatives, you pushed Scotland to demand more autonomy! Now it is for all of us who live and work here to make a success of devolution, to uphold the qualities for which Scotland is well regarded and to make progress to improve our society and environment.

I have revisited the country of my birth and seen extraordinary similarities. The beautiful countryside, the good qualities of the ordinary people are marred by petty political spoiling tactics and the damage that remote decision making causes. There are reasons for hope and pessimism in many a small country.

On the subject of racism, I can give you my own very personal experience. I think I have been very lucky and generally accepted. The truly Scottish family I have married into have not only never given me any cause for upset, they have taken me as one of their own. I have not had to earn this.

I have experienced racial abuse ranging from trivial childhood taunts to sly cowardice, but only rarely. I think my obvious participation in Scottish culture deters strangers from questioning my rights as an individual. Indeed, I have received an especially warm reception when abroad, and from Europeans in particular, because of the Scottish connection.

What can I give back to my adopted country? Just to be a participating person in the community of this country, including self-criticism as well as celebration, acknowledging the past as well as progressing forward.

# Isla Dewar

*Isla Dewar is a novelist. She was born in Edinburgh and now lives in Fife with her husband, a cartoonist illustrator. She has written six novels, one of which has been adapted for the screen. She is working on her seventh book.*

I blame it on the potato. The famed fatalistic Scottish outlook – that mix of sudden surges of pride and outright pessimism – can be put down to a vegetable. Or rather some of the nutrients it contains. The Scots are naturally fatalistic. Is it ingrained Presbyterianism makes us so swift to embrace doom? It was all John Knox's fault. I don't think so. I think we were like that before he came along. We were ripe for his preachings. Look at all those tiny cottages in backwater glens, facing away from the view. It might be they turned their back on the driving winds, rain and snow, but other civilisations in similar dire climes coped. It might be they were occupied by people who toiled in that view, and were sick of the sight of it. But, it seems to be more, that Scottish thing, you shouldn't enjoy yourself, totally, sensually. You'd get your comeuppance for doing that.

Blame the weather. It can be dreich (no other word gets it better). Blame the diet. Despite the fresh veg and fruits, the olive oils I see people buying in supermarkets, we have the reputation of having one of the worst diets in the world. We apparently live on mutton pies and deep-fried Mars Bars. Fact is, up till about 1707, while the clan chiefs may have dined in some splendour, the vast majority of Scots ate exactly as their ancestors had done for thousands of years. Very little meat. Their fish was usually salted or smoked. But mostly what they ate was made from oats. There was virtually no vitamin C.

Early eighteenth century, enter the potato, and that vital vitamin. It was vitamin C that caused the whole upheaval in Scottish history when the potato was introduced into our diet. After some initial protests (there were riots in Argyll), we couldn't get enough of them. Then in 1846 came the blight, and horrendous starvation that opened the way for the opinion that the population of the Highlands was too big for the area's resources. And that gave power to the elbows of those who thought they should be cleared to make way for sheep. Of course the reason why the Highlands were (it's hard to believe now) overcrowded was the potato. The sudden flush of vitamin C into our dour systems had caused the population explosion that led to thousands of people moving into the towns and cities, where they would often deny themselves that their children could be educated. Scotland became famed for its education system. It was in school that I had the beginnings of my awareness of being Scottish. Seven years old, steaming slowly, in an overheated classroom, white-knuckling my ruler, I discovered what shilpit, peelie-wally beasts the English were. They apparently cheated at Culloden. At everything they won, in fact. While the Scots were tough, hardy and artful. My teacher, a stocky man, who kept his trousers in place with a tweedy tie knotted firmly round his waist, was nationalistic to the point of racism. He wouldn't get away with his ebullient political incorrectness nowadays, which is a pity, for he filled his pupils with a fervent pride in their Scottishness. He backed his claim of the Scots as the master race with lists of achievements and inventions, asserting that everything beneficial to humankind from the fountain pen to penicillin to the bicycle had a Scottish brain behind it.

But there was an undertow to this fervour. A glorifying of fatalism. Martyrdom was good for you. Pampering yourself in any way whatsoever would lead to your downfall. The maxim behind this was the oft repeated: what's for you will not go past you. This was usually coupled with: as long as you're happy. That's the main thing. This was drummed into me by my mother who said, 'Well, John Logie Baird may well have invented the television, but was he happy?' I didn't know. But suspected he wasn't.

Through all this, I was smacked on the side of the head for using national words I love.

Wabbit – so much more than tired. It's aching and wilting.

Breeks – no, not mere trousers. But trousers that have become beloved.

Baffies – only the uninitiated think they're slippers. Slippers are but apprentice baffies. Baffies are worn, warm. You feel the comfort as they enfold your feet, and know you're home.

Being Scottish, then, was a baffling mix of pride, enforced to the point of propaganda, and shame at the language that I loved to speak.

In the mid-seventies, during the first run at devolution, all this was discussed in newspaper columns with much chestbeating. Scottish angst was exposed. And we learned to deal with it, laugh at it. Though we didn't get our parliament. Well, the English cheated.

At last we have. Young though it is, I have faith it will prove worthy. We have music, literature, art that is celebrated throughout the world. I live in a country I love, in a landscape that thrills me. Proud? You bet. But really, for me, and all the Scots I know, being Scottish is something that I enjoy.

# Owen Dudley Edwards

*Owen Dudley Edwards was born in Dublin on 27 July 1938 and lived there until 1959, after which he studied and worked in the USA for six years. He came to Scotland in 1966 with his American-born wife (née Bonnie Lee), making their first home in Aberdeen. Since 1968 they have lived in Edinburgh. His next book is* British Children's Literature in World War II.

To be Scottish is to belong to an imaginary country. That is an enviable condition of citizenship.

The country is ancient, diverse, multi-vocal.

Its monarchs (when it had them) were rulers not of Scotland but of the Scots. It is a people's country.

Its Declaration of Arbroath in 1320 is the oldest nationalist document in history, and it asserts a people's right to rule themselves for which it chooses rulers whom it repudiates if they prove unworthy.

Unworthiness above all lay in accepting subordinate status to another country, which then meant England, and later might have been France, and in various imaginations might from time to time have been Russia, America or Ireland.

I put in Ireland because it is my birthplace, and birthplaces, or ancestral roots, sometimes claim noisy priorities in loyalty. Some Scots found that circumstances cast doubt on the Scottishness of some Irish-descended Scots. The question may not have been asked politely, but it was not inappropriate. Ireland did mean more to many Scots of Irish origin than Scotland, especially when they would not admit to themselves that they would not return to Ireland. But the whole paragraph can be rewritten with equal truth when we substitute 'England' and 'English' for 'Ireland' and 'Irish'. All Scotland asks of the English and Irish is to know they are in Scotland.

The mountains break the country into fragments and the islands multiply themselves into myriads and a people consisting of peoples was born.

Arthur's Seat bathes in the multitudes of my fellow Edimbourgeoisie in amiable majesty, and if the most prominent posterior upon it was not the once and future king's, it could have been: the oldest surviving poem from here is in Welsh, Aneirin's *Y Gododdin*.

Nobody knows what language first produced the name whence 'Edinburgh' derives.

The king may well still sleep somewhere under the Seat, legend having testified to his slumber among his knights somewhere, and Wales being much more firmly peripatetic than Brigadoon.

*Regnum quondam et futurus*, if not *Rex*.

I am of Ireland, and Bonnie Lee, my wife, is of the United States of America, and we made our first home here after our marriage thirty-five years ago, and found it meant that neither of us significantly oppressed the other with our cultures since Scots culture was ours together to discover, absorb and invent.

Both of our countries of origin like to think of themselves as demotic in somewhat different ways: hers is the land of Lincoln and Woody Guthrie, mine the land of Eoghan Ruadh Ó Súilleabháin and Oscar Wilde, four demotic voices.

But Scotland identifies itself by a demotic voice: Burns. Scotland in the twentieth-century reinvented itself with a demotic voice recovering from the national symbol at Burns Supper, Hugh MacDiarmid's *A Drunk Man Looks at the Thistle*. A nation asserting superiority is an improvement on other spellings, and a linguistic manifesto in sublime art arising from acute hangover is an agreeable change of nightmare from which history is trying to revive.

For us anyway, Scotland offered a culture adopting us and into which our children were born, without problems of allegiance to improbable heads of state or governments of sufficient transparency, since the preoccupations of these entities were not with the imaginary country or the uncrowned people.

For me to be a Roman Catholic in Scotland was at first to be a second-class citizen, on much better terms than my ancestors had been in eighteenth-century Ireland, but second-class status for Scottish Catholics vanished when the Scots took the Pope to their General Assembly Halls and the Pope spoke better Scots-Gaelic than English. Anyhow, Scottish Presbyterianism and Scottish Roman Catholicism are very similar – formerly in their puritanism, today in their populism. Their clerics elbow their own way forward rather than dignify the state by reliance on it. They do very much the same thing as one another, such as when the Church of Scotland defied the Secretary of State and hosted a constitutional convention to demand real devolution, and the Catholic Bishops told the devolved parliament it should scrap nuclear weapons regardless of having so far been given too narrow a remit.

In any case, I discovered I had become Scottish long before I arrived here. To be Scottish was to enter the world of Scottish imagination. To be Scots is to be told by Aneirin and Gavin Douglas, William Dunbar and John Knox, William Robertson and Robert Burns, Walter Scott and Robert Louis Stevenson, Arthur Conan Doyle and John Davidson, J. M. Barrie and Sorley Maclean, James Redpath and James Connolly, Helen Cruikshank and Muriel Spark, John Buchan and David Daiches, Hugh MacDiarmid and Norman MacCaig, Michael Grieve and Dorian Grieve that you are welcome, and make yourself at home.

# Kevin Dunion

*Kevin Dunion has been Chief Executive of Friends if the Earth Scotland since 1991. He has travelled extensively with Oxfam and as the head of FoE International, campaigning on global environmental issues. He is formerly the editor of* Radical Scotland *magazine, and is author of* Troublemakers: The Struggle for Environmental Justice in Scotland *(forthcoming).*

Lipsmacking, Glasgow kissing, *Trainspotting*, glo'al stoppinn', Sunday Posting, tartan tatting, first footing, wanderlusting, bloody minding, faither kenning; wha's liking Scotland.

I live now on the Firth of Forth's shore at Cellardyke, Fife. It used to be said that there were old folk here who, year after year, never bothered to walk the few hundred yards into the contiguous and thus rival community of Anstruther. At the same time among their midst were sailors who were famous for having raced tea clippers from the Tropics, and whalers who brought back huge jawbones as entrance arches from the coldest waters. Scotland is like that – hame'll dae me, and at the same time surprised to still find yourself here.

I have travelled all over the world, and have always lived in Scotland. To be accurate, I have only lived in a geographically compact portion – Clackmannanshire, Fife and Edinburgh. My affinity is with people who have grown up among mines and engineering works, huddled around the grate in impossible-to-heat homes or stranded in car-dependent housing schemes. Campaigning or holidaying means I am no native stranger to rural, Highland or island Scotland. But, strange to think, I have probably been more often to Amsterdam than Aberdeen in the last ten years.

As an environmental campaigner I have been informed and inspired by what I have seen overseas. For a start environmentalism does not emerge from a common mould. To be an environmentalist in Estonia was to be a nationalist as the Soviet occupation was the biggest despoiler; in Bulgaria Greens were at the heart of the democracy movement as Cold War communism ravaged the air, land and water; in El Salvador it is to be a peace campaigner, as there can be no popular activism if leaders are cowed by death threats. In the Philippines it is to stand up for indigenous people as Western concepts of property sweep aside cultures which did not claim ownership but only rights to use natural resources. For me, it is impossible to be a Scottish environmentalist and not confront the circumstances by which the quality of life of people in our own poor communities is conditioned or compounded by a degraded environment. Scotland's landscape is more than the picture-postcard hills, glens and lochs, but also cratered opencast mines, mountains of wastes, and the lands contaminated as a legacy of our glory days of being a workshop for the world.

Scotland, you learn, is not unique – rather it has a distinctive experience of universal themes. The environmental injustice faced by those living next to derelict landscapes and polluting industries of central Scotland can find common cause and inspiration from poor and black communities in the USA; crofters with family memories of internal clearance should find empathy with the peasants who are fighting dispossession to make way for cattle ranching in Honduras.

Post-devolution internationalism is dangerous territory and we are reminded that foreign policy is out of bounds, as if communication with the wider world was univocal, channelled through official emissaries in full feathered fig. If our political leaders step beyond our shores it is seen as irrelevant or grandiose. A meeting in Birmingham is business; in Barcelona it's a junket. Being Scottish, we find it difficult to imagine what on earth we have to contribute to big issues such as globalisation. Yet we have made a mantra of wanting our economy to be world class, without looking around us and debating whether it might be better for us and the planet if we focused on stimulating local markets and services.

I take pride in coming from an internationalist Scotland. Not the past colonialism of tea planters, or missionary-geographers. Not the tartan tat and nostalgia, which can afflict a diaspora. (I have run a mile from a St Andrew's Night dinner dance in Bulawayo, and in any case, given my Italian family roots, I wonder what is the Bertolini tartan?)

Instead I admire my contemporaries who were medics in Nicaragua and in Beirut, or teachers in post-revolution Mozambique. There was purpose in Brazilian trades unionists coming here to compare the health effects of working in aluminium smelters; or women's rights activists from Chile learning about women's aid refuges. Now we have people travelling to make the voice of the global citizen heard at international summits on climate change or trade. The common language has been of people challenging the consequences of being on the political, economic or social periphery. I like to be where extremities meet.

Being Scottish for me has always been about being distinctive not apart, being inquisitive not declamatory, and engaged not self-absorbed.

# Donald Findlay

*Donald Findlay QC was born in Cowdenbeath in 1951 and was educated at Harris Academy, Dundee University and Glasgow University. He has been an Advocate since 1975.*

When given an open invitation to write a piece about being Scottish, it is important to define one's starting point.

I come from Cowdenbeath. My nationality is British. I would not expect my dog to eat haggis. In common with most men, I look like a big jessie in a kilt, a garment long since relegated to the far-flung reaches of my wardrobe. Tartan looks best on unwitting tourists with more money than sense. I consider bagpipes should only be played on a heather-clad hillside as far from civilisation as possible.

Our climate is dreich. Summer is usually a Tuesday afternoon, and I miss it.

Our football team is a source of national despair rather than pride. The Tartan Army are not Scottish ambassadors but a bunch of eejits who will go anywhere for a booze up.

'Flower of Scotland' brings a tear to my eye, but then again cringing invariably does. It reminds me of the story of the Irish team that lined up under Jack Charlton. As the anthem sounded a player remarked, 'I hope ours is better than that,' bringing the response, 'It is ours!'

The prospect of independence appals me. Even as the Chairman of the 'No No' campaign at the time of the referendum it gives me no pleasure to note that the Scottish Parliament is the glorified toon council some of us always knew it would be. The level of debate is an embarrassment and English as I know it seems to be a second language for many of the members. Worse still, it is an expensive body which has contributed little to the life of our people.

But am I proud of being Scottish? Deeply! So what for me is the essence of being Scottish?

Our country is as dramatic as it is beautiful, but there are many stunning places in the world. For me, it is the unique spirit of the Scot that makes us what we are and separates us out from every other race on the face of the planet. Like an elephant, it is hard to describe but you know it when you see it. It is a complex and illogical mixture of thrawn, frugal, introspective and parochial with generosity, vision, compassion, genius, wit and an insatiable desire to know what lies over the next horizon.

For a small nation our contribution to the world around us is immeasurable. From science to exploration, medicine to the arts, Scots have been pioneers, innovators, inventors and original thinkers. The great names are known to all, Watt, Fleming, Bell, Smith, Logie Baird, Livingstone, Walter Scott – a truly endless list. How many countries can claim that people will gather in Russia to celebrate their national bard?

But these traits are not confined to the great of the land. Travel to the four corners of the earth and there you will find a Scot. Sit in a bar in an obscure backwater of a country known only to university students of geography and a Scots accent will greet you like a long-lost friend. Quite why the owner is there will remain shrouded in mystery, but if he is not running the place he will know the man who is! You will also find yourself buying the drinks all night and thanking him for the privilege.

The Scot is unfazed by any challenge. I used to marvel at the Rangers supporters who would get on a bus, the luggage masquerading as poly bags, and head for places they had never heard of. Some years ago, two of the Bears turned up for a friendly game in Israel. When asked how they had achieved this, they replied casually, 'Biblical tours.' When asked what they thought of the Holy Land, the profundity of the response was undeniable. 'When you've seen one Golan Heights, you've seen them all!'

The Scot will always give generously of his best, inadequate as this may be. I recall asking for directions in Inverness. A local, having greeted me with that most esoteric of salutations, 'It's yersel,' informed me that my destination was up the hill past the white house with the red roof, only it wasn't there any more!

We are ever ready to improve ourselves. A colleague of mine, a man noted for thrift, had a young advocate working with him in a long and complex trial. After the verdict, he inquired solicitously, 'And what do you feel you have learned from me?' The lad thought for a moment before replying, 'The value of a pound!'

I delight in the way we treat all our fellow human beings as equals. Status, power, even wealth, mean little to the Scot. I vividly recall parking my car in Aberdeen, dressed in the full regalia of black jacket, striped trousers and the bowler hat when I was approached by the attendant, a man to whom humour was clearly an alien concept. 'How much to park for the whole day? I will be in the High Court,' I inquired with what I thought was a suitable degree of pomposity. He looked me up and down, yon way, and put me firmly in my place with the rejoinder, 'But fit if ye get time and dinnae come back fir yer car?'

I am convinced that the true Scot genuinely believes that man to man the world o'er shall brithers be for a' that. It is that, more than anything else, that makes me proud of my fellow Scots and proud to be one of them.

My own philosophy of life, and one I heartily commend, was provided by a Scot.

There was to be a dinner at 10 Downing Street. Alas the Civil Service could not work out the seating plan, being confronted by such problems as the comparative status of the Prime Minister of Ruritania and the King of Transylvania. It was decided that Sir Alec Douglas-Home would know. After all he was not only Prime Minister, he was a toff. The Cabinet Secretary explained the dilemma but was baffled when the PM shrugged it off. To a plaintive, 'But Prime Minister …!', Sir Alec responded, 'Those who matter do not mind, and those who mind do not matter.'

Not bad.

# *John H. Fitzsimmons*

*Father John H. Fitzsimmons is parish priest at the Church of St John Bosco, Erskine, Renfrewshire, and priest of the Roman Catholic Diocese of Paisley. He was former Rector of the Scots College, Rome, and former Chair of ICEL (International Commission for English in the Liturgy). He is a graduate of the Gregorian University, Rome (Ph.L., 1959), and graduate of the Biblical Institute, Rome and Jerusalem (LSS, 1965).*

## 'It is never difficult'

It was P. G. Wodehouse, I believe, who wrote:

> It is never difficult to distinguish between a Scotsman with a grievance and a ray of sunshine.

For some odd reason we Scots have been portrayed as pugnacious and only grudgingly honorary members of the human race, ready to make allowances for others. There is another fallacy on our own part, and that is that we are friendly, open, welcoming, and have not a trace of racism in any of our bodies. As ever, *virtus in medio stat*, i.e. the truth is somewhere in the middle.

I am a product of the industrial south-west of Scotland, born just after the outbreak of the Second World War. My earliest recollections of life on this planet are of air-raid shelters, ration books, and all the 'romance' of life in a tenement building in the West End of Paisley. Looking on the bright side, at least it was not the East End. I got to support the Ferguslie cricket team, not the Kelburne.

My father's people came from Armagh in Northern Ireland: as might be expected they were fiercely republican in their view of their native land. Never, to the best of my recollection, did I ever hear mention of violence and the IRA and all that; I assume we all had enough on our hands with Hitler and Hirohito. Those were the days when men and women were coming back to a country that was trying to give substance to the old promise ('A Country Fit for Heroes') which had so deceived their parents in 1918.

My mother's people, on the other hand, originally came from Val de Loire in France. They were Protestant Huguenots; I am indebted to various distant relatives for tracing the family tree. So it was that my mother was baptised as an Episcopalian, brought up as a Presbyterian, and eventually became a Roman Catholic.

Never, ever in their lives did Mum and Dad describe themselves as anything other than Scots, and I was taught to do the same. Actually I was not taught; I took it in by osmosis.

I am an only child, but I cannot say that I was 'spoiled'; there was nothing there to 'spoil' me with. I was educated to within an inch of my life, in the days when the Scottish education system was the envy of the world. The Roman Catholic Church continued this process, both in Rome and Jerusalem. Renfrewshire Education Committee (as it then was) saw to it that I was well provided for, possibly recognising a 'Lad O' Pairts'.

I have never been anything but grateful to my native land because it made me what I am. However, there are times when I wonder if we Scots have not yielded to the temptation to settle for the image of what we once were and refused to grapple with what, in fact, we still are. I never cease to be amazed by the insularity of our American cousins; but at least they live on a continent, and might be forgiven for not seeing beyond it. My problem is with Scots (and, sometimes, I have caught myself at it) who cannot see beyond the confines of this small country of ours. This has nothing to do with nationalism in politics; it has everything to do with a ferocious attachment to a land which is beautiful (but all too polluted), maddening (weather-wise), sophisticated (and primitive at the same time), capable of great things (and forever falling on its face).

Of all the doctrines associated with the European Union, by far the most attractive is subsidiarity. It means this: never interfere from above if those below are managing fine by themselves; if they get into trouble – then help them out. The Roman Catholic Church invented the idea; unfortunately it has not begun to learn how to practise it. The same might be said of our beloved restored parliament. I look forward to the day when I can wake up to find the Executive does *not* have an 'initiative'. Maybe then we will get down to carrying forward some of the initiatives we are juggling with already. If this means a moratorium on all public utterance from politicians – and church leaders, for that matter – then not only 'So Be It' but 'Praise Be To God'.

# Douglas Fraser

*Douglas Fraser has been Scottish at least since his birth in Edinburgh in 1964. Educated in Scotland, India, England, Wales and the USA, he returned to Scotland to be a journalist for various newspapers, currently as Political Editor of the* Sunday Herald.

Something or somebody else must be to blame. The boss. The rich. The poor. The central belt. Lairds. Edinburgh lawyers. Subsidy junkies. Catholics. Protestants. The poll tax. The current Scotland football manager. Men. Wummin. Lanarkshire politicians. People who blame other people.

But mainly, we like to blame the English. We define ourselves by what we're not. And above all, we're not English (except, confusingly, for the 7 per cent who are). Yet the English can barely define themselves. They are only just learning the difference between being English and British, figuring out whether there's more holding them together than warm beer and cricket, and reclaiming the St George Cross from racist bootboys. So we're stuck with the paradox of defining ourselves by not being a people who don't know who they are. That way we can blame them for pretty much everything, including both our identity and our lack of identity.

But to misquote that great patriot Mel Gibson, we shall only be truly free when we cast off the yoke of Anglophobia. He forgot to mention that we should stop binge drinking and exercise more. For the start of the third millennium, with our sparkly new parliament, it seems as good a time as any to focus on the ills in our own land.

And the main ill? The weather. Obvious when you think about it. We have lots of weather and lots of vocabulary for it – dreich, smirr, drookit – though curiously no words for scorching sunshine. Weather is central to who we are. We have a BBC forecaster called Gale. A former Scottish Television weatherman is now a Member of the Scottish Parliament, the reassuring pastels of Lloyd Quinan's old map now turned red with radical nationalism. Billy Connolly became a national icon by singing the praises of welly boots.

Growing up in Edinburgh, it seemed only natural that the wind whipped through you in any season, that haar could descend in June while the rest of the country dug out its twenty-year-old summer gear and turned a shade of painful puce. Our summer holidays were Hebridean, a parental pilgrimage to initiate the next generation in the soul of Scotland. Known as white settlers by locals – though they were pretty peelie-wally too – we learned survival skills; stocking up sufficient Milanda bread in case of cancelled ferries, or stretching a game of Monopoly over several rain-lashed days. But the key skill was finding Radio Four among the offerings from Hilversum and Luxembourg on the long-wave dial – this in search of the shipping forecast. The ordinary forecast let you know what had already passed overhead on its way to the mainland, but the shipping forecast offered up the raw data of meteorology, in an incantation of sea areas heaving with great highs and lows, gale warnings and barometric readings. From Viking and Forties clockwise round the softies' bits in the south, to the mighty engine rooms of Scotland's weather. Straddling Malin and Hebrides, we awaited the worst that Rockall could throw at us from the west. No icing in south-east Iceland, a voice in London would reassure, before reporting the visibility at Tiree. Thirty-eight miles was the ultimate. Next stop, heaven.

Aged ten, a different summer adventure took me to Toronto, where relatives laughed as I set out in beautiful sunshine clutching my cagoule. Subsequent holidays have taken increasing numbers of us to sunnier climes, waking each day to the novelty of … another perfect Mediterranean morning. It's there that we have begun to realise that life doesn't have to be as it is. The contrast has taught us how much we are a people shaped more by that great mass of water to the west than by the great ocean of people to the south. We are required to accept whatever the mighty north Atlantic throws at a coastline it has already deeply eroded. The Gulf Stream is our main import. From the palm tree-fringed lagoons of the Caribbean, past the fog banks of Newfoundland, it warms, waters and wallops us. Life without it would be unbearable, though life with it isn't exactly ideal either.

That maritime climate gives life only one certainty – the good times can't last.

Just as every cloud has a silver lining, every ray of Scottish sunshine has a cloud. A blue sky this morning will probably not even last until dusk, and the chances of it returning tomorrow are remote. Good times never go unpunished. In the words of Alistair Reid's poem, 'Scotland', 'We'll pay for it, we'll pay for it, we'll pay for it!'

That is our mindset. Life in Scotland is accompanied at all times by preparation for things to get worse, for the rain to fall on our nation's parade. We carry through our lives a tartan scarf, a cagoule and a grudge.

# Simon Frith

*Simon Frith is Professor of Film and Media Studies at Stirling University.*

## Not Being Scottish

I moved to Scotland in middle age and expect to live the rest of my life here. I voted for devolution and don't spend much time worrying about my identity. Scotland is certainly a different country from England (rather than being, as the BBC would have it, a British region) but that is primarily for geographical rather than historical reasons. I'm yet to be convinced that there is such a thing as 'Scottish identity' although there is certainly a Scottish obsession with how Scottish-ness is represented, and people in Scotland do seem more than usually concerned with their own national myths.

Scots' most self-deluding belief is in their native competence: the myth of the Taciturn Engineer, one might call it, after a familiar Scottish figure in British films, the man who gets on with making things work while everyone else is posturing. In her *Sunday Herald* column of 18 November 2001, Muriel Gray cites a book by Arthur Herman, *How Scots Invented the Modern World*, 'a stirring and moving account of how western Europe's poorest nation created our world and everything in it'. In his speech to Scottish Financial Enterprise's 2001 dinner (reproduced in its entirety in *Business am*, 1 October 2001), Ian Ritchie notes that 'The fact that all current leaders of the UK's political parties in Westminster – all three of them – were born and educated in Scotland doesn't particularly surprise us. It is normal to hear leaders of industry, finance and medicine around the world speaking with Scottish accents or sporting Scottish names.'

The other side of this story, of course, is that these canny and inventive Scots had to leave their country to make their mark. In Ritchie's words, 'For hundreds of years the Scots with get up and go have got up and gone.' Why should this be? If it's Scottish culture/religion/education that has produced such good entrepreneurs, why don't they flourish in their own country? The answers vary. For Muriel Gray, the problem is the *other* Scotland, 'small-minded, backward-looking, bigoted and parochial' (and now the essence of Scotland's 'tabloid mentality'). For Ian Ritchie, the problem is 'a collective lack of confidence in our own abilities', a Scottish reluctance to take risks. For Andrew Neill, the problem is the dead collective hand of the Scottish establishment, Tory and Labour, religious and secular, stifling bold thought and the pursuit of self-interest.

For an outsider, though, such arguments are confusing. How is it that the typical Scot is simultaneously innovative and cautious, free-thinking and bigoted, scientific and parochial? It may be the function of myth to resolve contradictions, but at some point reality should intrude, and what is obvious to anyone moving to Scotland from elsewhere is that Scotland does not have the best education system in the world (or even in the UK), that it does not have the best health service in Europe (but possibly the worst), and that its legal system is as blinkered as it is self-satisfied.

What's more, there is precious little evidence of the Scots' supposed administrative competence. Every month a different Scottish institution is shown to be badly run: West of Scotland Water and the Scottish Football Association, Glasgow Caledonian University and the University of the Highlands and Islands, the Scottish Qualifications and Authority and the Beatson Oncology Centre, numerous health and police authorities, Scottish Tourism, Scottish Ballet, Scottish Fingerprints, and so on and so on. The trouble with devolution is not that the politicians aren't up to it (because all the good ones went to Westminster) but that the civil servants aren't (because they have yet to emerge from their colonial cocoon).

I came to Scotland to co-direct the John Logie Baird Centre. Baird is another kind of mythical engineer, the unappreciated genius, the inventor of television who despite the tireless PR work of his champions is still 'not properly recognised'. By chance I went to school with the grandson of the man who developed the more efficient form of television that the BBC eventually adopted. Isaac Schoenberg made television work, while as the inventor of public service broadcasting it was John Reith, rather than John Logie Baird, who made the single most important Scottish contribution to twentieth-century history. There isn't a John Reith Centre.

The peculiarly Scottish element of Reith's approach to television and film was his belief that media citizenship should be rooted neither in politics nor commerce but in education and a dedication to the public good. There is a significant Scottish tradition here (John Grierson, Dennis Forman, Stuart Hood, Jeremy Isaacs, Alasdair Milne) which makes me pleased to be in a Scottish media studies department. But all of them left Scotland, of course, and just as well they did. Not because the Scots are small-minded, unconfident or conservative, but because they just can't make things work.

# Sandy Grant Gordon

*Born Glasgow 6 May 1931. Rugby School 1944–9. Queens'
College Cambridge 1949–52. National service Royal Artillery
1952–4. William Grant & Sons Ltd Scotch Whisky Distillers
1954–96.*

Like most Scots, I have a keen interest in my forebears, who they were, and
what they did in their time. My father came from a family that had worked a
croft in the remoteness of the Upper Cabrach in the foothills of the Grampians for
many centuries. A few years back, my wife took a pair of my shoes to a cobbler for
repair. The man looked at the shoes and asked my wife, 'What does your husband
do for a living? He's got shepherd's feet.' If my physique has been so moulded by
my predecessors, it is hardly surprising that my outlook on life bears the same
imprint. I am very much the man who has been taken from the bog, but the bog
remains in the man and I am proud of it.

From my mother's side, I was named after my grandfather Alexander Grant.
He in turn had been named after another Alexander Grant, who with two
brothers had fled from Culloden on the losing side and gone into hiding. One of
the brothers later found his way down to Lancashire with his family and in due
course his two sons prospered in the cotton business and were noted for their
benevolence and generosity. They were immortalised by Charles Dickens as the
Cheeryble brothers in *Nicholas Nickleby.*

This mirrors the experience of the many Scots who have left their native land
to seek better prospects abroad, and, who by dint of hard work and an ability to
get on with other folk wherever they found themselves, succeeded in a great
variety of enterprises. It is now recognised that the overwhelming majority of
Scots went abroad because they wanted to, and were not forcibly ejected. This

means that for three centuries there has been a drain of our more enterprising citizens going abroad to do great things all round the world, while those of us who stayed have not demonstrated as much skill in organising our affairs here at home. It is indeed a paradox that today in Scotland so much is being contributed to our national well being by those who have come from south of the border or from other countries abroad, and who have developed a love of our country every bit as strong as that of native-born Scots.

The developments of modern information technology have made it possible to run businesses from the more remote parts of our country where the working conditions are more congenial than in the main centres of population. There are already signs that this is beginning to start the process of regenerating some of our rural communities. In the central belt our new towns have been successful in getting new industries to take the place of the old heavy industries, which have now virtually disappeared.

We can now see the transformation of some the old derelict sites as at Strathclyde Business Park in North Lanarkshire, where the bings were flattened and a vibrant complex of factories and offices created with an excellent working environment in what used to be one of the dreariest parts of Scotland. Along the Clyde in Glasgow and on the sea front in Edinburgh the plans for urban renewal are well under way. We must hope that all this progress will encourage some of our ex-pats to come back to their homeland to participate in the rebirth of their nation.

While I have always had a passing interest in polities, I learnt long ago that I cannot stand the heat, so I have kept well clear of the kitchen. I am a separatist at heart, and while this is partly emotional, there are some solid arguments to support the case for Scottish independence.

First, I have learnt in the course of nearly fifty years of practical experience that Scottish industry is not well served by Westminster government. Furthermore, there does not appear to be any demand from the Republic of Ireland nor any of the countries of the Commonwealth that have secured their independence to return to their former state. Finally, would it not be better if we could look on the folk south of the border as good neighbours and not as our foreign masters?

# David Greig

*David Greig is a playwright and also co-founder of theatre company Suspect Culture. His work includes* The Architect, Caledonia Dreaming, *and* The Cosmonaut's Last Message. *He currently lives in Fife.*

I was once in Abu Dhabi, during Ramadan, and I was looking for a drink. There was none to be had. However, during my search I was told a story by a Scot who lived and worked in the city. In Abu Dhabi there had once been two hotel bars where the ex-patriots could congregate and take alcohol. There was O'Malley's, an Irish-themed pub, and MacGregor's, a Scottish-themed pub. Both pubs promoted the same Celtic twilight fakery, both served the same beer at the same prices, the staff were equally matched for skill and hospitality, but whilst O'Malley's thrived, full to the brim every night with drinkers from all over the world, MacGregor's had struggled, guttered and eventually burnt out. Even the ex-patriot Scots didn't really want to drink in a Scots-themed bar. In the mind of the drinker, it seems, Irishness represents conviviality, bonhomie, democratic wit and nostalgia. Scottishness, however, speaks of silence, violence, acid tongues and nursed grievances. It's just not something you want to be associated with on a Saturday night.

The Scottish cultural broth contains many ambiguous virtues. We're known to hold to old-fashioned moral values like socialism and religion but are prone to do so with the nit-picking certainty that comes of Protestantism. We are supposedly sage and economical with resources but in fact view everything through the actuarial eye of a nation of bankers. We are egalitarian but we yearn for the safety of mediocrity. We are enterprising but only when we leave the country. We are good losers but we revel masochistically in our own humiliations. We're unsentimental, or is it morbidly pessimistic? My partner's granny used to doom any proposed pleasure trip with the words 'There'll be nowhere to park.' The national reaction to the Miralles parliament building amounts to the same thing.

One need only consider our emblematic product – whisky. I love whisky. But how does it work? The first sip is fiery and hot and like the Proustian madeleine it brings with it memory. Not warm nostalgia but the harder edged memory – almost always a memory of loss. We drink more, hardening our tongue so we lose the flavours and we talk. But where champagne makes you flirty, whisky makes you clear headed – you're clear on one thing, where the wrong is. You can see it everywhere. Particularly in the man you're drinking with. His look, his demeanour, his damn attitude. Finally you've tanked the bottle. You don't even feel drunk. Until you try to stand up, then you fall to the floor, weeping like a jilted bride. This is our national drink.

No nation truly submits to generalisation. There can be no 'we' when writing about Scots. But to the outside world in this age of global branding we inevitably promote a certain image. There is even a government scheme to promote Scottish products abroad called 'Scotland the Brand'. So what is our brand profile? If people do think of us, the Abu Dhabi experience suggests they think of us as spreaders of mild unhappiness, as people who bring down the mood at a party.

For me, 'being Scottish' is simply a metaphorical kilt you wear when you go abroad. It's the expectations your hosts have of you when they meet you off the plane. You can choose to hide behind its comforting shared assumptions or you can lift it up and flash your cultural Calvin Kleins. You can present a Scottishness that is modern, European and young. The trouble is, by suggesting that Scotland is a vibrant nation of clubbers and web designers and so forth, you inevitably disappoint people. Every little country in Europe is a modern vibrant nation of clubbers and web designers. As globalisation homogenises European society the small nations are forced increasingly to hold on to the clichés as the only identity they have. Being Scottish is something I can't avoid but being 'Scottish' is a choice, sometimes I play up to it, sometimes I ignore it, other times I contradict it. Like a woman who sometimes chooses high heels, I know it's cheap but sometimes I feel like being cheap. If it gets you noticed.

# Robin Harper

*Robin Harper is the first Green to even be elected to a Parliamentary Seat in the UK. This success came after fifteen years' campaigning. Robin's previous career was as a teacher, and he has taught in a range of schools from Aberdeen to Kenya. His greatest love is music.*

Whipping winds that freeze your cheeks and bring tears to your eyes. Extraordinary skyscapes. Black clouds with stabbing rays of sunlight fanning out beneath them, laying a glinting golden path on the waves across the rippling wet beach to your feet. Processions of waves that seem to roll in from the distant horizon and then rear and crash upon themselves, sending jets of spume to hang momentarily above their inexorable progress. Seabirds wheeling on great tides of air. Every breath filled with the tang of salt and the rich dark scent of seaweed. The sounds of rounded rocks knuckling underfoot. My first memories – observing how the bleached pebbles on the fringes of Hoy took on a rich and glowing luminescence as they were covered by the incoming tide.

Being Scottish, for me, is an affinity with the landscape and the weather of Scotland as well as its people, culture and history. My first six years were spent in Orkney, making me Orcadian rather than Scottish. I certainly picked up no Scottish culture in my childhood. My parents are English and my accent, in those days, derived from our nearest neighbour's children, who spoke a very broad Belfast Irish. My elder half-brother David was brought up in Northern Ireland and still has a hint of a soft Northern Irish accent. My younger brother Euan is about as English as he could get, and was born in Cheshire. Why do I even consider myself to be Scottish?

My father served King, and then Queen, and country, in the Royal Navy for thirty years. When we left Orkney we stayed in London, Ceylon, London again before, in 1956, my father was posted to RNAS Lossiemouth. I came from that most English of institutions, the 'Boys Only Grammar School', to the co-educational Elgin Academy. I immediately fell in love with the school and several girls, one after the other. There were the same skies and the same winds I remembered from Orkney. I used to walk alone along the cliffs between Lossiemouth and Hopeman with the fulmars skimming the heather below the level of my knees. In a very strong sense I felt I was back home, but the language and the customs, the poetry and the dancing, and subtle differences in the humour and relationships all had to be learnt. Another year in London followed and, despite the fact that I gained the sixth form prizes in History and English and the possibility of a place at Oxford, I elected to apply for Aberdeen.

In my first year I shared digs with the late Arthur Argo, who used to play me 78 rpm recordings that he'd collected of north-east bothy ballads. At first I couldn't understand a word. Six years later, I had learnt the guitar and the Scots language, and was helping Archie Fisher to run Kirkcaldy Folk Club, a performing arena for all the top singers in the Scottish traditional music renaissance of the 1960s.

By 1965 I had three elements of being Scottish: I was born here, the environment was imprinted on my soul and the music and poetry were in my heart. I had gained a sense of Scottish history – a sense of a nation that has done itself more damage than has ever been inflicted on it externally, and of a culture that is genuinely distinctive.

I know I am Scottish because I cannot bear us to be defeated in any sport by any other country, although it is quite acceptable on the odd occasion to lose to the Welsh or, at a pinch, the Irish, our companions on the Celtic fringe. I was associated with the campaign for a Scottish parliament for twenty years, and yet I don't mind when people think I'm English. I was brought up to be English, but whenever I'm asked either here, or south of the border, or anywhere else in the world to define my nationality, I will say Scottish.

Is this important? I certainly don't say it because I feel being Scottish is inherently better than being anything else. I say I am Scottish because it defines me – politically, culturally, emotionally, more accurately than Orcadian, English or European. If I felt any of the latter three definitions were any more accurate, I would be equally proud and happy to adopt them. Deeply and profoundly, there is no other landscape that affects me like the landscape of northern Scotland. A stiffening of the sinews, an immense awe and a little cold crystal ache in the corner of the heart.

# Christopher Harvie

*Dr Christopher Harvie is Professor of British and Irish Studies at the University of Tübingen in Germany. He holds Visiting Chairs at Strathclyde and Aberystwyth, and is Honorary President of the Scottish Association for Public Transport. He has published and broadcast widely on Scottish, British and European history. Edinburgh University Press and Polygon at Edinburgh have published* No Gods and Precious Few Heroes: Scotland Since 1900 *and* The Road to Home Rule, *with Peter Jones. His most recent book is* Scotland: A Short History, *from Oxford University Press.*

## A Letter from Christopher Harvie to Tom Devine

Your letter inviting me to contribute to *Being Scottish* arrived when I was worrying about the very problem. *The Scotsman* told me to observe St Andrew's Day, and in revenge I was making a mental note of some Scottish contributions the world could do without: whisky, football, tobacco, the œuvre of Irvine Welsh, *Braveheart*, the Loch Ness Monster and Rupert Murdoch. A place which lived by peddling addiction? On cue, I found a grubby copy of Alex Trocchi's *Cain's Book* in a bookstall. Our man, Glasgow Italian, is out of his skull with heroin, after bad sex and worse food, in a barge on the Hudson. Manhattan glitters on the horizon with its 'electric castles'. He's talking to Beckett, Camus, Whitman and God. Cain *is* there, the farmer who kills his herdsman brother, the primal social criminal doomed to wander – like Byron, the Master of Ballantrae, Lanark. The chances of redemption are low. Amazing that Trocchi lasted until 1984.

We won't get away from electric castles or Middle Eastern murderers for months, maybe years. For some this invalidates the Scots' douce progress towards governing themselves. But Cain is also kin (Cain=Kin, maybe?) to Grassic Gibbon's megalith men, whose ploughs ended the pastoral Golden Age. So we won't get away from Scotland, either. 'Scotland small? … Our multiform, infinite Scotland *small?*' This almost sensual fascination with the place: qualities of light, stone, water, grass – in Stevenson or Edwin Muir, MacDiarmid or Alasdair Gray – hit the exile. Particularly in Germany, which had nationalism horribly burned out of it, but where the technology and society are being developed which might stop us making the twenty-first century our last. But it needs partners. Scotland is more than a personal correlative; it might be a place of redemption. To use Patrick Geddes' terms, folk, work and place once intersected there, in the eighteen and nineteenth centuries, creating a synergy which changed the world. They could still help reorder it.

Empathising with the place isn't easy. I still find it difficult to speak Alexander Gray's 'Scotland' (1928) without emotion:

> For this is my country,
> The land that begat me,
> And these empty spaces
> Are surely my own,
> And the folk who toil there,
> In the sweat of their faces,
> Are flesh of my flesh
> And bone of my bone.

This, and not the doleful 'Flower of Scotland', ought to be our anthem. Gray was an economist; his Scotland a man-changed land. His 'ghosts/ Of the marsh and the moorland/ Still ride the old marches,/ Despising the plough' suggest that nomadic element: reiver, drover, pedlar, seafarer, mercenary, scholar.

The twentieth was Cain's century: territorial politics provoked two tremendous wars. North Britain, where the elite thought it lived in a global civil society and therefore didn't need self-government, broke in the slump of 1921. The multiethnic kingdom had earlier survived by continual renegotiation: hence the Declarations, Covenants and so on. Now it became Edwin Muir's 'difficult country/here things miscarry'. Muir kept off drugs, though his Glasgow was as awful as Trocchi's. Rather desperately he fashioned a Christian–Jungian Scotland to domesticate Cain and refashion 'place', trying to check a synergy which had got completely out of hand and turned local chances and resources into something global, uncontrollable.

Muir didn't like Motherwell. You're from the Loaning, I'm from Manse Road, in a town whose steel built the world's greatest ships. Then industry disappeared and Muir, getting a foretaste of this in 1935, despaired in his *Scottish Journey*. Cain again, evicting the great herd? You have been more methodical and optimistic: 'measuring the distance', in Raymond Williams' words, involved in people's transitions from rural life to and through the Motherwells – from Highland and Lowland, Ireland and Italy – and into our late forming democracy. The other half of the equation means reconnecting Scotland with the technology and institutions that allow and contain synergy. Coming from an Irish background is valuable: no one whose history includes the 1840s is going to be complacent about 'invisible hands' or, with Ireland's remarkable career since then in mind, despairing about the ability of people to recover and excel. For you, the seductions of Englishness operate only at low power, while the Scots *bourgeoisie*, and I sense them at my elbow, wanted Cain's country, the 'high laughter, loveliness and ease' of the south – college, club, mansion, bank. They often succeeded, overtaking those who were slumped in their comfortable embrace. Did this help Scotland much?

Not a lot, I think. New Labour is probably its last gasp. What passes for its intellect looks north rarely, and comprehends less. Both of us will see our Scotland as hybrid or, as Alex Salmond puts it, 'mongrel', and that also holds for its future: 'Scotland plus …?' On one side there's the openness and resilience of America, something that Henry McLeish plainly finds inspiriting, along with most Scots and Irish. On the other there's Europe: a politics of conservation and negotiation and adaptation, masked by difficult tongues, and terrible precipices when things go wrong. Whitmanite liberty versus Carlyleian work, maybe – but remember the two were once linked, not least through a print-capitalist culture which (largely Scots-run, imperially marketed) could only be called British. Given peace in Ulster, and a Council of the Islands for starters, Britain can be repositioned, I hope, as an alliance of friendly states, and America has become more Europe-like, more diverse; 11 September has only emphasised how its innocence has given way to circumspection. That may help.

The fascination of Scotland is to see this 'flyting' between cultures acted out as something fricative and many-voiced. What Seamus Heaney calls 'the music of things happening' has made being Scots at the beginning of the twenty-first century continuously absorbing. Such privilege means work.

# Gerry Hassan

*Gerry Hassan is Director of Big Thinking, an independent think tank, and has produced a number of books and publications including* Tomorrow's Scotland *(Lawrence and Wishart, 2002) and* The Almanac of Scottish Politics *(Politico's Publishing, 2000).*

## The Long Journey to be Scottish

It was a long time before I realised I was Scottish.

I had a political sense of the world formed by left-wing values long before Scotland ever really entered my mind. I first became aware politically as a small child against the backdrop of the 1972 and 1974 miners' strikes, the blackouts and the general Dunkirk spirit of our backs to the wall that it all inspired. To my parents, both politically aware self-educated working-class people living in a decent, prosperous council estate on the outskirts of Dundee, my father in the Communist Party, my mother, a community activist, the Heath government was the most right-wing nasty form of politics you could imagine and opposed everything they held dear (full employment, looking after those in need).

When the SNP broke through electorally in the seventies, at first I did not understand what they were about. My gut reaction was to ridicule and belittle them as not a 'real' party compared to Labour and the Tories. What I do remember is a sense that they did not play the simple politics of left and right, and that they dared to challenge Labour in its council heartlands, where it had been unopposed for years.

Feeling particularly Scottish did not really register high on my radar. It was not, if I were being honest, until 1987, when in my early twenties, with the poll tax, Scots Tories representation halved at the election and 'the Doomsday Scenario' that I began to think of Scottishness as an important part of my identity – and my political identity.

I realise particular parts of my experience are unique to myself, but a broader political community on the left had a similar journey. It seemed to me in my seventies childhood that Scottishness was something archaic, like an ageing relative or drunk at a party that might embarrass you: the White Heather Club, bad Hogmanay celebrations on the telly, tuneless folk music. By the late 1980s Scottishness had become to me a kind of political resistance to Thatcherism. This was imbued with a moral superiority in relation to the English. They embraced Thatcherism; we rejected it. We opposed tax cuts, privatisation, council house sales; they embraced it. People sang Proclaimers' records and meant them: 'What Do You Do When Democracy Fails You?' was the musical equivalent of *A Claim of Right*.

Fast forward to the beginning of a new century and this seems ridiculous. However, from a future vantage point some of today's certainties might seem a little questionable. Contemporary logic, at least defined by the *Daily Record* and *The Scotsman*, is that Scotland cannot sustain a grown-up democracy and a proper parliament. Unique among nations on the face of the earth, the Scots cannot govern themselves. We have dullards as MSPs, Labour numptiedom everywhere, a country hijacked by the Section 28 homophobes – you get the picture.

We need to get a proper historical perspective on this. My 1970s Scotland was a hangover from the 1940s and 1950s and already out of date. The Scotland of Scottish country dancing, rotary clubs and an anglicised Toryism (represented for me by my Uncle Douglas from Carnoustie) was withering away, and being replaced by a more diverse and dynamic Scotland. In the 1980s, my Scotland became a world of black and white certainties, where the Scottish centre–left consensus stood relatively united in opposition to Thatcherism. And twenty-first-century Scotland seems to me just as prone as previous eras to stereotypes and simplistic views of a complex world.

Developing a story about contemporary Scotland, reflecting the good and the bad, is crucial. We must learn to celebrate success. What is wrong with Billy Connolly, even Sheena Easton? Success does not equal selling out, or have to mean ostentatiousness. I remember telling a Las Vegas taxi driver from Bulgaria last year (he hated everything Bulgarian) about the Scots' hatred of Sheena Easton (while going to a Sheena concert). Do you know, he just could not understand it, and at that moment I realised how small-minded and petty Scots can be.

We have to be utterly driven in our ambitions to root out poverty, inequality and ill health. If Easterhouse can shock Iain Duncan Smith, then why cannot our hundreds of Scottish politicians be motivated to do something about it? And we should get rid of some of the ideological blinkers: yes, Red Clydeside and the urban kailyard writers, but, broader than that, post-1989, socialism as a grand narrative is over and Scotland is no exception, while the politics of nationalism are more complex. Finally, what about some heroes and heroines for Scotland beyond centuries-old ones like Bruce, Wallace and Burns: reflecting the diversity of Scotland's talents, its dreamers, visionaries, and economic, civic and social entrepreneurs?

Creating a modern story about present-day Scotland is a prerequisite to getting much right about this country. We should note with alarm the absence of a modern Scotland from the international stage, and this is not a 'fundie nat' point about independence allowing us to rejoin the world. The Scotland that is presented to the world is the Scotland I was revolted by as a child: the tartan, the kitsch and so on – all supported by millions from Scotland the Brand and the week of Tartan Day horrors in the States.

Scotland has to break out of this straitjacket and speak to the world with its authentic voice. For this to happen we need a more mature relationship with the English. It is true, no matter how unpalatable it is to some, that as Scotland has become more Scottish, it has also become more anti-English. That does not make me Andrew Neil. However, there are so many excuses for anti-English prejudices from the Tartan Army and their fellow travellers: one being that England has racist, xenophobic, hooligan fans. Well, so do we, and are we saying that is all there is to England?

Andrew Wilson SNP MSP is right when he challenges us on this. Intellectually Scots should support England at football, and get over our inferiority complex. However, emotionally I am not sure that I can do it, given we are all a mix of various prejudices and gut instincts. But you know what, if the prize were a more confident Scotland at ease with itself, its southern friend and neighbour, and with a modern, international presence, I am willing to reach out and try.

# Joy Hendry

*Joy Hendry is a full-time writer, poet, playwright, broadcaster and editor since her student days of the literary magazine* Chapman, *now approaching its 100th issue. Over the years she has been involved in various aspects of Scottish culture – language, theatre, education, and the move towards greater political autonomy. She also lectures at Queen Margaret and Napier Universities.*

## Personal Reflections on Being Scottish Today

In the last month before writing, two 'celebrity' Scots have died: Hamish Henderson and Her Majesty the Queen Mother. Both Scots, both very similar in many ways although so different: one, *the* pillar of the British Royal Family, the other, *the* man of the Scottish folk revival and one of the several pillars of the Scottish literary renaissance. A staunch republican, I wonder what Hamish thought of HM the QM? It was one subject we never discussed, and, despite his unashamedly rabid republicanism, I'm not sure what his thoughts would have been.

What did they have in common? In relation to HM the QM, it is expressed as 'the common touch'. Hamish had it too, although in his case better put as 'the mankind touch'. An officer aristocrat to his core, he was nevertheless one of the squaddies, as muddy to his boots as any Jock in his ken. If we Scots have anything to offer to the international community, it is that 'mankind touch', the instinct, impulse, compulsion even, to touch, embrace and join with common humanity whenever and wherever we encounter it. Our natural exuberance as a nation, often inhibited on home ground, is loosed on foreign soil and we become mixers and messers; we don't go around in a clannish bubble, taking our nationality with us as a shield to keep out all comers, as many other nations do – we go native, and in going native we lose ourselves, and become ourselves. Exiled at home, perhaps, but the world is our oyster.

The painful transition we have been undergoing in Scotland, throughout the twentieth century in particular, is learning to be at home at home. Scottish identity has been a problem for us, for we have been exiled from ourselves in profound ways. After the gradual disintegration of Scottish identity over a period of centuries, all that was left of Scottishness was empty patriotism, and empty icons – degraded commercial images of ourselves. The reclamation process was, falteringly, underway at the beginning of the twentieth century with Robert Louis Stevenson and George Douglas Brown, and with poets like Violet Jacob and Marion Angus. Since then we have had Hugh MacDiarmid, Grassic Gibbon, we have had John Purser's *Scotland's Music* on Radio Scotland, showing us the reality of our Scottish musical heritage, both traditional and classical. We have had a renaissance in the visual arts, in interest in our history and much else. We now have our own parliament. Bit by bit we have been breaking down the self-exile, as we have clambered on hands and feet back towards self-knowledge.

Identity has been a problem, especially over the last thirty years, as up and coming writers wished to distance themselves from what they saw as the narrow, very male and challenging stance of writers like MacDiarmid. My generation of writers wanted to be the beat poets, or link in with American or Caribbean poets: they were afraid of their Scottishness because they did not know it. They saw it as an obstacle to their reaching through to an international literary market. But that was *then*, up to, say, ten years ago. This is now. Back in 1983, in *Chapman* issue 35–6 (as I write we approach issue 100), I asked writers of all different political and literary persuasions to consider the conundrum posed by Edwin Muir in *Scott and Scotland* (1932) as to whether Scotland was a 'predicament for the Scottish writer'. Though dubbed 'the loonie issue of *Chapman*' at the time, it caused a storm in the correspondence columns of *The Scotsman*. So diverse were the contributors, from Alasdair Gray to Christopher Whyte, from Joyce McMillan to George Byatt, that no one could accuse me, as editor, of having any political agenda. I felt like prefacing the issue by adapting the conventional proviso: *anyone who thinks the views expressed herein are the views of the editor needs their heid examined.* I got blamed for it all, but that's what happens to editors.

It was also incredibly stimulating. Maybe it was the pinch of salt needed in the Scottish intellectual brew, but it certainly seems that that issue marked a watershed.

After the wilderness years between the 1979 referendum and then, summer 1983, we were no longer sitting back, passive, defeated. Something had moved. It continued to move, with increasing pace. One of the hottest debates was about identity, between those who wanted to talk about it and those who didn't. And the debate was about whether we should talk about it, very largely. Fuss about nothing, surely? But no. Serious, deadly serious. Many things started to happen … schools, Irvine Welsh, *Braveheart* – not to mention four terms of Tory government, which left even the most unionist of Scots feeling that whatever was at home could never be at home unless . . .

So have we come home to a real fire? Since the mid-1990s, there has been an increasing lack of need for us to talk about Scottish identity. Why? Well, we are more ourselves, and know more about ourselves – even the most socially and culturally excluded of us knows more *in some respects* than their predecessors thirty years ago. There is less and less the need to talk about it, because we can *be* it, and, more importantly, *do* it. Whatever it is. If *Scottishness* is at last set free in the blood, it can express itself, without striving for disingenuous and rationalising articulation.

The death of Hamish Henderson in particular somehow encapsulates it all. Last night, outside my local chippie, I met an acquaintance on the street who had been enjoying a drink or two. Somehow, the word 'spirit' was mentioned. 'Here's to the spirit!' he said, after no more than one minute's conversation. Going up the steps to the chippie he looked back at me and challenged: 'You know what I mean?'

'Yes,' I said. 'The spirit of Hamish.' We had not been talking about Hamish Henderson. I did not know that he even knew of Hamish either personally or by repute. I do not even know that acquaintance's name, but for once I supplied the right answer. We have been at least partially restored by great figures like Hamish, no longer self-exiles.

Yes, Hamish, it is that spirit, the 'mankind touch', maybe even *pace* the Queen Mother, the 'common touch' which so transformed the British monarchy. It is that strange ability of our contorted, oppressed and self-oppressing nation to reach across oceans, classes, to cross untraversable mountains, that is one of the touchstones of 'being Scottish today'. And we don't need to talk about it nearly so much any more. Because we are being it; we are doing it. 'Great John McLean has come hame tae the Clyde.'

# Richard Holloway

*Richard Holloway was born in Glasgow in 1933 and brought up in the Vale of Leven. He was ordained into the ministry of the Scottish Episcopal Church in 1959 and became Bishop of Edinburgh in 1986 and Primus in 1992. He was Professor of Divinity at Gresham College in the City of London from 1996 to 2000. He is the author of twenty-three books and is a Fellow of the Royal Society of Edinburgh.*

When I was growing up the thing I regretted most was that I did not have a really Scottish-sounding name. My granny on my father's side was a Buchanan, but my grandfather was English, so I was stuck with the prosaic surname Holloway rather than the romantic Buchanan, which would have suited my temperament better. To my distress, there was no Holloway tartan in those wee books of Scottish clans I used to thumb through in the local library. It only made matters worse that my pals all had the right kind of names. Most of the families in the Vale of Leven were either Scottish or Irish, though we had a few Galonis and Biagis, part of the colourful Italian diaspora that has made such a contribution to Scottish culture. A working-class boy from an industrial town, my problem was that I was a Scottish romantic. Our towns straggled loosely along the banks of the Leven, the river that flowed from Loch Lomond out into the Firth of Clyde, fifteen miles further south. I was magnetised by the massive presence of Ben Lomond on the other side of the loch and hardly interested at all in the swarm of textile factories and dye works that lined the river. My father worked long, punishing hours in one of those dye works and came home a different colour every night. But I lived in my imagination, bewitched by the flickering Celtic twilight I compulsively read about in the novels of Maurice Walsh. Yet how could an authentic Scottish hero operate under the byline Holloway?

Another source of ambivalence was my religion. I belonged to the Scottish

Episcopal persuasion, 'the English Church' to everyone who did not belong to it. You could tell people till you were blue in the face that we were an authentic Scottish denomination and one that had paid dearly for its loyalty to the Stuart cause, but it made no difference – we were the English Church, the lairds' Church, the Church the toffs went to. Looking back, I wonder if it would have made a difference if I had been a quarter Irish rather than a quarter English, and I suspect it would. It was the Englishness of the connection that was the problem. I don't remember being taught it by anyone, but we picked up the notion from somewhere that England was our problem, our original sin. There was a permanent tension in our relationship. One of the ways it came out was in the jokes that were told. I remember hearing one at a Christmas pantomime in the old Metropole Theatre in Glasgow. The comedian told us that, sitting in a tea room, he listened in on a group of English visitors complaining about Scotland. 'Their towns are kill this, kill that – Kilmarnock, Kilsyth, Kilpatrick.' He got back at them: 'Aye, and yours are all mouth – Plymouth, Portsmouth, Yarmouth.' Great gale of appreciative laughter from Glasgow audience.

I need not give the details here, but I left Scotland at fourteen to study for the ministry – in England. A new kind of ambivalence emerged, this time about appearing to be and sounding too Scottish. I discovered that the English actually quite liked the Scots, though in a humorous, patronising sort of way. The fact that we were clearly not a problem to them, only made our problem with them more vexing. I started to experience the reaction that follows all neuroses like a shadow – self-mockery, self-contempt – till the day came when my nation's anguish no longer bothered me. When they leave Scotland, Scots are geniuses at assimilation. Yes, they have their Saint Andrew's societies and their Burns Clubs, but they rarely become professional Scottish exiles, probably because they are too busy getting on with life. It was the ones that stayed at home who were the problem, because they were still obsessed with the primal offence that was the source of all our woe.

Jump half a century and all is changed, changed utterly. Whether or not you think devolution has been politically successful, there is no doubt in my mind that it has been an enormous psychological success. Almost at a stroke it has wiped out our complex about the English. The proof of our coming of age is the fact that it is only the Scottish Tourist Board, or whatever it calls itself today, that bothers any longer with the old myth of a Celtic paradise that was only destroyed when the serpent from the south slunk into its midst. Now we think of ourselves as a vibrant part of a complex and changing European culture, and it feels good.

Though I did not realise it at the time, my own story has retraced the human adventure, which has been a movement from simplicity to complexity, from dourly clinging to one tribe and its ways to the gradual recognition that living alongside others and learning from them can be exciting, and not just in the kitchen. Geneticists use the term hybrid vigour to describe the enrichment that occurs when different races mix their genes. Of course, confronting change and increasing complexity can be disconcerting, which is why there is a debate going on at the moment about the new multicultural society that is emerging in Scotland. Personally, I am exhilarated by it. I love the fact that I can try a different ethnic cuisine every night in the week, if I want to, and that some of the strongest Scottish accents I hear come from Asian faces. I like the colour and verve of the new rainbow community of Scotland to which I now belong. The sooner all the tribes of the world are mixed together, and we are all a nice coffee colour, the better. Come to think of it, I am now even quite chuffed that 25 per cent of my genes are English. Even so, I'd still rather be called Buchanan than Holloway.

# Hamish Horsburgh

*Hamish Horsburgh was born in Haddington in 1943 and was educated at Knox Academy and Daniel Stewart's. He completed a pharmacy degree at Heriot Watt and has spent his working life building up the family pharmacy business. He is married to Heather and has two grown-up children; all are partners in Horsburgh Chemists. He now prefers to spend more time with his granddaughters Katie and Anna than dispensing prescriptions.*

I am British. Scotland is just one of the countries that make up the British Isles, as Bavaria is a state in Germany or Tuscany a province in Italy. Before the Romans landed in our country we were all British, so it is very much in that way that I see my homeland today.

The greatest thing that happened to Scotland was the succession of James VI to the English throne and then just over 100 years later in 1707 the Union of the Parliaments with the ending of Scotland's parliament and the Union of Scotland and England into one country ruled from Westminster. This ended centuries of fighting and heralded a peaceful future, not withstanding the two Jacobite uprisings. Rule from London does make me feel remote from the real power but it is not as bad as possible rule from Brussels. The reopening of the Scottish Parliament in 1999 is I'm sure meant to dispel this feeling, but at the end of the day the important government departments like defence and social security, not forgetting the ability to impose taxation, remain in London. Perhaps Members of the Scottish Parliament should think of themselves as councillors of a large region like Yorkshire instead of treating Scotland as a separate country. A sense of despair for Scotland overcomes me at the mention of an independent Scotland.

A sense of pride in your homeland is fundamental to all of us. Scots are correctly proud of their beautiful lochs and glens, the firths of Clyde and Moray, the Western Isles, their cities of Edinburgh and Glasgow as well as the picturesque villages like Dirleton and Crail. Scots have pride in their fighting traditions, not just on the terraces of Hampden but also from the long tradition, common in poor countries, of joining the army in famous regiments like the Royal Scots and the Argyll and Sutherland Highlanders. Scots feel emotional when a pipe band passes because of a pride in their history very much interconnected with tartan and soldiers and tradition. Traditions are important to create an identity, which we all recognise, and that makes us different from the English, just like our Bavarian or Tuscan counterparts.

Scots believe in the basic right for all to have free education. Although penniless, our new government will try to achieve the aim of totally free education at all levels from nursery school through to university.

Cynically, most Scots live in Scotland because they are here but they would really rather be somewhere else, but don't have the nerve to move until forced to do so. Scots take great pride in their role of Empire building, which they undertook with skill and ability. Scots settled in Canada, Africa, Australia, New Zealand, but most of them did so because they were forced by circumstance to do so, whether caused by famine or poverty. The infamous Highland Clearances are emotively brought up regularly, but most Scots fail to understand that this was a pan-European problem and not one solely affecting Scotland. Of course there are exceptions, with explorers like David Livingstone, who learned his exploration skills from spending a lot of time being lost on Scottish glens. However, it is the Scots who have emigrated who seem to be the most ardent about their Scottish identity, hanging on to their vision through folk tunes and paintings of the Monarch of the Glen. They will also be fully paid-up members of their Caledonian Society. Too many myths surround Scottish history. The Bonnie Hills of Tyree are flat. Macbeth was one of Scotland's great kings. Bonnie Prince Charlie wasn't.

The concept of Scotland as a nation is felt more when Scots are abroad and realise the extent of influence of their forebears. When at home there is not that feeling, except of course when facing the Auld Enemy at Murrayfield.

Hollywood's movie *Braveheart* evoked many of the Scots' anti-English feelings and the sense of being treated as an underclass. The film did, however, emphasise freedom. This word keeps cropping up, but what does it mean? Freedom from whom? Many Irish in Northern Ireland want to be free of the British. If they unite with Eire then there will be those who want their freedom from the Irish. Within this context there must be common sense. We have political freedom. We have a free press. We have religious freedom. Freedom of religion gave us Scots Presbyterian Christianity and through this much of the Calvinistic outlook of taking oneself too seriously, unlike continental Catholicism, which seems to encourage folk to indulge themselves at the cost of a few Hail Marys. However, the truth is that our freedom has really only been achieved since we became part of the United Kingdom and not in the days of William Wallace or Robert the Bruce, although their influence will have shaped what we now accept as freedom.

Scotland is a good place to live. Fortunately the air we breathe is fresh from the Atlantic. Scots do feel that they live in a healthy place where we have ready access to open countryside, which is there to be enjoyed by all. So why do we have the dreadful record with heart disease and cancer?

What does it then mean to be Scottish? I think that Rab C. Nesbitt would summarise most Scots feelings as, 'It's no bad.'

# Tom Hunter

*Tom Hunter built Sports Division from nothing into one of the UK's premier sports retailers over a fourteen-year period, employing 7,500 people across over 250 stores. He sold the business in 1998 for £290 million; his stake was valued at £260 million. He established the private equity vehicle West Coast Capital in 2001. Tom is an ardent supporter of fellow entrepreneurs and passionate about making Scotland a more enterprising nation. He is Chairman of the Entrepreneurial Exchange and recently personally bequested £5 million to support the Hunter Centre for Entrepreneurship at Strathclyde University.*

When you travel the world and say you're a Scot the overwhelming reaction is a smile, a brief synopsis of our awesome history and a slap on the back. You are an instant friend, the proud keeper of the indelible mark on history that our Scottish ancestors delivered. We are known around the globe for delivering many, many groundbreaking inventions and great leadership – Andrew Carnegie was not only the world's wealthiest man, he also set the foundations of modern-day philanthropy through giving his entire wealth away. Whether it's Dolly the Sheep, William Wallace, Rabbie Burns or the telephone, we are known throughout the world as honest, trustworthy and imaginative people, a nation to be proud of. But what is Scotland to me?

First and foremost it is forever home, a place where we as a nation can continue to make a great mark upon the world in which we live. But we do need to move on from being suspicious of wealth and we do need to give more back, following the lead Carnegie gave us – we should create wealth to effect change for the good of all our people.

A couple of years ago I met a young offender who had converted his crime skills to setting up a very successful business. He had been led into crime because he didn't really have a chance to see the other opportunities available to him, but when he did, boy, did he take the chance. All of us deserve that chance. And that's what Scotland is about – it is a land of opportunity with an almost unsurpassed heritage, a stunning landscape and a creativity that needs to be unleashed. We are a people, largely, of great integrity and honesty, but too often we miss seeing opportunities and instead view too many hurdles in our way. We can, I believe, lead the world as a small but innovative nation, we have guts and determination and yes we often fail – particularly it seems at football. But we always pick ourselves up, dust ourselves down and get back on the pitch. Maybe one day we'll win the World Cup; we will certainly never stop trying, and that is the mark of a true Scot. Sure it's painful when we lose, whether that's in business or in sport, but the fact is we Scots never give up trying.

To the outsider we may sometimes be the land of tartan, mountains and whisky, but is that such a bad thing when more or less all Americans either claim Scottish or Irish heritage? Importantly that's my point – I could never imagine trying to claim any other heritage than that of my birthplace, Scotland, because I can think of no other nation I would want to belong to, nor can I ever recall a fellow Scot contemplating such a thing. We are Scots through and through and if we stand shoulder to shoulder we can achieve far more than we do today as a nation that is focused upon giving opportunity for all, where we lead by example and help others as they help themselves. Our culture really does have to change. We remain too dependent on the government – it won't change anything, we as a people will. And we continue to fear failure when in and of itself it is a worthy learning experience.

I worked long hours for nearly twenty years before selling my first business, Sports Division. Many pundits at the time had me retiring to a beach in some exotic land. Today, I'm building more businesses and I hope, in my own small way, that I'm giving something back. If I ever retired to a beach, and let me tell you that's unlikely, it would be one on the west coast of Scotland.

Being Scottish is something you can never give up, no matter where you are on the planet. We Scots are, for the best part, honest, imaginative, creative and kind. We Scots will stubbornly go on creating positive indelible marks on the history of the world because that's what marks us out as Scottish – we never give up on making our mark.

# Craig Hutchison

*Craig Hutchison is a counsellor and trainer specialising in working with lesbian, gay, bisexual and transgendered people as well as with men who have been raped, sexually assaulted or abused. He previously volunteered with a telephone helpline for three years, and also provided training to Lothian and Borders police on sexuality awareness. He was a founder-member of the 'Pink Panthers', a gay-rights activism group and has been involved in several campaigns and direct actions.*

## Not One of the Boys

It was football that finally decided it. Being quiet and studious at school was one thing, but not liking the 'beautiful game' was quite another. Whereas before I might just have been considered a bit strange, now I was a fully-fledged poof. I was absolutely, definitely *not* one of the boys. The only attraction I had to football was for Ally McCoist's legs.

Being 'one of the boys' was pretty central to the Scottish concept of masculinity when I was at school: drinking, sex and football seemed to be the main stars around which manliness revolved. It was made clear to me pretty early on in my school days that manhood was an exclusive club and that I was not a welcome member. You couldn't just be a man – you had to *prove* that you were. You had to earn your macho badge as a result of your spitting and shagging prowess. Being gay made me an outsider in the eyes of others – somehow not properly a man and certainly not 'one of the boys'. I was to be reminded of this every school day.

Belonging to a gang of some description seemed more vital than oxygen at Broxburn Academy, but I certainly wasn't welcome in any of the existing groups. Like animals in the wild the other kids could smell my difference and they turned on me. I was spat at, attacked and verbally assaulted nearly every day. No gang wanted me as a member so I joined the anti-gang, falling in with a group of punk girls from the year above. Becoming a punk singled me out even more but this time I was making a deliberate choice to be different. I was rejecting them before they could reject me. In my imagination I was the Nietzschean hero and they were the plebeian *Das Mann*. It was a way of coping with being ostracised. It is only now with the benefit of hindsight that I can appreciate the irony of being told it wasn't okay to be a gay punk by little heterosexuals who thought I should listen to 'proper' music like Wham, Culture Club and Kajagoogoo!

It's a long time since I was at Broxburn Academy and I would love to think that things are different now for young lesbian, gay, bisexual and transgendered people, but I know that they're not. I regularly speak to teachers, community workers and school students who tell me that the most common insults they hear young people direct to one another still include 'poof', 'lezzie', and 'faggot'. And the recent Section 2A debate was a chilling reminder of just how many people there are in Scotland who don't like queers and don't want us near their children. I wonder if they believe that we spring full-grown from the head of Zeus: there surely can't be lesbian or gay young people in our schools and they certainly can't need protecting from the other kids! But there are and they do: I've spoken to too many young people bullied or ostracised because of their sexual orientation. Sadly, I don't think that young lesbian, gay, bisexual and transgendered people at school now are in any better a position than I was way back then.

I do think that adult Scottish society has moved on and that we are a bit more tolerant of difference (I use the word deliberately as I don't believe we value diversity, I think we merely tolerate it), but in the playground the pack still rules. So why the hostility? Why homophobia? In my opinion it has a lot to do with gender – there are very strict rules about how boys and girls should be and people from sexual minorities are thought to be breaking the rules. Young men in particular are so desperately keen to prove their masculinity that they need to establish a pecking order from most masculine to least, and the devil take the hindmost.

I think Scottish manhood is in a pretty sorry state at the moment: some things are changing while some things stay the same. Scottish men are caught up in the whirlwind of change and the dust hasn't settled yet. So how do we define a man? Not by the existence of a penis (I was grateful to be taught that lesson by some of the transgendered people I have met over the years). Not by his heterosexuality (because I am as much a man as anyone else). Not by the amount he drinks, his bravado, his sporting ability or by his dubious attraction to *Scotsport*. So what is left when we strip away the tinfoil macho badges? A person of the masculine gender. Full stop, end of story.

I think that homophobia in schools will continue to exist as long as young people need to prove themselves in order to be accepted as a member of their gender and peer-group. In the meantime I think we need to be doing more to support and protect those young people who are made to feel that they don't fit in.

Oh, and just to let you know: I am one of the boys now. But our little gang prefers *Sex and the City*, Prada and champagne to *Scotsport*, Adidas and lager. But I now know that we don't need to prove our masculinity to anyone.

# Billy Kay

*Writer and broadcaster, Billy Kay was born in Galston, Ayrshire, in 1951. He is the author of* Scots: The Mither Tongue *(Mainstream, 1986) and editor of* The Complete Odyssey *(Polygon, 1996), an oral history collection based on the acclaimed radio series. He has produced and presented over 200 radio and television documentaries on Scottish culture.*

My sense of Scottishness was wrought primarily in a working-class family in 1950s Ayrshire. Intellectual dimensions were added studying Scottish literature at Edinburgh University, and international perspectives gained from travelling round the world and speaking several foreign languages, but my first identity is as a Scots-speaking Lowlander from the Burns country. His brilliant poetry and songs were ingrained in the local culture, and it was a source of community pride that we spoke the same dialect of Scots as the poet. My father taught me stories from Scottish history ... Galston had sheltered Bruce before the skirmish at Loudoun Hill while my grandmother lived in Stand Alane street – the words uttered by Wallace when his followers deserted him in the face of an approaching English force – 'I stand alane.' Cultural, as opposed to political, nationalism was absorbed by osmosis. The socialism of the mining communities was another major influence, so along with pride in being Scottish there was a strong sense of egalitarianism; we were nae better than ither folk, but we were gey shuir we were as guid as onybody!

Given that background, you will understand how moved I was when Sheena Wellington sang 'A man's a man for a' that' at the opening of the Scottish Parliament, and consequently how scunnered I was to see certain MSPs reduce the debate to have a question on Scots included in the Census to the level of comic capers. As someone whose work has always promoted cultural diversity, making programmes about minorities like Lanarkshire Lithuanians or Ayrshire Spaniards, whom very few people knew existed, I was pleased to see that the lobby pressing for a question on religious identity in the Census had succeeded. I found it bitterly ironic, though, that if I had belonged to a religious or ethnic minority, the same MSPs would not have dared trash my mither tongue. I stand alane with the many hundreds of thousands who use Scots as their first language, yet see it given scant recognition from our major institutions.

However, as most MSPs and most Scots have not been educated in their own culture, ignorant attitudes abound, and the Scottish cringe is everywhere. I collect examples: the education convener in a Labour fiefdom who replied to the proposal that Scottish studies should be an integral part of his schools' curriculum, 'Oh, no, we live in a multicultural environment!' Apparently every culture was to be taught except the native one! A few years ago when I asked a Fife headmaster if Scottish literature was encouraged in his school, the reply left me almost speechless: 'No, this is not a very Scottish area.' Can you imagine an English or Irish headmaster making such a statement? It shows how far we have to go in renewing Scotland after centuries of self-inflicted cultural colonialism. I have actually heard educated Scots argue that no Scottish history from before 1707 should be taught in our schools, as it only foments 'dangerous nationalism'. The Catalans reckoned it would take three generations after autonomy for a similar 'slave mentality' to be replaced with cultural and political self-confidence. With us, it might take a bittie longer!

Yet on the occasions I feel alienation from my countrymen, I hear MacDiarmid's humorous response to the same conundrum:

> 'Mercy o' Gode, I canna thole
> wi sic an orra mob to roll'
> *'Wheesht! It's for the guid o your soul.'*

It micht be for the guid o my soul, but I dinnae like whit it duis tae ma heid.

I do feel, nevertheless, that Scotland is inevitably moving towards being at one with itself, and that the positive values ingrained in the culture will survive and thrive as we gain political maturity. At the core of the culture is the tradition defined by George Elder Davie as 'democratic intellectualism'. It has been there for centuries, and has affected positively our perspective on the world, with our working-class culture especially enlightened and liberal compared to most societies. My wife's first experience of Scotland was an airport taxi driver who quoted huge passages of Burns' poetry on the way into the university hall of residence. A fellow student there was astonished to discover a rose and beautifully handwritten lines from 'My love is like a red, red rose' lying on his bed, placed there by the woman who cleaned his room. The foreign students at the summer school realised they were in a very special cultural environment. I am constantly being made aware of that, too, and realise its immense potential.

Having made documentary features for over two decades, I have interviewed almost 2,000 people from different walks of life, and I never fail to be impressed by our human kindness in adversity, our rampant egalitarianism, our wild, dark humour, the power of our stories, music and songs, our insatiable thirst for knowledge, our passionately shared desire for sense and worth ower aw the earth tae bear the gree, an aw that. For aw that potential to bear fruit is something definitely worth waiting for.

# Charles Kennedy

*Charles Kennedy is the MP for Ross, Skye and Inverness West in the Scottish Highlands and the Leader of the Liberal Democrats. He was born in Inverness and brought up and educated in Fort William.*

Hugh MacDiarmid once wrote some beautiful lines about Scotland and Scottishness:

> The rose of all the world is not for me,
> I want for my part only the little white rose of Scotland,
> That smells sharp and sweet,
> And breaks the heart.

Beautiful … but wrong. That is introspective, self-regarding, solipsistic Scotland, turning its back on the world and stumbling into a Celtic twilight – a temptation for Scots, I know, but one that should be resisted.

My Scotland is one that is outward-looking, generous, engaged with the world – a world to which the Scots have given so much more than they have ever taken in return. It may no longer be true – as it was said it used to be – that if you opened the hatch of any sea freighter anywhere in the world, and shouted 'Jock', you'd always get an answer. But there is a Caledonian community in virtually every major city in the world.

The interesting thing about the Scottish diaspora is that it is almost entirely voluntary. From the Middle Ages there was a tradition of mobility in Scotland, and close links with the continent, to which young Scottish clerics and doctors travelled regularly. The Auld Alliance was as much a matter of culture as economics or politics. The Scots left their native land driven by ambition rather than poverty. This flies in the face of Scottish legends about the Clearances, but Tom Devine, Director of the Research Institute of Irish and Scottish Studies at Aberdeen University, has researched the subject, and concludes that of the two million Scots who emigrated to America between 1850 and 1939, 90 per cent were Lowlanders and city dwellers seeking a better life abroad.

Devine compares them to the Irish, most of whom were forced out by famine or rapacious landlords. The result is that while the Irish retain a misty, sentimental fascination for what they still regard as a lost homeland (and which perhaps accounts for their otherwise inexplicable capacity to ignore the true nature of the IRA), the Scots are much more hard-headed, entrepreneurial – and successful. They may have a romantic attachment to their roots, but they're not particularly anxious to come back, unless for a holiday.

But that's what is appealing about them. They would not particularly jibe at such famous insults as 'The noblest prospect which a Scotsman ever sees, is the high road that leads him to England' (Samuel Johnson) or 'There are few more impressive sights in the world than a Scotsman on the make' (James Barrie). They might even regard them as compliments. This is what makes them such curious, compelling people. They can be patriotic, even mawkishly so, but they often cherish their myths as much for the tourist trade as to give themselves an identity. I know Scots who prefer wine to whisky, ciabatta to haggis, and who don't much like the sound of bagpipes. They are an internationalist people, for whom a global world is perfectly designed.

It means that someone like me can be, simultaneously, and with no sense of contradiction, a Highlander, a Scot, a Briton and a European. I felt as at home doing a graduate course at Indiana University as being an undergraduate in Glasgow. It is why I so utterly reject the idea that Scottish Members of Parliament should in some way be restricted in the issues they can debate or policies they can vote upon. Scotland may have its own parliament again, but it is still an integral part of the United Kingdom. Indeed I can almost sympathise with the English feeling a little threatened when they see how many Scots took Dr Johnson's high road to positions of power and influence in London.

Yet, while dispersed across the land or across the globe, the Scots retain a very clear sense of their Scottishness. Is it not remarkable that during those 300 years when there was no parliament in Edinburgh, yet Scotland maintained so many of its particular institutions and symbols, in education, the law, medicine, not to mention literature and culture and accent? Remarkable … that just a few million people, stuck on one of the most remote fringes of a continent, should have gone forth to colonise the world, and still preserve their distinctiveness at home.

The little white rose of Scotland may still smell sharp and sweet, and I hasten home to its aroma as often as I can, but equally I am proud to know that the rose of all the world is shot through with tartan, too.

# Mark Kennedy

*Mark Kennedy is a Development Worker with the Scottish Gypsy/Traveller Association and a Gypsy/Traveller.*

In my opinion many of Scotland's people have as yet not seen any real change as a result of the Scottish Parliament. It is true that there is more access to MSPs and that parliamentary committees have become a feature of Scottish politics, and that there are a number of MSPs who are looking to make a difference to those they serve. This said, there are still too many Scottish MSPs who are bound by Westminster and who hold on to old ideas. This is not only my opinion – it is also borne out by my experience in dealing with those in power. In my working life I see their collective refusal to let go of the need to control what they don't understand.

I am a Gypsy/Traveller – a term that has only recently been adopted in Scotland, and which has come out of a deep sense of frustration and despair. Many like me have grown up being racially abused, discriminated against, and had our culture and our traditions slowly squeezed and negated by those who still can't deal with cultural diversity, who do not truly accept that Scotland is a land of peoples of different colours, religions, cultures and traditions. This despite the fact that these people were born in Scotland, and in some cases may have come from generations of people born in Scotland. Yet they still can't feel Scottish because they are not able to celebrate their own cultural heritage, as is the case for most of Scotland's Gypsy/Travellers.

Writing as a Gypsy/Traveller leaves me open to the accusation of being subjective and biased. Many people are of the opinion that I am too emotional and unreasonable, and that I am a very angry man. To which I would answer 'guilty'. Strange term, 'guilty'. I have spent my entire life experiencing the settled community's reaction to my culture and tradition – from being a child and having men coming through the night to burn us out, to a school system where my culture was ignored in classes but had to be defended in the playground, where being a Gypsy/Traveller was a curse, and to fit in was to hide who you are. What shame that creates. The consequences of being from a culture like mine can be seen around the world – the culture becomes lost; all that is valuable is lost in trying to fit in. Today they call it mainstreaming, but it has had many names. It means, 'Be like us and we will show you how you can avoid displeasing the majority; it doesn't matter if you lose your identity and become displaced, as long as you fit into one of our little tick-boxes'.

Many who read this may well be offended by what's on the paper in front of them and will be quite willing to dismiss this as the writings of a bitter and twisted human being who has an axe to grind. Whether that is true or not – and I may not be in the best position to defend myself – I would offer the following observation. Over the last decade alone in Scotland there have been many studies on Gypsy/Travellers. One was carried out by the University of Dundee and Save the Children. The findings of this study (which made grim reading) showed that Gypsy/Travellers were the most discriminated against people in Scotland, and that the record of most public bodies was poor in relation to Gypsy/Travellers. As a result of this study the Parliamentary Committee for Equal Opportunities investigated the level of service provided to Gypsy/Travellers and how well they were treated by public bodies. Their inquiry took nine months and evidence was taken from all those involved in the Gypsy/Traveller industry. Based on the evidence gathered, a report was produced in June 2001. With it were thirty-seven recommendations to the Scottish Executive covering a range of issues, including ethnic status, housing, health and education.

For many in the Gypsy/Traveller community, myself included, the Equal Opportunities' report and recommendations were seen as an important move forward in improving the lives and conditions of Scotland's Gypsy/Travellers and it was hoped that these parliamentary recommendations would be as readily adopted, with the same willingness, as a set of recommendations that had been made in regard to Gypsy/Travellers by a state quango the year before. Sadly this was not the case. Though the quango's recommendations were not debated in parliament the Executive has used them to form policy about Gypsy/Travellers in Scotland. The Equal Opportunities' report has for the most part been ignored by the Scottish Executive. This has obviously trickled down to most public authorities, and when the report was debated in December 2001 in the Chamber, the racist and discriminatory views and language were disgraceful. I sat in the public gallery ashamed and angry that I was being subjected to what the Equal Opportunities Committee has reported.

Scottish Members of Parliament are above the law – they can say what they like and have the protection of parliament. I don't have that protection. I can't say what I like about people without having to accept the consequences of my actions. After the debate letters of complaint were sent to four of the five political party leaders and to the Presiding Officer. I also complained to the First Minister personally and to the Leader of the SNP at the Holocaust Memorial Day in Glasgow, where Gypsy/Travellers were excluded from the platform and from lighting a candle for the 500,000 Gypsy/Travellers whose lives were lost in the Second World War.

Despite there being a whole range of laws in Scotland to protect its people, and some to protect ethnic minority groups, there are none that truly protect the rights of Gypsy/Travellers. The Executive view is that there has never been a legal test case and so there are no Gypsy/Travellers in Scotland, and that they can't make a decision on it as it is a matter for Westminster. Yet the first known legal case surrounding a Gypsy/Traveller in Britain was in the city of Aberdeen, on 8 May 1527. It is the opinion of this writer that as long as the Scottish Executive and some of those who have the protection of the parliament refuse to take seriously the plight of Scotland's Gypsy/Travellers, their culture and traditions will slowly disappear.

As a Gypsy/Traveller born in Scotland I will leave you with this fact: the US State Department Human Rights' report highlighted the Parliament Equal Opportunities' Committee work in respect of Gypsy/Travellers in 2002. The response of the Committee Convener, Kate MacLean MSP, was as follows:

Whilst it is gratifying that the hard work of our Committee is being recognised on the global stage, it is worth bearing in mind the report represents an international recognition of our failing to adequately safeguard the rights of Gypsy/Travellers in today's Scotland.

# John Laird

*The Lord Laird of Artigarvan is a Cross Bench Member of the House of Lords. He is a former Member of the Northern Ireland Parliament and is currently Chairman of the Ulster Scots Agency, which was created as a result of the Belfast Agreement of 1998. The Agency's function is to promote Ulster Scots culture, history and language throughout the island of Ireland.*

## Proud to be Ulster Scots

By today's standards they were anything but politically correct – but then who was, 400 years ago? The border reivers, from whom the majority of Ulster Scots people who live on the island of Ireland are descended, were that type of people.

I can trace lines on both sides of my family back to the border region in the early seventeenth century when King James VI, or, as some would have it, James I, moved the reivers out of the area. His idea was to make one kingdom of the island now known as Great Britain as well as using the displaced to hold the Irish in check in the north-eastern part of Ireland.

The reivers were hard men who owed their allegiances to no king or authority except making money – hence the word 'freelance'. Ireland was a disappointment to many, too wet, too much trouble with the locals, and a place where rights for those not in the established Church were few and far between.

As an Ulster Scot growing up in Belfast, I was always conscious, like so many Ulster Scots, that I was not Irish. Not aggressively – I just felt alienated and in my time nothing was ever said or done by the Irish which would make me feel Irish or select Irish as a nationality when confronted by an official form.

I used to muse on the strange position that I was in. My people have lived in the island of Ireland for almost 400 years and yet feel deeply attached to Scotland.

I think that this, if it reflected on anyone, reflected badly on the native Irish population. To be of that branch of the Scottish people who had been grafted on to the plant of Ireland is to hold different yet similar feelings to the totality of Scottishness. The result was the creation of a people who naturally intermarried with the Irish and who added their culture and music to the local melting pot.

I, in common with the majority of Ulster Scots, have a burning admiration for the quarter of a million who moved on from Ulster in the eighteenth century for North America. Their descendants, who now number 22 million, played a vital life-giving role in the creation of the modern USA.

From an early age my brother and I were told stories of daring by Ulster Scots figures in the USA, where they are called Scots Irish. Frontier men like David Crockett, Kit Carson, Sam Houston (Houston, Texas!) were favourites in a time when Western movies were in fashion. The political importance of the Scots Irish who created the American Declaration of Independence and the seventeen Presidents who are of Ulster Scots stock were the particular interest.

The overriding desire of Ulster Scots has always been freedom of expression. Political alliances have always been weighted against that vital requirement. Being reared in Belfast clearly meant support for the Union of the United Kingdom. For many, including my family, political expression of Ulster Scots is to be a Unionist. I feel that, compared with anything else on offer, remaining British is the way in which we are allowed to express ourselves.

I suspect that at a day-to-day level my life would seem much more Scottish than Irish. The use of Ulster Scots language so similar to Scots always made those from the 'mainland' at home. Interest in music of a Scottish flavour is second nature, as is the importance of Hogmanay – a night of particular significance to my late father, a man who always referred to his church as the Kirk and for whom a highlight was to attend it in his kilt.

Interestingly in sport, too, an important point occurred. Despite having a range of friends who play rugby for Ireland, the support of my family for that team is qualified. Scotland is always first choice and Ireland only next. The names of Scots players sound more natural to us than the Irish ones: Ferguson, Stewart, Murray, White and Redpath were names I came across on a daily basis. I know no one called O'Gara!

A people and a nation are not defined by the land on which they live. They are defined by what is in their minds. Those of us who are Ulster Scots and who live in Ulster see ourselves as part of the Scottish family. Proud to be of a particular and identifiable past. Proud to be Ulster Scots.

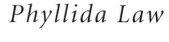

# Phyllida Law

*Phyllida Law is an actress. Born in Glasgow, she and her actor daughters Emma and Sophie Thompson divide their lives between London and Argyll.*

My father was wounded in the First World War. Highlanders, he said, were easy targets for the enemy because of their white spats. An order to dirty them came from High Command. This was countermanded the following day by the Clan Chieftain, Cameron of Lochiel. No man in his regiment was to muddy any part of his uniform. That's very Scottish. We are dangerously clean.

Gertie Mackay in our village was sent to stay with her auntie after Christmas every year in order to help her clean the house for the New Year. The grates were polished with Zebo, the fires set, and there were seven washing waters for the walls, she said, and vinegar in the final rinse. Our Mrs Lauder scrubbed the legs of any table before she attacked the top, and used Harpic to polish the brass bath taps. At one time travelling anywhere in the world and seeing little hands turned to claws by rheumatism, you knew they belonged to a Scot.

If the First World War changed my father's life, the Second changed mine. I was an evacuee and have remained so ever since. A displaced person. The theatre is the perfect home for such a one. When my academic ambitions faded we never told my grandmother. She was the doughty widow of a Scots minister who thought the theatre was 'the work of the Devil' and I was afraid that if she learnt my shameful secret she would do some violence to my mother. My married aunts still got a sermon if they came home after midnight on a Saturday, thus defiling the Sabbath. Grannie called her five daughters 'painted females with a drink in one hand and a cigarette on the other'. Aunt May always kept her sherry glass behind the bread bin.

While waiting for auditions to all the drama schools I had ever heard of, I took coffee and tea under my mother's bed and only appeared in public at supper-time when I could reasonably be expected to have returned from lectures at Glasgow University. From my hiding place I watched Grannie's little black shoon tottering around the room as she turned out a gas fire here, a light there. She liked to turn the electricity off at the mains after 9.30 p.m. and if we complained she said she had a Degree in Electricity. Had she been born a generation later she might very well have achieved one.

The auditions I took had to be for drama schools in England. There were none in Scotland. There are now. I suffer from bitter retrospective envy. My accent was ironed out for Shakespeare's sake. I worked at this assiduously with no notion that it would be considered treasonable, and I think it still is. It can work both ways of course. I once got a bad notice from Bernard Levin for playing Mistress Overdone (a bawd) in *Measure for Measure* with a Glasgow accent. I doubt it would be cause for comment now, though I sense irritation in certain southern quarters that the House of Commons sounds so Scottish.

Abroad, being Scottish is a trump card. I have learnt to say 'I am Scottish' in several different languages and I always tied a tartan scarf to my rucksack.

One advantage of working away from your roots is the bliss of returning. With precision timing and an aeroplane I can catch each season twice in one year. But I miss the Royal Scot, the mighty exhalation of steam at the summit of Shap, and the guards calling out in the dark at Carstairs. The absolute certainty that I would never reach my mother at the barrier in Glasgow Central without someone talking to me. Calling me 'lassie'.

We lived in one of those tenements with 'wally closes tiled to the top for the Toffee Noses'. There would be soup. Lentil soup with the ham bone. (If life was a little flat my mother said it was 'like lentil soup without the ham bone'.) There would be baps, a pan loaf with a burnt bottom and a gold crust, mutton pies and potato scones, tender little home-made pancakes and floppy crumpets from Hubbards in Great Western Road, quite unlike the peely-wally objects that pass for crumpets down south.

Down south. It seems to me that in every country there is a north–south divide. A sense of economic inequality. Some element of suspicion and disapproval. At least we don't have passports. Yet. The border is manned by the midge, as efficient as the teste fly, in repelling barbarian hordes.

Then there is the matter of climate. Mist can cling round your ears for weeks till even the sheep get depressed and park themselves mumpishly on the nearest stretch of tarmac. Being Scottish, I happen to know the mist will lift one day. Being Scottish, I've seen what lies behind it.

# Helen Liddell

*Helen Liddell was appointed as Secretary of State for Scotland on 24 January 2001. She has been MP for Airdrie and Shotts since 1997 and was MP for Monklands East from 1994 to 1997. She was educated at St Patrick's High School, Coatbridge, and the University of Strathclyde. In her spare time, Mrs Liddell enjoys cooking, hill-walking, music and writing – her first novel* Elite *was published in 1990. Mrs Liddell is married to Dr Alistair Liddell and has one son and one daughter.*

## Being Scottish: A Reflection

For me, being Scottish is as much about the contradictions in our national character as about the individual qualities that bind us together and for which we are justly renowned. For without those contradictions we would not be the people we are.

As a people we are complex yet straightforward. We are compassionate yet thrawn. Romantic yet practical. Generous yet prudent. Innovative yet fiercely traditional. Outgoing yet introverted. Collectivist yet ruggedly individual. Civilised yet austere, and scornful of the trappings of culture. Our Celtic, Pictish, Norse and Saxon genes struggle within us, almost visibly at times, for supremacy. It is tempting to cite these contradictions as evidence of a national schizophrenia, yet to my mind they are most definitely a strength, not a weakness. Indeed, in my opinion, this hybrid vigour forms the basis not just of our uniqueness as a people, but of our enduring success. And the increasing ethnic diversity of twenty-first-century Scotland promises to enrich that blend still further.

One might imagine that a people harbouring within them such a maelstrom of conflicting traits would not be easy to represent to the wider world. Yet one of the things that has most impressed and encouraged me in my travels as Secretary of State has been the sheer strength of Scotland's image … and the ease with which people throughout the world have identified the positives in the Scottish character. Indeed, some of the traits within ourselves that we Scots find hard to come to terms with are perceived by others as attributes that do us credit.

Complexity is our overarching characteristic, but we are also undeniably straightforward. People know exactly where they stand with a Scot, and that has won us a reputation also for integrity. In a world of ambiguity and sometimes double-dealing, we are renowned for getting straight to the point … sometimes very bluntly indeed.

Compassionate we certainly are. Scots have a reputation not just for identifying with the underdog and for caring, but of putting that compassion into practice, at home and worldwide. For us as a people, society and community are concepts we particularly cherish. But that doesn't mean we are a pushover. We can be awkward customers and at times downright thrawn. There's nothing we relish more than digging our heels in, even when it might suit us better to compromise. But when an issue of real principle is at stake, we will stand firm to defend it. That streak is ingrained in Scotland's history.

Over the centuries, most Scots have never had much. But we have always been willing to share what we had with the less fortunate, and we remain so today. I take particular pride in the commitment of so many Scots to helping the world's poorest countries, both practically and financially.

Yet we are also renowned, caricatured even, for our carefulness with money, a quality that the Chancellor of the Exchequer – a Scot – has successfully refined into 'prudence'. A powerful strand of austerity runs through us, an austerity born as much of hard times as of Calvinism. Our renowned ability to manage money – and to do so honestly – has made Edinburgh one of the world's leading financial centres.

Romantic – we are certainly that, and incurably so. The memory of Bonnie Prince Charlie and the work of our poet Robbie Burns. And with scenery like ours, how could we be otherwise?

Romantic, yet practical, for we are great at making things work. We may have our heads in the air, but our feet are firmly on the ground. If you want something done, a Scot will find the way. We can claim great inventions from the steam engine to the lawn mower, from the telephone to the television, from radar to Dolly the Sheep. We may not have invented the wheel, but it was a Scot who put a rubber tyre on it.

Here's one final contradiction: we contrive at one and the same time to be immensely proud of our country and its attributes, but reticent about singing the praises not just of the Scotland of castles, whisky, golf and the pipes, but of the modern Scotland of vibrant cities, a new political culture and exciting trends in fashion, computer graphics and much, much more. For the Scotland we love is itself a land of contradictions, reflecting the nature of its people.

# Baroness Linklater

*Baroness Linklater founded the New School, Butterstone, Perthshire, in 1991, a school for educationally fragile children. Created a Life Peer in 1997, Baroness Linklater speaks on penal matters and education. Trustee for the Social Development Sector of the Esmee Fairbairn Foundation, she also chairs their new initiative 'Rethinking Crime and Punishment'. Honorary Doctor of the Queen Margaret University College, of which she is a Foundation Patron, she has also recently been created a member of the Scottish Committee of Barnardo's and a Chancellor's Assessor for Napier University Court.*

## On Being Scottish

I was born and raised in the hills of central Perthshire, above the village of Dunkeld and about three miles from the tiny village of Butterstone. The house is called Riemore, and it used to be a – very modest – shooting lodge, so it is in a landscape of hills, heather and trees of extraordinary beauty. The view from the house is of a hill called the Deuchary, and it is one which after nearly sixty years I can never tire of or get used to. Behind the house is a small wood and the sound of wind in the trees is one I can never tire of. The landscape is deeply familiar and ever changing. To many who visit us it feels like the back of beyond, but to me and my family it is the centre of the universe. In short it is the place where I am absolutely rooted and that is something I regard as the most enormous privilege. Wherever I have lived my life – and principally that includes the first twenty years of my married life in London – there has never been any question of where I come from. That is, for me, the starting point of being Scottish. I could never, and did never, feel I was a Londoner in any way at all. Equally, despite a strong love of Caithness, where my mother's family comes from, and where many wonderful holidays have been spent, the core of being Scottish is not associated with Scotland generally, but very specifically my part of Perthshire. It's a visceral attachment which in some way defines who I am – although precisely how I couldn't possibly say.

When I was sent away to boarding school – to Dorset no less – I think I can vaguely remember being rather tiresome about my Scottishness. I was a bit wilder, I tried to tell them, different from the others, while of course being cringingly unconfident inside. I then went to Paris to the Sorbonne for a year, where I quickly discovered that to say to the very insular Parisians that I was Scottish, not English as was usually supposed, made all the difference to how I was viewed by those I met: 'Ecossaise! Ah, c'est différent, ça' was the sort of response. So my pride in my nationality was endorsed and underlined. At university in England, I was more tarred with the brush of my maiden name – Lyle – as it was tainted with the blot of capitalistic activity to do with sugar and, no doubt, slaves. So although also thoroughly Scottish capitalists from Greenock, the Scottish part escaped censure.

After many very unsuitable boyfriends, I actually chose a Scot of whom my family approved, and so did his family of me – initially at least. My father-in-law, Eric Linklater, with whom I got on extremely well, used to go on about my 'Norman nose' (which never sounded all that flattering), which gave him pleasure on the basis that all the Sinclairs originally came over with the Normans (St Clair), thus closing the circle with my French connections and demonstrating through this a living example of the Auld Alliance.

All this was inherited by our children, who, despite being born and initially educated in London, also always 'knew' in some way that they were essentially Scots. They used to wind down the window of the car as we drove north each holidays and when we crossed the border breathed in 'real air'. They wore kilts to children's parties, to the amazement of other Islington mothers, and seem to feel about Riemore as I do. Given that they would disagree with me on most things as a matter of course and knew that I was wrong nine times out of ten, I can only assume that their feelings of rootedness comes from somewhere other than me. But I am so glad that they feel like that now.

Now, whether in the House of Lords (where I am Secretary of the Scottish Peers Association, which entails organising a cross-party gathering each year) or discussing applications to the Esmee Fairbairn Foundation, of which I am a

Trustee, my Scottishness is, amazingly, still a factor in how I go about my business. Of course, in the Lords, it is all mostly irrelevant with the advent of devolution (and I played my little part in the passage of the Scotland Bill) but my colleagues on the Foundation good-humouredly tolerate what they always assume is going to be a bias whenever a Scottish matter is raised. I don't object, and am just grateful that this allows my bias free range.

Today, my husband and I are back at Riemore, my father having died a year ago. He lived up there in the hills, alone for six years after my mother died, in the place of which he knew every inch and which represented the core of his being. He was a difficult man in many ways, who didn't like the idea of handing things over or losing control or authority over things. The result is that this place where we are all rooted is now going to need a lot of work, input and tender loving care – and money – if it is to survive. We have very little of the latter, but plenty of the former, and this includes my husband too. We are doing all the things people in our position have to do, which is to look desperately for ways and means to turn what my father always cheerfully called a 'non revenue producing asset' into a place where at least enough revenue can be generated to continue to make it viable. Common sense and reason may seem to argue that anybody in his or her right mind wouldn't even consider such a proposition. But what ties us to this place is not rooted in common sense and reason, but something much more important, far deeper and more binding than such sensible reactions, and this is what we are committed to. We have a grandson now, who may have less Scottish blood in his veins as his mother is a New Zealander, but on whom Riemore may come to weave its magic since it is roots we are talking about.

All this, and above all this place, is what my Scottishness is about.

# Jacqui Low

*A graduate of Edinburgh University, Jacqui Low began her career working in local radio in Dundee. From there, she spent five years in the Scottish Office as a Ministerial Press Officer, primarily in the area of Industry and the Economy. A spell in Standard Life's press office followed, after which she moved to become Head of Communications and Research at the Scottish Conservative Party. In 1995 Jacqui was appointed Special Advisor to then Secretary of State, Michael Forsyth, and was the first woman to hold the post in Scotland. After the 1997 election, she set up her own communications consultancy, Indigo (PR) Ltd, to specialise in reputation management using PR and strategic communications.*

I don't think I have ever questioned what makes me Scottish, any more than I question the colour of my hair or eyes. Being asked to consider such a notion has made me examine the very fibre of my being – and how many of us can explain that?

What I can't say is how much have I been moulded by genetics, parenting and environment versus some deeper, older and unseen influence. How much is learned and inherited behaviour – and where has that inheritance come from?

I am probably a typical Scot, not a 'heart on the sleeve'-type person, preferring to see myself as practical and reserved. But the sound of the pipes playing 'Highland Cathedral' can bring a lump to my throat and cause a welling-up of pride. I don't know why and can't explain the effect, but it's real.

Then there's the fact that, as someone who regards herself as a Unionist, I struggle to overcome my aversion to cheering on England in any sporting event – but I can when the same people wear the GB badge or even local team colours. I know there is no rational reason for such an attitude but, even so, I can't help it.

What is clear to me is that there isn't such a thing as a template for a Scot today. I, living in our increasingly cosmopolitan capital city, feel like a neutered Scot. It may be that I have had my Scottish rough edges smoothed away by years of cross-border forays and trips abroad so that whilst I have the accent and the address, can I honestly say my experience of being Scottish today is the same as that of someone in the Western Isles? Or in Stonehaven, Leven or Dumfries?

It may be more to do with the fact that Scotland itself is fragmenting, that the divisions aren't so much running through our society as along the geographical boundaries of our regions. This has always existed but now things like the economic effect of the Scottish Parliament is adding substance to the perception of a growing gap between Edinburgh/Glasgow and the rest of Scotland.

Almost imperceptibly, there feels like the beginnings of a two-culture Scotland as there are less and less shared national experiences to shape us. One will be populated by Scots like me, who feel empowered, mobile, who have a good quality of life and who can see a role for themselves in helping to realise the potential of this country in a global economy. The other will include those left behind, those whose opportunities are limited and who see and feel no difference in Scotland today from twenty years ago, because their horizons are unchanged. It is a danger we must all be alive to.

For now, we are a nation that has many constantly changing faces. But can we claim this makes us any different from any other country? We can be spectacularly petty at times, especially in politics when the cheap shot can carry more weight than a well-constructed argument. The 'wha's like us?' arrogance lies at the root of many of our country's spectacular sporting failures. Yet, in times of crisis, we can be rock solid and resilient; in adversity, we pull together. If in trouble, a Scot will rarely run away and is more than likely to stand his or her ground.

Against that, we build up successful people – especially those who triumph against perceived adversity – and then work just as hard to knock them down. It's what I describe as the 'kent his faither, clapped his dug' syndrome.

If you have the audacity to rise above your station in life, don't worry, your countrymen will put you back in your place. And, yet, there is genuine admiration among Scots for the many who have made it, but only for those who continue to respect their roots. That's why Sean Connery has survived his exile but Sheena Easton hasn't.

However, even those comments are said slightly tongue-in-cheek, because there is more substance to us than that. Scots have given the world freedom from pain, the means of global communication and the deep-fried Mars bar. Watching and listening to television and radio reports from around the world, I smile when I hear the interviewee has a Scottish accent. I take pride in coming from a culture whose influence on the world has been disproportionate to its population. Long may it continue.

Maybe being Scottish is just a state of mind. If it's about tartan, the kilt, swooping eagles, golf courses, Scottie dogs, couthy humour and a chip on the shoulder, it doesn't match up with my Scotland of dive-bombing pigeons, traffic congestion, urban foxes, innovation and an indestructible spirit.

For me, being Scottish is simply what I am.

# Bashir Maan

*Bashir Maan, born in what is now Pakistan in 1926, is a leading member of Glasgow City Council, President of the National Association of British Pakistanis and Chairman of Strathclyde Joint Police Board.*

I was born in a quiet farming village called Maan, in rural India, forty-five miles south-west of Lahore. My ancestor Ladha Maan, according to the family legend, left his homestead near Delhi on the orders of the Mughal emperor and founded the village, where he was made chief of a sizeable area taking in twenty-one villages. I am eleventh in line to Ladha.

My father's share of the family land was very modest due to our laws of inheritance. However, it was fertile and very productive and he usually rented out his holding and lived on its income. He himself received a very rudimentary schooling but was determined to educate his children.

When I finished my primary education in the village school at the age of ten I was sent to a high school about 180 miles away. It was a trying experience at that tender age but, looking back, I think it was that early ordeal which developed in my personality, confidence, perseverance and a sense of responsibility.

I was the first from my village and my family to go to university. During my student days the struggle for the independence of India and the campaign for the establishment of Pakistan was in full swing. As a Muslim student I fully participated in both movements and learned much about politics. India won its freedom and Pakistan came into being on 14 August 1947. For the next two years I helped to organise the resettlement of thousands of Muslim refugees from India in the various villages of our area and this gave me a taste for community-based work.

I arrived in Glasgow from Pakistan in early 1953 for further education and attended the Royal Technical College. There were then about 500 Asians, mainly from Pakistan, in Glasgow. They were mostly peddlers living in self-imposed segregation, perhaps for security reasons, and suffering from endemic racism, mostly institutional. I became so involved in helping them and fighting against racism that I had to abandon my studies.

During these endeavours I found Scottish people generally friendly, considerate, willing to listen and help. I was surprised to notice that while just walking about the streets complete strangers from the other side of the street would often greet you or nod their head and pass a remark about the weather or just say 'Hi!' with a smile.

I learned my lesson not to ignore anybody I come across soon after I arrived here. One day I went to visit a friend at his flat in a Gorbals tenement and as I was climbing up the stairs, keeping my head down, a woman was walking down. Noticing that I was not paying any attention to her, she stopped as we crossed each other and said, 'Listen, young man. In this country we don't just pass by people. We say good morning or good evening or just nod at them with a smile.' God bless her, that motherly admonition has stood me in good stead and won me many friends over the years.

My work for the community brought me into contact with the local politicians and officials. The co-operation and consideration I received from them convinced me of the inherent tolerance and the genuine concerns of the Scottish people for the deprived and marginalised Asian community living among them.

Increased contact with local politicians introduced me to politics, and in 1964 I was persuaded by my Scottish Labour Party friends to join the Labour Party. I think, perhaps, my sense of belonging to Scotland began to develop from then on without my realising it. That realisation dawned on me suddenly in 1970, when the people of Glasgow elected me as one of their city councillors, with an overall majority against three indigenous Scottish candidates.

My sense of being Scottish matured in the late eighties when I was involved in research for my book, *The New Scots*. I discovered that the Scots were a mixed race, and almost everybody here, like me, had come from some where else. Scotland's oldest constitutional document, the 1320 Declaration of Arbroath, states that 'the chronicles and the books of ancients' show the Scots to be a migrant people of mixed ethnic background. The Celts, who make up the majority of the present population of Scotland, are descended in part from the Aryans and so are the people of northern India, from where I come.

These facts strengthened my feeling of affinity with the Scots and of my being Scottish. I came here as a migrant, a stranger. Scotland welcomed me and gave me respect and honour – far more than many of its own. My nearly fifty years of living in Scotland has taught me much and has given me much more.

As a Muslim, among other moral values, my faith teaches me to be kind and congenial, to be forgiving and tolerant. Scotland, however, taught me to practise those values and to greet even strangers with a smile. Though very much aware of my Pakistani origins, I now feel privileged in being Scottish and part of a nation that has given so much to the world in education, in knowledge and in humanity.

# E. Mairi MacArthur

*E. Mairi MacArthur has worked abroad as a bilingual secretary and at home in the voluntary sector, in the environmental movement and on research into the history of Iona. Now self-employed, she runs a small part-time publishing venture and is involved in a variety of oral history and storytelling projects in the Highlands.*

It made a memorable place to play, yards from the front door. In the grassy precincts of St Andrews Cathedral you could dodge around the great pillar-bases of the nave and peer with fearful anticipation into the mossy depths of the holy well. Robert the Bruce, no less, came here for the consecration ceremony – though much more impressionable on young minds was the White Lady, as you scurried past her haunted tower on the seaward wall. Sometimes, at weekends, we tagged along to my father's workplace, the venerable University. There was the thorn tree planted by Queen Mary, here the polished hush of Parliament Hall, where the Scottish Estates once met, and finally a labyrinth of shadowy, book-lined corridors ideal for hide and seek, though known officially as the library stacks.

In summer the family decamped, to the island of Iona. As crows, our flight would have been almost directly due west. Instead, we were content to chug cross-country on several different railways, catch the night run out of Glasgow Buchanan Street on the old West Highland line and board a red-funnelled steamer at Oban pier. The holiday playgrounds included a green rampart strewn with bobbing harebells but which at one time enclosed a monastery of great renown. In full view lay a medieval Abbey first patronised by the Lords of the Isles.

Only gradually did it dawn that the two spots between which my childhood zigzagged held considerable significance for the country at large. The town of my birth and upbringing was written about in magazines and bore the name of

Scotland's patron saint, while my father's island home cropped up in school lessons about St Columba. By coincidence, my two native heaths were steeped in events and personalities that helped to shape the nation. Only now, perhaps, do I fully appreciate that privilege.

There were no great proclamations or reassurances about being Scottish. It seemed straightforward enough that we were distinct from our neighbours, if only in matters of language and accent which I could hear for myself. On Iona, in the 1950s, there was still plenty of Gaelic. In St Andrews, Scots was all around and though we did not use it as a family my first book, at two months, was Hogarth's *Scottish Nursery Rhymes*. 'Puddy in the Well' and 'Cheetie-Poussie-Cattie-O' retain a comforting familiarity to this day. England, and London in particular, seemed far away and quite exotic. The first trip, as a teenager, to the city where Big Ben chimed was genuinely exciting.

Why, then, does the matter of 'being Scottish' now feel much less clear-cut? At times, in fact, it can be plainly discomfiting – those unnecessarily mediocre radio programmes, that casual anti-English jibe masked as jovial banter – or just bemusing; is the nation really in such thrall to footie as the pervasive coverage implies? And I'm definitely with those for whom there are many Scotlands. Whenever I meet anyone rooted in a locality, whether by heredity or by choice, and who can talk of its place-names or customs or characters, sing a few verses composed there or relate a little of its lore, then that particular patch of land comes alive. Far from being parochial, such narratives pick up on human themes that are timeless and universal and they can, of course, be heard all across the planet. The ones I have been lucky enough to absorb happen to have a context within Scotland.

A distinct sense of being Scottish comes, perhaps, from two simple factors of geography. I never like to be for too long too far from the sea, and I always like to mark the turn of the seasons. I recall a tall, black-gowned headmaster who toured the classrooms one autumn with a genial reminder to stick with our own proper Hallowe'en and not to bother with that bonfire-night business. The Christmas of today does little for me, its jingly trappings too crass and intrusive. However, to the bafflement of many friends (by no means all non-Scots) I obstinately cherish the old notion of Hogmanay, with its clearing of desks and hearths, its conviviality and fireside cheer and looking to the future. The public fire festivals may have gone, bar a few, though their regular reinvention down the ages is hardly surprising in these dark northern climes.

I live on neither of my childhood coastlines now but in the heart of the Highland hills, under the brow of a vitrified Iron Age fort. Who knows how exactly the people of Knockfarrel identified themselves, but no doubt they created their own story for their own time and place. And I'd like to think that the depths of each winter brought some kind of celebratory ritual, and a flame in the night sky.

# *Bridget McConnell*

*Bridget McConnell has been Director of Cultural and Leisure Services, Glasgow City Council, since August 1998. She is currently a member of the Board of the Royal Scottish Academy of Music and Drama and is Chair of the Scottish Association of Directors of Cultural and Leisure Services. Bridget is married with two adult children.*

## Personal Reflections on Scottish Identity

1. All my life, and without really thinking what it means, I have described myself resolutely, and without hesitation, as being Scottish. Being Scottish has always felt more than a mere accident of birth and geography; it is the context in which I have defined myself and made sense of my world.

Some of my earliest memories are not just of the plethora of events and incidents which every child has – but significantly of a real sense of respect and hunger for education among family, friends and the wider community. Starting school, learning to play musical instruments, going to university, all were made to feel like the whole point of being alive! This was at least in part due to the air of optimism arising from the Wilson government of the 1960s, with a real sense of health, education and housing services being made genuinely available to the majority for the first time in history. Equally, I am sure, this was the direct result of my parents' and my grandmother's passion for education. In particular my grandmother, who lived until she was ninety-nine, was determined that her family would benefit from education in a way that she had always wanted for herself, but because of material circumstances was never able to do. Losing her only son and her husband to accidents in the coal mines, she had a burning anger about the opportunities lacking to so many young men and women because of the inequalities in society. Having been born in the last year of the nineteenth century and into a time when the vote was not available to women and education for women was extremely limited, she nonetheless believed that women should take advantage of education and develop a career wherever possible. Throughout my school education I was well aware that Scottish education was viewed as the best in the world and it was a direct consequence of that widely held belief that I never once considered doing anything other than completing my education and taking up employment in Scotland.

Graduating in the 1980s, determined to pursue a career in arts administration I was regularly advised that I would never succeed unless I either took up work outside of Scotland or arts administration training in London, as Scotland's culture and cultural infrastructure was not significant enough in its own right to provide the relevant quality arts experience. However, I soon discovered that this was simply not the case. Taking up employment initially with Tayside Regional Council at Dundee's Community Arts Centre, I found in local government a rich tradition of cultural activity supported and developed by local authorities that challenged elitist definitions of arts and culture, enhanced the role of the voluntary sector, developed new partnerships and nurtured personal and community confidence and pride in local traditions, achievements and abilities. Underpinning all of this was a fervent commitment to widen access to arts for all. As was later noted in the country's first ever charter for the arts published in 1993 by Scotland's Arts, Film, Museums, Libraries and Information Councils and COSLA, 'local authorities were the structural pivot of cultural life in Scotland'. Throughout this period there were unique cultural achievements indicating a new self-confidence in Scottish culture at home and abroad. For example, the establishment of the Scottish Youth Dance Festival, the renaissance of Traditional Music and Gaelic Culture, and the establishment of major new museums and arts centres in Glasgow, Dundee, Edinburgh and elsewhere; writers such as James Kelman, Jeff Torrington and Irvine Welsh winning national and international recognition, writing not only in English but in Scots; a new generation of visual artists such as Stephen Campbell and Adrian Wiszniewski; and bands such as Texas and Travis, to name but a few!

Significant as my post of Cultural and Leisure Services Director of Glasgow City Council is – and the only woman on the Glasgow City Council's Management

Team of twelve Chief Officers – I am acutely aware that I am more often perceived as the wife of Scotland's First Minister. Although I have always resisted the role of politician's wife there are some things as the First Minister's wife I am happy to have influenced, if only in a small way. For the first time ever, Bute House will be part of the Doors Open Day programme, giving the public unprecedented access. (There will even soon be a sign on its gates indicating for the public that it is the residence of the First Minister, providing assistance to confused tourists!). Already students from further education colleges have been providing catering services for official dinners, and students from the Royal Scottish Academy of Music and Drama and other institutions have been providing entertainment for official functions at the House. This may not seem much in itself but is none-theless symbolic of the fact that government in Scotland, local as well as national, and its institutions belong to, and are accountable and accessible to, the people, and that government is proud of its young Scottish talent and will showcase and support their achievements wherever it can.

2. On a very personal level, being Scottish has given me a sense of belonging to something greater than myself – a sense of belonging to both a history and a future, as much as I belong in the present. My family history, like many others, is part of a wider dynamic in society which influenced political, institutional and social developments, the most significant probably being the establishment of the Scottish Parliament. It is a fact of history that political parties in a democracy only succeed if they reflect society's will and interests and the Scottish Parliament is a direct result of the people's will for more responsive and more effective govern-ment. And it will only succeed if it reflects their aspirations and their humanity. For example, the current disquiet about the state of the National Health Service is one which everyone seems to have a view about and most have direct experience of. My own father died in April 2001 shortly after a diagnosis of lung cancer, and whilst there was genuine support and compassion from health professionals, nonetheless the overall verdict from the family was that much more could have, and should have, been done.

My parents and grandparents represent to me the large number of Scots, especially women, who are unknown and whose lives are unrecorded but are the ones who collectively, and through the ways they lived their lives, brought about the great social changes of our time. The public demand for a successful Health Service, along with other modernised and high-quality public services, is a continuation of that Scottish tradition.

3. Scottish identity in the opening years of the twenty-first century cannot be defined by any one organisation's or individual's experience or analysis alone, but rather as a sum total of the many diverse experiences, histories, views and cultures that have shaped, and continue to shape, modern-day Scotland. My sense of being Scottish is not an introspective one but rather an outward-looking one – and I believe that is the case for most Scots. Just as Scotland today has been influenced and transformed by many different cultures throughout history, equally our own indigenous Scots and Gaelic traditions are shaped by developments in other parts of the world, in particular North America. Recent celebrations of Scottish culture in the United States demonstrated that Scotland has not only an increasing confidence in itself, but is comfortable with, and sees no contradiction in, its 'Scottish-ness' being represented in all its diversity, by either tartan and shortbread, or young rock bands and comedians.

4. This confidence in Scottish identity and evidence of a national renewal was probably most recently in evidence for me at the Queen Mother's funeral, with the heads of the UK's devolved governments sitting alongside the UK Cabinet and heads of the Commonwealth Nations, the sound of the distant Highland pipes and drums leading the funeral cortege to Westminster Abbey, mixing with Bach's organ music inside, which created a magnificent new sound, at once strange yet hauntingly familiar – a new music with distinctive Scottish notes, reflecting and symbolising a reconfigured United Kingdom.

# Jack McConnell

*Jack McConnell was born in Irvine in 1960 and grew up on the Isle of Arran. He was educated at Arran High School and Stirling University, where he served as President of the Students Association. Mr McConnell is Scotland's third First Minister and is MSP for Motherwell and Wishaw. He is married to Bridget and has two children.*

In our hearts, but also in our heads.

From our past, but also finding contemporary expression.

'Being Scottish', feeling Scottish, is more than simply emotion, history, culture or democratic expression. 'Scottishness' may be a bit raw at times, but it reflects a rich tapestry of all that binds us together. And in the twenty-first century it must surely be a confident and more settled identity than at times in our chequered past.

Emotionally, being Scottish fills me with both pride and an element of guilt.

Pride in our role in invention and cutting-edge technology – the telephone, television, penicillin and today's cancer research. Pride in our positive and friendly reputation, recognised and applauded throughout the world. Pride in our legal and education systems, distinctive and used as models throughout the countries of the Commonwealth and beyond. Also pride in our contribution to government, ideas, literature and democratic developments outwith our borders.

Yet, guilt, too, that Scots abroad were involved historically in obscene acts of cruelty and exploitation. Scots played a crucial role in the development of the slave trade, and there is our shameful history of sectarianism in central Scotland and elsewhere. Anger when I think of the persecution and decay allowed over the centuries in our rural areas.

Visually, Scotland conjures up images of breathtaking hills and glens, beautiful lochs and rivers – unique images that thousands of people throughout the world marvel at. But images also of shipyards and mines, factories and farms, the industries that have shaped our past, and in many ways our character too.

At school my history lessons might have been full of kings and queens, but Scottish history is about the people – and it is those people who embody what our Scottish roots mean to me.

We picture our plaid-clad ancestors stalking the dramatic mountains and glens of Glencoe in ferocious conditions. Cities and towns where big families lived in cramped and appalling conditions on top of each other. Where women had lots of children, when many died young; an age where men grafted hard in the heavy labour industries and let off steam by going to the football on a Saturday afternoon. Times when families lived close by, and bringing home an opened pay packet was more than your life was worth. But also times when much earlier than elsewhere in the world it was possible for those born into ordinary families to join the education system, develop talents and improve lives.

Throughout my life, I have been fortunate enough to have lived in three very different parts of Scotland.

I grew up on a farm in the middle of the island of Arran and I went to a small rural school. I was always aware that any disadvantage of distance was overcome by the strength of family and community, and by the simple pleasures of growing up in such an area. I then moved to the former market town of Stirling, went to what was Scotland's newest and most dynamic university, and saw Stirling become one of the country's most modern, dynamic towns.

Now I represent and live in industrial Lanarkshire, in a constituency which was probably dealt the single most devastating economic blow in recent history when the Ravenscraig steel mill closed. This was a community based on steel and heavy industries, but it has achieved the challenge of developing new skills and employment to regenerate the area in recent times.

Scotland is all these and more. New cultures joining, integrating and influencing. Our cultural life in renaissance and a freshness about the contemporary expression of our traditional music and song. A new parliament, providing democratic expression for our national identity in a modern context.

But being Scottish for me has nothing to do with not being English. Our new Parliament and system of government can settle that old tension, developing a new relationship with the United Kingdom and allowing us to concentrate on the actions of government rather than the location of the decision makers.

Most young Scots today have a huge ambition and drive. Their aspirations give us the chance to develop ourselves as a nation where we are not continually looking over the border but moving on ourselves, comfortable inside the United Kingdom.

In my time as an MSP, I have seen enthusiasm and excitement at the opportunities for our young people today. They and their families are aware and willing to grasp the many chances available to them, and they are becoming increasingly confident, looking to the wider world for those opportunities. But today, as throughout our history, our Scottish identity encourages us to do better still. Far too many Scots do not have either the opportunity or belief in themselves to take up those new challenges, to enjoy and benefit from the successes, to live life to the full and to be fulfilled.

My 'Scottishness' may encourage me to wear the tartan, to put the pride above the guilt, to work tirelessly to make our new democracy work, but that identity makes me want – more than anything else – to see all our citizens make the most of life, to live long and happy lives, and to look after each other as well as ourselves. That is what Being Scottish means most to me.

# John McCormick

*John McCormick took up the position of Controller at BBC Scotland in January 1992. Born in Ayrshire, John McCormick is a history graduate of Glasgow University. He is Chairman of the Edinburgh International Film Festival; Board member of Scottish Screen; Lay Member of Court, University of Strathclyde; and Board member of the Glasgow Science Centre. He was awarded an Honorary Doctorate of Laws from the University of Strathclyde in April 1999; an Honorary Doctorate of the University from the University of Glasgow in June 1999; an Honorary Doctorate from the Robert Gordon University; and appointed an Honorary Professor of the Department of Film and Media Studies, Stirling University. He is a Fellow of the Royal Television Society.*

I'm writing this in the weekend that we celebrated the retirement of a great Scot – Bill McLaren. It was a very Scottish occasion. Not for Bill the black-tie dinner with the great and good. (And, of course, the greatest and the best would have all wanted to meet and say farewell to Bill McLaren.) No, after Bill put down his microphone at the end of his commentary at the Melrose Sevens he allowed us to have a gathering in Hawick Golf Club, a gathering of family, friends and the people from BBC Scotland who had been closest to him in his broadcasting work. No great ceremony. No fuss. A relaxed occasion, full of fun. Close. Unpretentious.

For me it sums up something special about being Scottish. Bill was never a man to be sidetracked from the task in hand or seduced by the distractions of fame or the baubles that can go with it. He is a man to be respected because he knows instinctively what is true and what is worthless. Rooted in his community in the Borders, his reputation is truly global and yet he could say – and mean it – that 'a day out of Hawick is a day wasted'. Bill has a true sense of himself as a Borders man.

Being Scottish today is, for me, being part of a country that has a truer sense of itself than the Scotland I grew up in during the 1950s.

I was born in Ayrshire, exposed in school to no Scottish history and no Scottish literature, apart from Burns. Scott and Stevenson came at home from my father, and it was also my father's great interest in the movies that had an enduring effect. We went every week but the Britain I saw represented on the screen bore no relationship to how my family lived. It was a land of English country houses, all with drawing rooms with French windows, looking out on large gardens, in films almost all of which seemed to star Margaret Lockwood. My father preferred the Hollywood version. It may not have been any more realistic but, as he said, the Yanks knew how to write a script. So the great cultural influences of my childhood were Burns, Humphrey Bogart, Spencer Tracy, Katherine Hepburn and Jean Arthur (his favourite).

Through the 1960s and into the 1970s the key cultural influences, however, were, in the main, English dominated in publishing, film making and broadcasting. Cultural messages come from so many different sources but there is less chance now of the Scottish voice being drowned out by the English or American as in the 1960s. And there are many different Scottish voices. Through the 1960s BBC Scotland was selling to the UK tartan and bagpipes wrapped up in shows like *The Kilt is My Delight* and, famously, *The White Heather Club*. But it was also the time of breakthroughs in drama, with Pharic MacLaren's memorable production of Grassic Gibbon's classic *Sunset Song*. And we shouldn't forget that, today, Robbie Shepherd's programmes on Radio Scotland featuring Scottish country dance music are among the station's most popular. They are an important part of contemporary Scotland for a lot of people, just as much as the TV series *Tinsel Town* or Lynne Ramsay's films *Ratcatcher* and *Morven Caller*.

Today, across the board, there are opportunities and outlets and investment that weren't there twenty-five years ago, opportunities to have work published, music performed or films produced which are distinctively Scottish. Work created by people living and working here in Scotland, drawing on their own experience but not constrained by it. We are in some ways only at the beginning of this process to ensure that creative talent can be encouraged and supported and developed away from the overheated south-east of England.

The Scottish Parliament is also intertwined in all of that. I don't think there's any doubt that a feeling of cultural self-confidence contributed to the sense of optimism that led to the creation of the Scottish Parliament. And now before its first term is over we're 'ca'ing the feet from it' and wondering if we did the right thing. Now that's very Scottish. The 'Mother of Parliaments' has had centuries to establish itself. No such timescale for us. In terms of historical sweep an instant judgement is in danger of being made.

So, for me, being Scottish today means being part of the generation that helps to ensure that this parliament is one that a small self-confident country deserves. Cultural and political self-confidence can be a potent mix. It's up to all of us to make sure we don't let it slip away this time.

# Neil MacCormick

*Sir Neil MacCormick MEP QC(hon) MA LLD hon LLD, FBA FRSE is on leave of absence as Regius Professor of Public Law and the Law of Nature and Nations in the University of Edinburgh, and is currently (1999–2004) a Member of the European Parliament (SNP) for Scotland, and a Vice President of the Scottish National Party. His most recent book is* Questioning Sovereignty: Law, State and Nation in the European Commonwealth *(Oxford University Press, 1999, paperback edn 2001).*

Seldom if ever have I felt such exhilaration as on 1 July 1999, on the occasion of the formal opening of the Scottish Parliament, and the celebrations throughout Edinburgh on that mild July evening. Everybody around was happy, and everybody positive. We hadn't got a parliament to score a point against somebody else, but just to affirm ourselves.

Donald Dewar's achievement and John Smith's unfinished business? Yes, and I would take nothing away from either of them, for they were both my friends over many years. But for me it was even more John MacCormick's unfinished business. The Scottish Covenant of 1949 with its two million signatures was ultimately redeemed by the referendum of 1997.

The Covenant itself resulted from a falling out within the SNP between those who wanted a strict political party (the continuing SNP) and those like my father (the Scottish Convention) who hoped to pose the issue of Home Rule as a cross-party and above-party idea. Both views turned out to be right in the end. Without the persistent SNP threat to Labour, the consensus articulated from 1988 through the Constitutional Convention from 1988 would probably not have borne fruit. The broad-based alliance for the referendum of 1997 was what it took to get the thumping majority needed and achieved.

My father and mother were both involved in the National Party from the outset in 1928, through the then recently founded Glasgow University Scottish Nationalist Association. Without John MacCormick's diplomatic if useful chairing, no party would have emerged at all. The merger with the Scottish Party six years later to create the SNP was, for good or ill, primarily his achievement. Others from that date included the formidable Eleanor M. Dewar, aunt in due course of her brother Alisdair's son Donald, and 'courtesy aunt' to a numerous brood of young Mac-Cormicks. One who never quite forgave John MacCormick his departure from the Independent Labour Party into the ranks of nationalism was Archie Smith of Tarbert, a student contemporary in the University Labour Club, who stayed there, but later went on to become headteacher of Ardrishaig School, and father of John Smith.

Being Scottish certainly involves tangled roots and connections, incest almost. This is all to do with being a citizen of a small country, with its own strong networks in education, culture, the law, medicine, music, journalism, the arts and sciences, and whatever else.

In the European Parliament, we are a 'region'. 'How is it in your region?' they ask benignly. Probably a translation of the German '*Land*' is what they are striving for. If so, 'country' would be nicer. Anyway, there is a real dislocation of sensibilities. Everybody I know at home – and most people in England also – thinks of Scotland as a nation, indeed one of Europe's ancient nations.

How Scottish am I, and what kind of Scottish? My father's family were intensely Highland, from Mull, Iona and Glenurqhart, Gaelic-speaking, song-composing, pipe-playing, bards and (in case of Great-Uncle John) Gaelic novel-writing. When I was at school in Glasgow, at the High School in Elmbank Street, I would go to Great-Uncle Neil's on the way home, up a grimy tenement stair to a spotless home. He and his brother Dugald, retired sea captain and Australian adventurer come on hard days, taught me the practice chanter. I learned not just of piping but of an imaginary landscape, the Ross of Mull in the great days of the nineteenth century when the quarries were turning out majestic pink granite for monuments everywhere, and for foundations of docks and of lighthouses like Skerryvore. I still don't speak Gaelic properly, but I have a toehold on the old Gaelic culture, from the stories of the tunes I learned, and the words of pibroch songs.

My mother's people were contrastingly Lowland and Scotch-spoken, from

Fife and Lanarkshire, with some Ulster-Scots flavouring. They were medical people and merchants, with some house building in the Townhead going back a couple of generations (they lived in the flats that they built, no purpose-built slums these, though the arrival of the railways changed all that). In the summers, we ran wild for a month in the huge garden of my grandmother's Bothwell home after our July holiday in Mull or at Tayvallich.

We were an essentially Presbyterian family, I suppose, but we were not sharply aware of it, for we were far removed from any kind of orangeism, and were brought up in a free-thinking way outside of the dour dominion of the Kirk. The divided schools made Catholic Scotland strange to us, much stranger than Jewish Scotland, until long after, essentially until university friendships broke barriers (and my brother became a convert). Getting to know Muslim Scotland has come much later. I am thankful to have lived at a time when having our parliament and our political institutions has cancelled any tendency to make Scottishness some-how a religious or confessional issue.

In my professional life, as in the European Parliament, I move in a completely international milieu, while remaining consciously an heir of the massively signi-ficant philosophical tradition of the democratic intellect and of Scots law. I hope that means that I am very Scottish, but not narrowly so, and that my highly liberal nationalism is the other face of my internationalism.

# Mukami McCrum

*Mukami McCrum is the Chief Executive of Central Scotland Racial Equality Council Ltd (CSRECL), responsible for the overall running of the organisation. She was born in Kenya and has lived in Scotland since 1973, having been educated in both Kenya and Edinburgh. She is a founder-member of Shakti Women's Aid, the first refuge for black women who experience domestic violence in Scotland. In addition she is a member of the following advisory forums and committees: UK Government Race Relations Forum; the Racial Equality Advisory Forum of the Scottish Executive; NLCB; Comic Relief Africa Grants Committee; and Responding to Conflict. Mukami has a deep commitment to justice, peace and equality issues at local, national and international level and actively campaigns against all forms of discrimination.*

I will start by telling you how Scotland became my country. I was born in Kenya of the Kikuyu people whose ancestral home is on the slopes of Mount Kenya. Among the Kikuyu, when a woman gets married she leaves her home and her people to set roots among her husband's people. Therefore, when I married a Scot, the Scottish people became my people and Scotland became my country. I was a young woman when I came to Scotland twenty-nine years ago, with my first-born baby just a few months old. From very early on I found the Scots, especially friends, relatives and neighbours, to be warm, caring and easy to get on with. However, it was not long before the other side of the Scots became evident. The side that did not believe that Scotland was my home.

I have lived in Scotland for most of my adult life, and, all things being equal, being Scottish for me should have been easy. There are so many similarities between the Scots and my people: our history, our patriotic pride and our dignity. I was brought up in the Church of Scotland tradition and my first encounter with Scots was through the mission hospital. If I close my eyes when I am in St Michael's Church in Linlithgow, it is like being in St Andrew's Church in Nairobi. The lush and fertile landscape that unfolds as I travel through the hills and valleys of Scotland takes me back to the country of my birth. On a sunny day it is like driving through the white highlands towards Nakuru or Nyeri. When I see politicians, and men in particular, believing in their own importance, and listen to mothers fussing about their children, I know immediately that if the words or remarks were translated into my mother tongue they would carry the same sentiment. If it was not for the rain, I could be forgiven for believing that I was back in Unjiru, where I grew up.

In school I was taught Scottish history and the parallels between our people were immediately evident. The clans of Scotland were as important to Scots as the Nine clans of the Kikuyu people. The clearances of the Scottish Highlands were about land ownership as were the clearances of the white highland that dispossessed my people. In my younger days I could beat many Scots at Scottish dancing.

For me, being Scottish is about a sense of belonging, identity and how others see me. While Kenyans often remind me that I am Scottish, not all Scots have come to terms with my colour and ethnic background. When I say that I come from Linlithgow, political correctness makes some people accept it, while others ask me, where do you really come from – a question my children, who are Scottish by descent and birth, are asked on a regular basis – and, might I add, strongly object to! For some people I was okay as long as I blended and did not assert my rights in any way. How does someone of my colour blend, I wondered? It was not okay when I insisted that my name was Mukami instead of the many derivatives or anglicised versions that were considered easier on the Scottish tongue.

I learnt too late that the Scottish people knew nothing or very little about my people, but I did expect to be treated as a human being. My Scottish teachers in Kenya never told us about the inherent fear and dislike that some Scots have for people like me. Yet I was taught about their greatness, sense of humour and about people like David Livingstone and Rabbie Burns who were noble, superior, brave, tolerant, hospitable, hard-working and kind.

My people have humour, too, but some Scots may not understand why some of my experiences in Scotland can make my African friends roll on the ground with laughter. My experiences are a mixture of moments of expressing happiness and joy, sorrow and sadness, and the occasional tear or two. Scotland made me almost lose 'myself' as I wrestled with forces compelling me to lose the 'chip on my shoulder' and replace it with shoulder pads. Clearly my colour and being Scottish were mutually exclusive and a challenge for many people.

Many little and big things conspired to create a sense of alienation. My first encounter with hostility was when I was pushed off the pavement on to a busy road and I had to struggle to keep my baby and myself from being run over by a car. The laughter from the young men who did this still haunts me. I still drive past the garage where the owner refused to change my flat tyre when I was six months pregnant. My husband had no answer when I asked why his people were so mean to me when my people had treated him like a king!

Then there was the spitting, bricks through my car windscreen, and the endless malicious phone calls. Abusive language and negative comments about physical appearance such as thick lips were always hurtful, but those were the days before collagen injections were fashionable. All this would have meant nothing if the system had protected my children from unfairness, ill treatment and systematic racial harassment at schools by pupils and teachers. When my son was little he was described as cute but it seems to me that society did not want him to grow up like other boys. As a young man, he could not participate freely in ordinary small-town life. At any moment in a Scottish pub, criminals of all sorts, including murderers, wife beaters, child molesters, can socialise without any trouble but the landlord would ban a young Scottish man of a different complexion for resisting abuse from fellow pub-goers. This is where being Scottish for people like me starts to wear thin.

Other comments were a source of amusement in a sad sort of way. A friend of mine was told that our natural colour was not special because it was not acquired like a sun tan. In other words, being born with a natural brown complexion is not as special as two weeks on the beach, tanning bed or lotion.

Being a Scot abroad has its own challenges. I get teased about my use of Scottish words with an African accent. My colleagues in other parts of the world describe me as the African woman who talks about Scotland as much as she talks about Kenya. Scotland does not know it but I have become the unofficial, unknown, unsung ambassador of Scotland. But I am careful not to behave like some Scots abroad. A few years ago in Australia, I offended an immigration officer of Scottish origin, who had tried to test my knowledge of Scotland, by telling him that, in reality, the only people who had a right to check my passport were Aboriginal Australians. He was not amused to be reminded that he was a migrant worker – a term reserved for people like me.

Will I still feel Scottish tomorrow and tomorrow and tomorrow?

# Finlay Macdonald

*The Right Reverend Doctor Finlay A. J. Macdonald is Moderator of the General Assembly of the Church of Scotland.*

'Play Kilmarnock!' 'Play Dunfermline!' 'Play Dundee!'
These are not a manager's musings on the fixture list but instructions issued by my grandmother. The Kilmarnock, Dunfermline and Dundee in question were not Scottish football teams. They were psalm tunes.

Granny would come from her 'hielan' hame' for extended visits. She was a great seamstress and would spend her days at the treadle sewing machine which shared a room in our house with the piano. As Granny sewed, her teenage grandson practised his Clementi and his Czerny. When practice was over I became a kind of ecclesiastical juke box. She would call out her favourite psalm tunes and, leafing through the split words/music pages of the Scottish psalter, I would play her requests. Forty years on I still think of the tunes with their numbers attached – Harington 66, Huddersfield 71.

Granny came from the village of Breanish in the parish of Uig on the island of Lewis. There she worked the croft and wrote Gaelic poetry. My grandfather had been the lay missionary there, with the Church of Scotland's Home Board. She was an early supporter of the suffragette movement and in between the psalm tunes she would hold forth on the iniquity of the Church's policy of restricting its ministry and eldership to men. 'Women were the first apostles of the resurrection!', she would inform her grandson. I am pleased that she lived to see the Kirk's first women ministers. She would have made a fine, if somewhat fierce, one herself!

Part of my own sense of 'being Scottish' certainly involves a familiarity and a deep affection for the Scottish metrical psalms. This is a rich heritage and one I cherish dearly.

Burns wrote with warm sentiment in 'The Cottar's Saturday Night' of the family at worship 'round the ingle':

> They chant their artless notes, in simple guise,
> They tune their hearts, by far the noblest aim;
> Perhaps Dundee's wild-warbling measures rise,
> or plaintive 'Martyrs', worthy of the name;
> Or noble Elgin' beets the heavenward flame,
> The sweetest far of Scotia's holy lays:
> Compar'd with these, Italian trills are tame.

Granny and I would agree!

My first parish was in Clackmannanshire. I recall conducting a Remembrance Sunday service in Alva, the congregation gathered in a dreich drizzle round the town war memorial. We sang the 23rd psalm to Crimond and you could feel as well as hear the familiar cadences rising and falling, mingling mournfully with the November mirk.

What a moment at the start of each day in the General Assembly when the precentor (who leads the unaccompanied psalm singing) takes up the opening psalm and a thousand voices join in vigorous praise of God! And on 1 July, 1999 the Scottish Parliament was itself reconvened with the singing of the Auld Hundredth.

The rendering of the psalms into metre and their setting to simple, easily remembered melodies was a vital element in the Scottish Reformation. The General Assembly, meeting in Edinburgh in December 1562, was clearly anxious to publish a selection of psalms for popular use, deciding to lend Robert Lekprevik, printer 'twa hundreth punds to help buy irons, ink and paper and to fie craftsmen for printing'. Thirty-nine years later another General Assembly, meeting at Burntisland, was to initiate the process which gave us the King James Bible. By such means the people were able to read and to sing the faith in their own familiar tongue. It was this same spirit which lay behind the Knoxian vision of a school in every parish, a system which enabled young people not only to be tutored in the Christian religion but to receive a general education which would open doors of opportunity, regardless of social class. This certainly has much to do with 'being Scottish'.

However, by the mid-seventeenth century puritan forces had risen up and under their influence the development of psalmody was eclipsed. The choice was limited to twelve approved tunes and no deviation from these was permitted. The liturgical historian Millar Patrick, in his *Four Centuries of Scottish Psalmody*, tells a bizarre tale from Bridge of Teith Church 'in the days when the tyranny of the Twelve Tunes still persisted'. He continues: 'New tunes were beginning to be allowed elsewhere, and one day the precentor, without authorisation or warning, broke into the novel strains of Bangor when the psalm was given out. The minister, Mr Fletcher, sat for a moment or two dumbfounded, unable to believe his ears, then rose, seized the pulpit Bible and brought it down with stupefying force on the head of the offender beneath him, and dared him ever to be guilty of such an outrage again.' This also says something about 'being Scottish'!

# Margo MacDonald

*Margo MacDonald is currently MSP for Edinburgh and the Lothians. Formerly MP for Govan, Margo was Deputy Leader of the SNP from 1974 to 1979. Her varied career also includes working as a barmaid, teacher and Director of Shelter (Scotland). She writes weekly columns for the* Sunday Post *and the* Edinburgh Evening News. *Margo is a Hibs fan and enjoys country and western music.*

I've always been Scottish, a Celt, never British. I identified more with the men who occupied the Dublin Post Office many years before I was born, than I ever did with Winston Churchill, the first national icon I remember … ironically, without whose bulldog qualities Scotland might have been a much less congenial place.

There was an unspoken reservation about the twentieth century's greatest Englishman among the adults surrounding me in the middle years of the last century: Churchill had been a great war leader, that was true but … As I grew up in the dying days of the Lanarkshire coalfield, I heard of the other Churchill, the man who sent soldiers against the miners of Tonypandy, and the man who, in common with his aristocratic class, thought England had won the war.

My home town was the regimental headquarters of the Cameronians. I learned there were no better soldiers in the British army than in the Scottish regiments. I couldn't stand the whole Union Jack bit, even as a wee girl. My heroes were Wallace and Bruce; they didn't start their battles with the reminder 'England expects … '; their symbols were the thistle, St Andrew's Cross and Lion Rampant.

I don't know from where my nationalism came. It must have been in the air I breathed because I have no memory of an event, or meeting, or of a book being either catalyst or defining moment. Being Scottish was simply what I was. Later, my nationalism meshed with other beliefs and assumptions. I was anti-nuke, anti-Vietnam War, pro-civil rights, pro-Hungary and the bitter-sweet Prague spring of

Alexander Dubček. With the beginning of political analysis came the start of a love–hate relationship with my fellow Scots. How could they claim nationhood yet not demand the sovereignty for which people elsewhere gave their lives?

I know now it's not uncommon for a people, a nation, to be without the political means of deciding their own priorities and, therefore, of being the ultimate guardian of their own interests, which, in our shrinking world, includes the ability to barter internationally and join, or not, international treaties or military actions. Apart from Scotland, I cannot think of one stateless nation which does not aspire to these de facto or internationally recognised powers. What sort of people are we that we should put up with an arrangement for governing and guarding our nationhood that few of us endorse without equivocation, rather than take responsibility for who we are, and for our contribution to humanity, global politics and economics?

Where do we position Scotland in the global village? In the kailyard, or shoulder-to-shoulder with small, progressive and respected peoples like the Scandinavians?

The ambiguity common among our unionist political establishment offers a third way: Scotland could be like Bavaria … only not exactly, because Bavaria's not a nation.

If the homogeneity created by the British state, and, more recently, by North-Atlantic popular culture hasn't destroyed the roots of distinctive Scottishness, the egalitarianism derived from Knox, or Burns, or, maybe, from that group of fourteenth-century landowners who challenged the God-given doctrine of feudalism, makes us a candidate for membership of the good guys' club of nations. And we like this self-image. It fits well with barely-remembered notions of modesty and moderation promulgated by the Covenanters, and the fierce independence of spirit that characterised Scots from north of the Highland line.

It's a myth. We're moderate, but only because we fear the consequences of pushing ourselves to the limit. Our independence has been eroded by our willingness to play second fiddle, while defensively asserting that Scots play that role better than anybody, anywhere. Why is there such a low ceiling on our aspirations for Scotland? Why are we content to let Secretaries of State, in London, make strategic decisions at the interface of morality and realpolitic which, were they made in a Scottish forum, would expand and enrich our national psyche?

For a minority of Scots, being British says it all. For most other Scots who eschew the label 'nationalist', being British has to be rationalised: Scotland gains more than she gives to the Union; Scotland is too poor to act independently of England; we punch above our weight in the world. This is where the honourable, independently-minded Scot gives way to the collectively cowed community that complains ineffectually when slighted, or disagrees with actions taken in our name, but is too scared to strike out for the far shores of shared international responsibility and self-respect.

Because we hadn't the courage or confidence to demand powers appropriate for a national parliament, disappointment has to be rationalised, so lack of ability among MSPs is instanced as proof Scotland couldn't run a sweetie shop let alone a country. That, more than the humanity and egalitarianism of our greatest poet-hero, defines the Scot at the beginning of the third millennium.

# John McGurk

*John McGurk is Editorial Director of The Scotsman Publications Ltd.*

So God is creating Scotland. And as he looks down on his work, he sees areas of rich seams across the central belt. ' Well,' he says, 'that's coal so that these Scots can keep themselves warm.' There in the Highlands, he observes clean, deep lochs and fresh running streams. ' That's the finest water,' says God, 'so that these Scots can make whisky, the best drink in the world.' Across into the North Sea, there are dark pockets running along the seabed stocked with precious fluid. 'That's oil,' says God, 'so that Scotland will be a nation of riches.' 'Aren't you being too generous to these Scots?' God is asked. 'Certainly not,' says God, '... just wait and see who I give them as neighbours!' And so it began.

I don't know when I first realised I was Scottish. Perhaps I was aged around five when my father, who had been a Royal Scots piper during the Second World War, would parade up and down our modest living room blaring out 'The Black Bear'. My brother and I would hide under the table with our hands over our ears. These days, when I take my own children every year to the Edinburgh Military Tattoo, and the massed bands strike up that powerful war-cry as the traditional climax to their performance, it brings tears to my eyes.

But it wasn't until my career in newspapers began to blossom that I began to understand what being Scottish was really all about. Although I had served a successful apprenticeship with a local county newspaper group in Midlothian, my attempts to work as a reporter in the old North Bridge headquarters of *The Scotsman* were thwarted at each attempt. In those days, you had to have gone to the right school in Edinburgh to join such an illustrious newspaper. So in 1974 I headed to England to work on the evening paper in Nottingham. Aged twenty-one, I was in an alien land with alien voices eating alien food – faggots always seemed to be on the works' canteen menu – while my new colleagues treated me with suspicion. That was the first time I knew I was Scottish, and I wanted to go home.

Yet when I did return north of the border to work in national newspapers in Glasgow, it was equally alien. I discovered that the west of Scotland was very different to the east. They asked me if I was the office 'Tim' and I didn't have a clue what they were talking about. The early years of the now demolished *Daily Record* and *Sunday Mail* building at Anderston Quay provided a very different kind of Scottish education, where 'bluenoses' reigned, where several 'hauffs' were mandatory at lunchtimes in the Copycat and where anti-English stories never hit the spike. I became Deputy Editor of both papers. Being from Edinburgh, I was regarded as being posh while in Edinburgh I was sure I had been regarded as being common.

Working in Scottish newspapers in the 1980s, at the height of Thatcherism, rammed home the archetypal image of downtrodden Scots at the hands of those English. The miners' strike; the shutdown of Ravenscraig; the further erosion of real shipbuilding on the Clyde; the protests over the poll tax; the loss of big business as our nation was sacrificed. How it would all change, we believed, if we got rid of those dreadful Tories and were able to run our own affairs. By that time I had eventually made it to North Bridge, ironically joining as Editor of the *Edinburgh Evening News*. A few weeks after the 1997 general election I became Editor of *Scotland on Sunday*. In the referendum campaign and then the historic Scottish election to follow in 1999, I was sure that devolution truly was the way forward, and, of course, said so. What happened then, you couldn't make up. We had three First Ministers in a year. As for our own Parliament, is this really what we'd fought for? Or are we a nation that enjoys having pain inflicted? Like a World Cup football match, we love to build ourselves up only to see ourselves being knocked down.

I like being Scottish. I would have been very disappointed if my children had not been born in Scotland. I enjoy our traditions, our heritage, our history and our reputation abroad. I like the size of Scotland, the beauty of the north, the humour of Glasgow and the village that is Edinburgh. Sadly, we are renowned for our unhealthy lifestyle (although we're making progress) and we're generally too quick to realise our limits. Too often we're too happy to make the best of what we've got when we could have settled for something better. It's a kind of 'never mind … that's the way it goes' Scottish mentality. But when God did create Scotland and the Scots, he didn't make a bad job … didn't he?

# Ian Mackenzie

*Ian Mackenzie was born in 1931, and educated at Fettes and the University of Edinburgh. He has been Assistant Organist and Assistant Minister at St Giles' Cathedral, Edinburgh, and Assistant General Secretary of the Student Christian Movement. Previously Executive Producer, ITV Religion, London, and Head of Religious Programmes at BBC Scotland, he is now a freelance writer, and preacher.*

Scottish scenery is talked of as if it was detachable, like a film set or computer graphic: a mountain, a loch, a winding road. But the chunks of physical reality that are home to 5 million humans are of serious diversity. Scotland is not a landscape, it is many landscapes. It is not a culture, it is many cultures. Is it, therefore, many countries? Of course. And as you can't live in a landscape without absorbing its physical components, you aren't going to grow up or grow old with a people without inhaling their prejudices.

I was born in Fraserburgh, a grey town which grew backwards from an outcrop of rock on the north-east corner of Buchan. By walking a few yards round a corner you moved from facing Scandinavia to facing the North Pole. In Buchan a tree was an event, as was a calm day. The North Sea churned over the harbour wall like a predator. I grew up with a sense of being on the edge of danger. As steam drifters lurched and plunged out to sea in wild gales, they were all too often on suicide missions to hunt fish. Then in the Hitler war Luftwaffe planes from Norway hurtled in under the radar to hunt us. But in peacetime I was aware of a benign edge. Ships from foreign countries called in; and in summer double-headed freight trains snaked several times a day out of the town for the long journey to London with fish for hotel breakfasts and protein for people even further away, starving in Russia.

It was a tough landscape. The people, too, were tough. Originally from the

Low Countries, they had tamed an unforgiving land to yield food and a living. They ploughed and they fished, they traded, and they spoke a Doric tongue with a crackling energy. Nor were their old ladies less fierce: they dabbled furiously in stocks and shares. When I was thirteen my father died and we left Buchan, I assumed forever. My parents, being Highland, had felt alien in the Doric culture. Highland aunts and uncles pitied me for having been beached on an abrasive shore. Brochers regarded most Highlanders as devious and lazy, charmers who would utter any lie to please you: my Highland relatives thought the Buchan folk allergic to subtlety.

For me then it was Edinburgh, for school, university, first jobs. I became attuned to the capital's smoothness. Yet, despite meeting many wonderful individuals, I didn't feel at home in Edinburgh. I missed the granite of Aberdeen and the mistiness of Inverness. These contrasting urban landscapes were not merely visual experiences. Aberdeen was on its own terms an exhilarating capital city to its hinterland. Inverness, now officially a city, was capital to an empire of islands. Its dreamy softness was incarnate in the lilting voices sleepwalking off the early trains from north and west, relaxing in gossip over coffee in the Station Hotel.

In mid-life, after some years working in London, I was asked to be the minister of the Muckle Kirk in the Blue Toon (Peterhead), the other, bigger sea town eighteen miles south of Fraserburgh. I returned to Buchan with foreboding, remembering a dark-streaked childhood in war storm and sea storm, and the dying of my father. I was astounded. I discovered Buchan as a new country. After Edinburgh and London, it blew me away: stupendous seascapes and skyscapes, vast sunsets, open weather, gaunt trees and brown earth as of *Sunset Song*. Its people were distinct, brave, funny, and shot through with poetry, struggling to absorb the vandalism of the oil boom and the Brussels' betrayal of the fishing industry. I don't see myself fighting for Scotland, but I might have fought for Buchan. As I might fight for gentle Galloway and its princess of a town, Dumfries. As I might for the kingdoms of Moray, Fife, Orkney, Shetland, Lewis. As I would for Loch Maree, Suilven, Arran, Kintyre. I've now lived long on the Clyde. For Glasgow I might fight, for it is the nearest to an urban Scottish heart, a true city state. I might even have fought for Edinburgh, if its new parliament had been set, as we all imagined it, on a hill, instead of crowding it in beside a part-time palace.

But best of all would have been to arrange for the new forum to move around Scotland. Given the chance to try a new kind of radically developed democracy, we blew it. We saw ourselves as just another political territory to be managed rather than as the many countries we are, each waiting for the release of its dreams.

# Sheila McLean

*Professor Sheila A. M. McLean LLB., M.Litt., Ph.D., FRSA, FRCPE (Edin), FRSE, is the first holder of the International Bar Association Chair of Law and Ethics in Medicine at Glasgow University and is Director of the Institute of Law and Ethics in Medicine at Glasgow University. She has acted as a consultant to the World Health Organisation and the Council of Europe. She has published extensively in the area of medical law, is on the editorial board of a number of national and international journals and is regularly consulted by the media on matters of medical law and ethics.*

It is surprisingly difficult to explain something so profound and innate as a sense of belonging to a particular country. In some ways, it is a little like suffering from a bipolar disorder – immense highs (when Scotland actually does something outstanding) and lows (when Scotland loses at rugby or football)! Equally, to continue the metaphor, being Scottish both includes and excludes others. It is the unthinking attribution of loyalty that possibly best describes being Scottish. Like many Scots, I am happy to remind the world of all of the things we have achieved, invented or discovered, but all too ready to forget the role Scots themselves played in the Highland Clearances or in slavery.

But the sense of belonging is much more profound than these examples would suggest. In the long run, it is about a deep, but subliminal, identification with a small piece of earth and its people. And, of course, it transcends the cultural or racial characteristics of these people. Everyone who lives here is accepted as Scottish irrespective of his or her original roots, and that is as it should be. However, this is also somewhat puzzling, as it seems to confuse the reasons for loyalty. It is not possible to define Scotland in terms that exclude those who have migrated to its shores – indeed, it is often impossible to identify anyone's heritage.

Scots have absorbed many different cultures and shaped them throughout the rest of the world. A visit to almost any country will reveal the pride which ex-patriot Scots maintain in their Scottishness even after many generations have passed.

Yet there are some things which seem to be peculiarly Scottish. A fierce dedication to education shaped this country and its people historically. An almost visceral commitment to social inclusion and the rights of everyone to have access to health care and other social services permeates the way we aspire to live. The introduction of a devolved parliament with considerable powers has served, in my view, both to facilitate involvement in these areas and to reinforce their importance.

In some ways, of course, identifying ourselves as Scottish is also exclusionary. It serves to prove that we are not English, or French or whatever, and somehow seems to be an important part of the collective psyche. Since this generally doesn't stem from hostility to others, it is difficult to explain why when asked I will always reply, 'I am Scottish,' rather than, for example, British.

There is also a kind of revolutionary aspect to Scottishness. Great thinkers, leaders and inventors have emerged from this culture, many of them radical, opinionated, almost anarchistic in their views. The stubbornness and drive that made them great is evident at all stages in their work. The thinkers of the Scottish Enlightenment perhaps exemplify this most clearly, with their radical and visionary approach, which has had such an intellectual and practical impact worldwide.

Of course, being Scottish is also about sentimentality. Which true Scot doesn't get a tear in the eye when the bagpipes swirl? Who doesn't look back at our history and feel him- or herself to have been a victim rather than a victor? Who doesn't deeply resent the worldwide assumption that the Scots are mean? Buying into the kilts and heather model is very much part of the experience of being Scottish, even if we know how far from the truth it actually is. Yet this romanticism lives in tandem with a more hard-nosed search for success, and possibly can be seen as a national flaw. However, without it, we would not be really Scottish.

For me, it is the ability to marry each of these apparently conflicting views of Scotland and being Scottish that sums up the character of the Scot. The ability to ignore the unpleasant and bask in the good that we have done is as fundamental as the ferocious support for our international sportsmen and women. Neither is likely to be rewarded, but both are strongly felt in the face of reality.

Finally, being Scottish is about being outward looking rather than parochial. It is unlike some other forms of nationalism, in that – whether intended or not – the Scots have always looked to other lands and other peoples for their opportunities. There may only be 5 million people here who call themselves Scottish but our peripatetic past means that there are probably many more than that throughout the world whose loyalty is to Scotland. Our links with Europe, in peace and in war, mean that parochialism is not an option. Being Scottish means having a powerful sense of common identity, but an equal appreciation of other cultures – something of which I believe we can be justly proud. In fact, pride is probably what sums up being Scottish. Whether misplaced or not, in the long run we have a strong sense of self-appreciation, which can be a positive characteristic so long as properly channelled.

# David McLetchie

*David McLetchie was born in 1952 and attended Leith Academy and George Heriot's School in Edinburgh. He studied law at Edinburgh University, where he gained an LLB (Hons) and he qualified as a solicitor in 1976. He has held numerous senior positions within the Scottish Conservative Party at constituency and national level and is now Leader of the Scottish Conservative and Unionist Party.*

I n common with all Scots, I am enormously proud of my Scots heritage and of the achievements of my fellow countrymen.

The Scottish people have always been outward looking and enterprising. We have contributed an enormous amount to many countries around the world as explorers, missionaries and philosophers. I was recently asked to list my three books of the year for a Sunday newspaper and one of my choices was *The Scottish Empire* by Michael Fry. This is an outstanding history chronicling the contribution of Scots to the British Empire. It shows clearly how in the past the Union and the Empire gave Scots a world stage on which to flourish in commerce, industry, law, medicine, science, the arts and politics. Indeed, England has been a much more civilised country since we took it over in 1603.

Alex Salmond claimed in his speech at this year's SNP Conference, in that characteristically understated manner of his, that Scotland 'invented' the United States of America. Whilst I might not have used those exact words, he is right to be proud of the fact that so many of the founding fathers were of Scottish descent. Scotland has produced more great men and women per head of population than almost any other country in the world. We have a guid conceit of ourselves and it is well founded.

However, I have never seen this pride in being Scottish as diminishing my equally strong commitment to the Union. For me there is no contradiction between being Scottish and British and different loyalties do not have to be divided loyalties. We do not have to choose between being Scottish and British – we can be both. This is best illustrated by using a sporting analogy – we support Scotland at football, the British team at the Olympics and Europe in the Ryder Cup.

This does not mean that I believe that everything in our garden is rosy. When one appreciates the scale of our past achievements and the prominent roles played by Scots in all walks of life in Britain today, it makes you wonder how anyone can contemplate a retreat into narrow nationalism. Yet that is exactly what many want to do, and in order to advance their case these narrow nationalists use arguments based on greed, grudge and girn, which are out of keeping with the best traditions of our country.

The negativity of the nationalist approach is combined with the arrogant belief that they are the true Scots and anyone who disagrees with them is guilty of being anti-Scottish or doing Scotland down. This leads them to reject any criticism of the way we do things as being 'alien to the Scottish tradition', an insular attitude that was one of our main concerns about devolution. This 'Little Scotland' mentality is a betrayal of our heritage and is out of keeping with the tolerant and open traditions which were the basis of the Scottish Enlightenment and which are arguably our greatest contribution to civilisation.

The values that I hold dear of freedom, independence, prudence and personal responsibility are in tune with the values of the Scottish people and are not exclusively those of any one political party. To my mind they are best represented in the values and principles of the Conservative Party

It is essential that we shed this 'Little Scotland' mentality as quickly as possible and return to our traditional role of looking outward, both to help other countries and learn lessons that will improve the running of our own. This will help us to combat the other main danger of devolution, which is that it will lead to outright independence. This is something that as unionists we believe would be deeply damaging and which we must constantly be on our guard against. It is why we must avoid the 'Little Scotland' mentality and do everything in our power to ensure that the devolution settlement works and is seen to improve the quality of life for everyone in Scotland. If the devolved Scottish Parliament fails then the only winners will be those who wish to break up the United Kingdom. That is why devolution needs the Conservatives to act as the anchors of the Union.

So our role is to continue to fashion a new unionism which recognises that we can be Scottish and British, equally proud of both our separate identities and at the same time of our shared identity and history.

# Duncan Macmillan

*Professor Duncan Macmillan, MA, Ph.D., FRSA, HRSA, is an art historian, art critic and gallery director. He is also Professor of the History of Scottish Art and Curator of the Talbot Rice Gallery at the University of Edinburgh. He is author of the definitive book on Scottish art,* Scottish Art 1460–1990 *(Mainstream, 1990), Saltire Society/Scotland on Sunday Scottish Book of the Year, enlarged edition reissued (2000) as* Scottish Art 1460–2000. *He is also author of a number of other books and monographs on Scottish art and artists, and of numerous catalogues, articles, essays on Scottish and European art, historical and contemporary. He was art critic of* The Scotsman *(1995–2000) and of* Business a.m. *(2000–2).*

I remember one summer many years ago taking my family on holiday to Spain. It was a summer of fierce heat and dreadful drought. We drove back from our holiday across Spain and France and England through a parched brown landscape, but then we came in sight of the valley of the Tweed and suddenly everything was green. What a lovely place we live in, even if, like a capricious lover, that beauty is often hidden by a frown and the landscape shows a very different, unkind face; whether it is the colour of the birch trees in winter against the snow in the Highlands, where I spent the most memorable part of my childhood and still have a home, or, in Edinburgh, where I have spent my adult life, it is the sight of Edinburgh Castle in winter, floodlit against a brilliant evening sky of the very palest blue, that landscape, the place itself and the feeling it arouses, are for me an essential part of being Scottish. That such things focus love of country is a natural, a universal thing, but the latter sight, Edinburgh Castle against the sky, is not the product of nature alone, but of humankind and nature. Likewise being Scottish is not just a matter of roots, of place, but also of what we do with what we have inherited in that place. It is a construct, not a passive thing, a matter of pride, certainly, but patriotic pride is not itself distinctive. It is another universal. Also it is really a tautology. Patriotism is a form of pride. So there is nothing special about being Scottish and being proud of it more than belonging to any other nationality, proper though it is. For your pride in your country to be more than the expression of the need for a sense of belonging, it needs to be a more articulate thing. You need to know what it is you are proud of. It is a kind of self-esteem, a proper sense of your own worth, which is as essential in nations as it is in individuals. For most of my generation this was difficult, however. How were you to know who you were as a Scot if, so far as it was taught at all, Scottish history began and ended at primary school and what you were given subsequently as a substitute was a diet of tartan kitsch? Mostly, too, primary school history added up to little more than a few names to be proud of, Robert the Bruce, William Wallace, heroes certainly, but remote and not much more than personifications of a vague and imprecise patriotism, ciphers, pegs on which to hang your unfocused sentimental pride. Perhaps I was aware, or became aware of how unsatisfactory this was as I grew up. Certainly after spending a year in France – and it was definitely because of the Auld Alliance that France had been my first destination as soon as I had the means to travel independently, I had just twenty pounds in my pocket – and two years as a postgraduate in London studying art history, I made a conscious choice to come back to Scotland and ignore the temptations of an academic career in London. My reason was that I wanted to do something for my country. I did not know what it could be, but gradually it became a matter of putting some flesh on the bare bones of that patriotic pride. This was for myself of course at first, but also in my chosen field for others too, I hoped, as I realised that Scottish art was something that we could indeed be proud of, but that it was a great tradition that was almost wholly ignored, not only elsewhere, but even in Scotland itself. It was part of our heritage to which we had no access. Instead we were told, and for too long we believed it, that we belonged to a purblind, philistine nation. But the more I learned about it, the more I realised that Scottish art was also an integral part of something much bigger, something close to the heart of what Scotland really is about and what it is we should be proud of as Scots. It goes back to the Reformation, perhaps it caused the Reformation. It certainly drove the Enlightenment and I hope it is not yet entirely extinct. It used to distinguish us from our southern neighbours as much as it united us with our friends on the continent. It is a willingness to see ideas as essential to the construction of human happiness, to see intellect and imagination as the truly essential tools for the building of a better world. George Davie christened this the 'democratic intellect'. It was once the force that made Scotland such a special place whose contribution to the world has hitherto been out of proportion to its size or wealth. This, a construct, is a matter of special pride and is certainly the foundation for our proper self-esteem as a nation. The democratic intellect has for too long been in retreat, however. My own hope was that the establishment of the Scottish parliament would reverse this. Donald Dewar understood this, I think, and bequeathed us a remarkable Parliament building that might still embody such ideals if it is properly realised. The prospect for that is not good, but perhaps we will surprise ourselves and through it demonstrate that as a society we still believe that the culture of ideas, the imagination itself, are not a luxury, an optional extra, but the bedrock of our identity.

# Douglas McNaughton

*Douglas McNaughton was born and raised in Perthshire and works in publishing in Edinburgh. When the weather's good, he can't imagine wanting to live anywhere else. He has worked extensively in the voluntary sector and washed dishes for the Queen. In addition, he has co-written several slim volumes of Scottish-themed humour. The following extract comes from one of these,* Scots Wha Hae! *(Goblinshead Publishing, 2001), and reflects the tone of a certain venerable Scottish Sunday newspaper …*

## The Guid Auld Days – The Twentieth Century

### The Sunday Scone – 1900

What's this craze for running about the streets? Children should be seen and not heard.

Time was, laddies would spend all day at their lessons, then read quietly in the evening.

Now it's all street games, fancy spinning tops and tearing about on carties they make out of scrap wood. The streets are hardly safe any more. If they're not doing that they're chapping on doors and running away.

And if that's not bad enough, they're thieves as well. Stealing apples from folk's gardens and cheeking the bobbies.

\*\*\*

### The Sunday Scone – 1930

Time was, laddies made their own fun. We had hours of enjoyment with a dandelion stalk. Slit the end and hey presto – a braw wee tooter. You could get a rare wee tune out of it, imitate birds, play tricks on auld wifies.

And there was more good humour then. Harmless wee jokes like chicky-melly – chapping on doors and running away. Or taking a few apples from folk's gardens for a dare. The bobbies never minded, they kent it was just laddie-like.

And when we'd done that, we made carties out of auld wood or played with spinning tops. That was all we needed. We were never bored.

And I mind fine, a tanner ba' would do us. Now they all want high-falutin' real footballs. Nothing but the best will do, it seems. They're never happy.

Aye. Changed days right enough.

\*\*\*

*The Sunday Scone – 1960*
Latest thing is, the cinemas are setting up clubs for the youngsters now. The ABC Minors, they cry it. It's even got its own song – 'All Pals Together' or some such.

What's happened to the guid old street games of yesteryear? When I was a lad, we played rare street games. Out in the sun all day long, or playing a game of fitba. Everyone knew each other. You could leave your door open all the time. And go away for a week's holiday leaving it unlocked. Safe as houses.

Now it's all sitting in the cinema watching these fancy talkies. Some of them are even in colour, I hear. And the big thing now is *Dan Dare* comics and *Superman* films.

Aye. Changed days right enough.

\*\*\*

*The Sunday Scone – 1980*
What's happened to good old-fashioned heroes? I mind when I was a youngster, Superman was the lad for us. He was someone you could look up to. Someone with true grit.

You would go to the cinema on a Saturday morning and just get in with a jam-jar. See everyone from your school there. Even had our own song. 'We are the ABC Minors, we come along on Saturday mornings … all pals together …' or something like that. Great days.

Now the laddies are all into this Evel Knievel and skateboards. And if it's not that it's these pop groups.

Aye. Changed days right enough.

\*\*\*

*The Sunday Scone – 2000*

Whatever happened to Evel Knievel? He was the boy. Our hero when we were laddies. Where is he now? Thrown aside, that's where. Along with all the braw pop groups of yesteryear.

Now the laddies are all into this World-wide Wrestling Federation and Eminem. And if it's not that it's this Britney Spears.

When I was a lad I would wake up and there was ice on the blankets. Never felt a thing. Didnae care a jot. These youngsters nowadays, they've got it made.

Aye. Changed days right enough.

# Kevin MacNeil

*Kevin MacNeil/Caoimhin MacNèill was born on the Outer Hebridean island of Lewis (Scotland) and is a widely published writer of poetry, prose and drama (English and Gaelic). He was educated at the Nicolson Institute, University of Edinburgh and Sabhal Mòr Ostaig. He is the first person from this country to win the prestigious Tivoli Europa Giovani International Poetry Prize and is currently living on the Isle of Skye, where he is employed as the inaugural Iain Crichton Smith Writing Fellow (writer-in-residence for the Highlands area of Scotland).*

## Keep Britain Tiny

Being Scottish is difficult when your passport, like mine, is a forgery. For state-sponsored forgery is forgery nonetheless.

Quite honestly, and through no fault of my own, there's not a fraction of a jot of a speck of a fragment of an iota of me that feels – or has ever felt – British. A world citizen, I am as embarrassed at being described as 'British' as I am of Scotland's own shameful role in 'Great' Britain's colonial past (I fully concur with the opinion that History shall judge Britain favourably for the way it dismantled an empire and not, God help us, for the way in which it acquired or fashioned it).

I am a Gael. I belong to a culture that has been systematically eroded; my inherited worldview is one that has been methodically diminished – and this, furthermore, with perplexing elements of tacit (*and* forceful) Scottish complicity. A language torn from its throat, a heritage humiliated, generations starved of their natural rights and robbed of their very sense of identity. Our cultural identity – essential for individual and cultural well-being – has been ruefully jeopardised …

My pride is a multicultural pride. I despise racism, and partly for that reason I agree with T. S. Eliot, who said:

It is to the advantage of England that the Welsh should be Welsh, the Scots Scots and the Irish Irish … If the other parts of the British Isles were wholly superseded by English culture, English culture would disappear too.

## No Man – not Even an Islander – is an Island

Being an islander, I cherish independence and loathe insularity in equal measures. Naturally, I have a problem with grand-scale insularity, for I don't think that 'cultural globalisation' is a myth as much as a danger. The worry that one day people in cities all over the world will be eating the same burger, reading the same lifestyle comic, wearing the same brand of clothing and speaking the same language is terrifying. Global culture comprises a vast multicoloured spectrum: the thought that it should be eclipsed by a single shadowy power is heartbreaking. I truly love America, but there are more than fifty stars in my skies.

We should celebrate unity-in-diversity, not unity-in-conformity. Scotland has always been multilingual and multiracial, and it is a source of pride to me that nowadays Scotland is more multicultural than ever. I see myself as respecting – and learning from – other cultures, while simultaneously attempting to do my best to preserve and nurture my own. If a single culture is represented by a hand, then cultures should be regularly shaking hands with one another, not arm wrestling.

Diverse close and lasting friendships I want, not an acrimonious marriage.

## Oops! I'm Scottish

The story is well known and all too plausible. James Boswell, on meeting Samuel Johnson, says: 'I do indeed come from Scotland, but I cannot help it …' It seems to me we are still – Gaels, arguably, in particular – lacking an essential confidence, a sense of lasting dynamism, which we might otherwise gift to those who will come after us. This is due, in no small part, to insecurities about our identity.

The questions 'Who are we?' or 'Who am I?' ought to be the most fluent, natural, satisfying and wholesome in the world, but these questions, in Scotland, are skewed. The answers to them are historically – and rigorously – blurred, to our national and individual detriment.

Those institutions which insidiously prevent us from answering such questions are causing damage, and they would catalyse something wonderful if they would only help us to learn about and appreciate our culture. (I'm thinking specifically about certain areas of the educational establishment and of the media.)

As far as the media and education are concerned, I open-heartedly request that we bring about not devolution but revolution.

I have had the privilege of travelling to many different countries to read my poetry (in Gaelic and English) and I always find that the people I meet in other countries have a greater fascination for Scotland's languages and cultures than we do.

'Wha's like us?' – It's hard to say when we don't fully realise who we are.

'We are who we are' represents the tentative beginnings of an answer, insofar as it (hopefully) pulverises that stickily unconscious acceptance of the notion that we are who we *were* …

## Time is a Blind Guide

We are our predecessors' myopic plagiarists. Too often we are backward-looking, misty-eyed and wistful even as nostalgia writhes Celtic-mistily around us, taunting us with insubstantial, outdated images. Moving steadily into the present, towards the future, we must make sacrifices, and I propose that the first sacrifice we make is to sling that kilt-hitching, bagpipe-wielding, whisky-guzzling, tourist-robbing haggis of our past into Loch Ness. We deserve better, and the people who come in their thousands every year to visit Scotland deserve better. Who would realistically choose to live in a present that is the past? It's not as if the Scots decided a few centuries ago to instigate a marketing campaign for self-promotion through self-parody.

My feelings are that despite the politicians (surely the only species who can smile and spit at the same time), ours is a great and commendably diverse nation. Let us therefore belong, first, to the world and let us, subsequently, belong to Scotland, for as James Grant wrote:

The world is neither Scottish, English, nor Irish, neither French, Dutch, nor Chinese, but human and each nation is only the partial development of a universal humanity.

The Scotland our world deserves is multicultural, vibrant, inclusive, forward-looking, confident … and independent within the context of our sister nations.

Let us be ourselves, and let us do good with dignity and, above all, with compassion.

# Susie Maguire

*Susie Maguire is a writer and performer who used to do stand-up and sing a cappella. She has acted on stage, film and TV, and written comedy and drama for radio and television.* The Short Hello *– a collection of stories including Marina McLoughlin's print debut in 'The Day I Met Sean Connery' – was published by Polygon in 2000.*

## 21st-Century Schizoid Girl

*Media studies graduate Marina McLoughlin spends an evening with her mentor, Susie Maguire. Susie huddles on the sofa nibbling shortbread, while Marina reshelves Susie's extensive collection of crime fiction.*

Marina: *… Barnes, Block, Connelly, Deaver … .*

Susie: *Ah – you can put him in the pile for the Shelter shop …*

M: *Okay. Dunant … Evanovitch … .Grafton … Harris, Harvey, Hillerman …*

S: *Fabulous, ever read him? Talk about sense of place …*

M: *Is that the Indians bloke?*

S: *The Navaho series, yes.*

M: *Wouldn't you love to go to there? Colorado, New Mexico … Gaze at those big red rocks, ride around in a jeep admiring the cactuses …*

S: *I. Cact –I. Travel doesn't really appeal to me that much – as someone or other said, wherever you go, there you are.*

M: *Och, travel broadens the mind, though.*

S: *Where did you go for your last holidays?*

M: *Mull.*

S: *Feel it gave you a whole new perspective on Scotland and its place in Europe and the wider world?*

M: *Well, I did actually. See, I got talking to this guy from Holland in the B&B, and there was a couple from Canada, and the two men that ran the place, one was from Yorkshire and one was German. They were dead friendly: we shared the same breakfast table and talked about culture.*

S: *Exactly.*

M: *Exactly what?*

S: *Wherever you go, there you are – we're all the same. It doesn't really matter if you never go to Germany or Holland or Canada now, because you've discovered that we all share the same things …*

M: *Marmalade?*

S: *Ideas, desires, perceptions, they may vary a little, but there's no major difference. Nationality is moot. Borders are pointless, we're all becoming a part of the same society …*

M: *That's not true. Just because you can get samosas in Glasgow doesn't mean you don't need India to exist.*

S: *Eh? Run that past me again?*

M: *If there hadn't been the Highland Clearances, you wouldn't get McDonald's restaurants ruling the world, would you?*

S: *What numskull have you been talking to?*

M: *It's something I was reading in the Sunday paper …*

S: *Spare me!*

M: *But we're not all the same, are we? We're all unique … look at you and me …*

S: *I'm unique, you're just a figment of my imagination …*

M: *… we have totally different ways of seeing the world. Scotland's identity is very important, and now we've got our own parliament and everything, people in other countries actually realise we're not the same as the English.*

S: *Name me one. Anyway, the major difference between you and me is that you grew up in Glasgow, think parochially and aspire to be cosmopolitan, and I've lived abroad, don't think of myself as Scottish, and wear tartan ironically …*

M: *I gave you that black-watch scarf for your birthday! D'you really not think of yourself as Scottish?*

S: *I used to tell people in France I was, when they called me English. Otherwise, no. There are enough pigeon holes in life …*

M: *School changing rooms …*

S: *No, you idiot, like 'Female', 'Feminist', 'Socialist', all that stuff. I don't want to think about labels, I'm not interested in joining anything, or representing anything …*

M: *You're independent …*

S: *Damn right …*

M: *Except when there's women's book prizes …*

S: *Don't get me started!*

M: *Sorry!*

S: *Anyway, that scarf was scratchy.*

M: *Genuine Scottish lambswool.*

S: *I'm allergic to wool.*

M: *Pity you don't get silkworms in Scotland, eh? Still, if you'd been born in China, maybe you'd feel differently about nationality …*

S: *Have you been drinking too much caffeine or something …?*

M: *I'm just saying, you know, you'd maybe talk about your culture differently, and be really proud to be Chinese, and you do love Hot & Sour soup …*

S: *You can be born in China and not be Chinese, just as you can be Chinese and be born in Scotland and not consider yourself Scottish … oh, how did this get started, for goodness sake!*

M: *You've even got a kimono …*

S: *That's Japanese, you blockhead …*

M: *Anyway.  Kerr, Millar, Mina, Muller … loads of these are American, Susie, how come?*

S: *Because I like them.*

M: *Would you like to be American, then?*

S: *No.*

M: *Would you like to live there?*

S: *No.*

M: *Where would you like to live?*

S: *It doesn't matter. The mind travels abroad, the body stays put. Where are you up to?*

M: *The Ps and Qs. Pelecanos … um … what next?*

S: *R for Rankin, then. Hurry up. I want a cup of tea.*

M: *Okay. S … .Scott, Manda … Manda Scott, who's that?*

S: *She's a Scottish crime writer.*

M: *Quite a few of them now, eh?*

S:  *If you'd stop hanging around expecting to be entertained, maybe I could get on with my own novel …*

M: *Right. Finished. Shall I put the kettle on?*

S: *Make that cocoa, I'm knackered. Want to watch* Newsnight Scotland?

M: *Only if Gordon Brewer is on. I love him …*

S: *Kettle!*


As Marina scurries to the kitchen, Susie lifts the last piece of shortbread from its tartan wrappings, and reaches for the TV remote.

# Martin Mansergh

*Martin Mansergh is Special Advisor to the Taoiseach on North-
ern Ireland, Economic and Social Matters. He studied at Oxford
University, where he became an authority on eighteenth-century
French history. He is married to a Scot and runs the family farm
in Tipperary with his brother.*

While I cannot count myself Scottish, I am proud of my wife's and my own
more distant Scottish heritage. Liz was born in Glasgow of a long line of
doctors. Her grandfather Dr Gavin Young, who with his brothers served in Scottish regiments or the Royal Navy during the First World War, lived off Sauchiehall
Street. His father-in-law Dr Kerr Love was a noted ear specialist, who treated and
corresponded with the famous deaf-mute Helen Keller. When Liz was small, her
father, 'Jock' Young, also a doctor, and her mother, moved to a terrace off
Morningside Road in Edinburgh.

After moving south, there were family holidays in West Kilbride, Arran, Kintyre and later Ardnamurchan, where they retired. Her great-grandmother was a
Mackenzie, descended from the MacDonalds of Keppoch. A stone on Culloden
Moor marks where the Chief of Keppoch fell in 1746. Many Highland clans
ultimately trace their ancestry to semi-mythical Irish High Kings, whose early
descendants formed the kingdom of Dalriada.

My great-grandmother, born Helen Ogilvy, came from Dumfries, a clan in the
second line at Culloden. My father's third name was Seton, being descended from
Isabella Seton. We have a copy of the portrait of George, 5th Lord Seton, and
family in the Scottish National Gallery in Edinburgh, in the study in Tipperary.
Staunchly Catholic, and a leading supporter of Mary, Queen of Scots, he gave her
refuge after the murder of Darnley. I have visited Seton Collegiate Chapel. Sixteenth

and seventeenth-century Scottish family history can be gloomy, containing, like *Macbeth*, dark nights of treachery and bloodshed.

St Columba, or Columcille, is a symbol of early Christian and Celtic links between Ireland and Scotland. Iona, in sunshine or in rain, with its royal burial ground is an evocative place. The Columba Initiative encourages cultural exchange between Gaelic Scotland and Ireland. 'The Council of the Isles' under the Good Friday Agreement evokes the medieval Lordship. In Europe, the word 'Scot' meant Irish, provoking a centuries-old debate over the degree to which Scottish identity derived from Ireland. The case has been more often understated than overstated.

Ireland and Scotland are in many respects a geographical, historical and cultural continuum, and make an interesting comparison. Not enough people from the south know Scotland. I discovered Scotland, when I met Liz, giving it the happiest associations. The Highlands are beautiful, like the west of Ireland, though more desolate, while Edinburgh is a great European capital.

The Union with Scotland was more successful than the one with Ireland. The intellectual quality of the Scottish Enlightenment was the equal of any in Europe. The Scots, like the Irish, emigrated to North America, Australia and New Zealand. The Clearances were traumatic, though not as extreme as the Famine. (In Ireland, the tenants eventually got rid of the landlords. In Scotland, it was more the other way round!) Scotland, like Ulster, and unlike the rest of Ireland, participated fully in the industrial revolution. The Irish navvy, celebrated in the novels of Patrick MacGill, played his part. Labour founder James Connolly was born in Edinburgh. He was shot following the 1916 Rising, by order of General Maxwell, a Scottish soldier, who did not comprehend the effect of his actions.

Gladstone had intended Home Rule all round, but was blocked. After waiting another thirty years, Ireland struck out for full independence. Scotland did not have the same reasons for doing so. Ireland slowly developed its democracy, laws, economy and culture, and today reaps the benefits. We welcome our growing links with devolved Scotland, which Donald Dewar pioneered.

Ulster does not have an exclusive franchise on Scotland in Ireland, but Scottish influence is strongest there. An effort is being made to build up an Ulster-Scots identity as a counter to Irishness, though they should be complementary. Who could object to the language or politics of Robbie Burns (except perhaps the

Lord's Day Observance Society)? One reads today claims that the Ulster-Scots (or Scots-Irish) helped found a new nation in the United States. Contemporaries founded the Society of United Irishmen with their Catholic fellow countrymen with a similar object in view in Ireland. Their ideal did not prevail, and a generation late the 'New Light' spirit was replaced by a return to the religious acrimony of an earlier age. Doubtless, a strong reaction against sectarianism will come, as happened in Scotland, and should dissipate some wariness in the Ulster/Scots relationship.

I have three personal wishes for Scotland – first, more regional airports (preferably one at Fort William); second, that someone would restore the boarded-up historic Mingary Castle at Kilchoan facing across to Mull; third, that a fast ferry be provided across the North Channel between Ballycastle and Campbeltown, and open up Kintyre to visitors from Ireland, and also that Caledonian MacBrayne would occasionally serve Lough Foyle.

# Alex Massie

*Alex Massie was educated at Glenalmond College and Trinity College, Dublin. On his return to Scotland he became a sports journalist for* Scotland on Sunday. *He is now Assistant Editor and chief leader writer for the same paper.*

Leafing through the *Scotsman Guide to Scottish Politics* (Polygon at Edinburgh, 2002) it was with some surprise that I discovered that no fewer than three MSPs had been educated at my old school. Since that school was, and is, Glenalmond this should not on the surface be enormously surprising. The school had after all been like the other Scottish public schools, a breeding ground for politicians and civil servants for more than a century. I was, nonetheless, surprised since Scottishness did not feature highly on the curriculum. Nor were we encouraged to stare into such deep pools. Set in spectacular scenery ten or so miles west of Perth, Glenalmond was an awkward place in which to spend five of one's formative years. That is no reflection on the quality of the teaching available, nor on the range of extra-curricular activities or muscular ethos that characterised the place, but rather a recognition that being educated in an environment that combines undoubted privilege and good fortune with an almost complete isolation from the rest of the world has its own set of disadvantages. Like the other major Scots boarding schools – Loretto, Fettes, Strathallan and so on – Glenalmond was an English school planted in Scotland pretending to be British. Its purpose, ultimately, was to equip its alumni with all they needed to assume minor administrative positions in the British Empire. If Empire and war were the two crucial components needed to forge a sense of Britishness then the loss of that Empire and the fading memory of the Second World War were bound to require

Britishness to be redefined. In such circumstances Scottishness would be up for grabs as well. So too would the purpose of the public schools, which, even in the 1990s, still drew large numbers of pupils from Kenya, South Africa and Hong Kong. The majority of my schoolmates might have been Scottish – and most would consider themselves Scots first and foremost – but we were not, in any real sense, educated in Scotland. The history curriculum, for example, demanded a reasonably in-depth knowledge of Tudor England but no awareness of Stuart Scotland. Similarly I cannot recall ever reading a novel by a Scottish writer (outwith one's own free time) during five years of English literature classes.

In part this was, of course, because the school chose to enter its pupils for GCSE and A Level examinations rather than their Scottish equivalents, but no effort was made at any point to balance this academic requirement. The distance we felt from our home towns and families was matched by our distance from Scottish history and culture.

If the curriculum was silently hostile to Scottishness then I'm afraid as pupils we were little better. Boys who arrived from Glasgow comprehensives (or even one of the Glaswegian day schools such as the High School or Academy) with distinctive Scottish accents were mercilessly barracked. A broad Glasgow or Aberdeen accent was in many, though not all, cases distinctly infra dig and some boys did their best to ensure they lengthened their vowels and adopted the polite tones of the World Service as quickly as possible.

Yet the very boys who affected to despise a broad accent would be as vociferous as any Kelso farmer in supporting Scotland at Murrayfield (following football was not out of the question, it just wasn't encouraged). Indeed I vividly recall travelling down to Murrayfield in March 1990 to see Scotland play England for the Grand Slam during which journey, as on countless other buses across the country that day, someone struck up the first droning bars of 'Flower of Scotland', whereupon the rest of the bus joined in with gusto: we had reckoned without the masters on board, however, who promptly ordered an end to the singing. It was never clear whether they objected to singing per se or just that particular song. Either way it was a curious start to the day.

It was certainly the case, however, that proclaiming support for the SNP or the cause of independence occasioned wry looks of amusement among the staff as though the entire concept was a priori ridiculous (left unspoken was the assumption that this was the sort of silliness one would grow out of in time). It was also normally, incidentally, left unsaid that real achievements could only be made outside Scotland. In other words, this was a school in Scotland yet not of Scotland, populated by Scots who when south of the border would grow tired of having to explain that they were indeed Scottish but who spent too much time (shamefully) looking down on other Scots who had not enjoyed the same advantages.

No wonder that former public school boys are so often viewed with suspicion by those who have had a more typical upbringing and education. Only a tiny minority of Scots receive such an education. That may not, for all these schools' undoubted strengths, be such a bad thing since it now strikes me that we were invited to admire and despise Scotland in all but equal measure.

Perhaps, in retrospect, that made it a very Scottish place to be educated after all.

# Donald E. Meek

*Donald E. Meek (b. 1949) is a native of the island of Tiree. He is currently Professor of Scottish and Gaelic Studies at the University of Edinburgh, and was Professor of Celtic at the University of Aberdeen from 1993 to 2001. At the time of writing, he was Chairman of the Ministerial Advisory Group on Gaelic. He has written numerous books and articles on many different aspects of Gaelic culture.*

## Reflections on a 'Queen'

Being Scottish is not something that I often think about. Being Scottish and feeling proud of it, as Scots are supposed to do, is for me an even rarer sentiment. I confess to having felt Scottish, and proud of it, only once. That peculiar sensation occurred in the year 2000. I was far from home; in fact, I was standing on the edge of the Pacific Ocean, in Long Beach, California, as the evening sun dropped in the sky. Even more significantly, I was positioned on the forecastle of the steamship, *Queen Mary*, now preserved as a floating exhibit at Long Beach. I had fulfilled a boyhood dream to see the *Mary* for myself. The great ship was even larger than I had imagined her to be, with her huge curving decks. From the bridge, I could not see her stern. Her massive funnels towered high above me. By late afternoon I had reached the forecastle, and, resting on one of the immense capstans, I looked upwards. There, in gleaming brass, sparkling in the rays of sunset, were the words 'Built by John Brown & Co., Engineers, Clydebank'. As I surveyed the curving wonders of her design, an unspeakable sense of pride suddenly softened my hard heart, and I rejoiced in the former glory of Clyde shipbuilding. Thanks to the American dollar, and to the sentimentality of those Americans who loved the old *Queen*, I had experienced that deeply elusive emotional moment when I almost – almost – found myself shouting, 'It makes me proud to be Scottish.'

Long Beach, California, is a far cry from the Hebridean beaches of my boy-hood in Tiree. It was from these sandy shores that I used to see passing ships, 'butting through the Minch in the mad March days' (apologies to Masefield) – puffers and MacBrayne steamers, all built on the Clyde. From these shores too I looked out to the mainland, and saw Ben Nevis and Ben Shiant and the Five Sisters of Kintail on the eastern horizon. How remote they seemed! Canada seemed closer, as I had a grandmother in a friendly-sounding place called Vancouver, who used to send me wonderful parcels filled with 'candy' and sweet-smelling books.

For me, Scottishness has been an acquired concept, initially as remote and inaccessible as those peaks. In my Hebridean boyhood, I was first and foremost Gaelic, brought up on an island croft, where cows and sheep and humans and the Gaelic language lived in happy harmony. Even the dogs barked in Gaelic, and understood no English. Scotland was some place far away in a big, blue school-book. I reasoned that those mountains on the hazy eastern skyline must belong to Scotland.

Scotland became for me a land of other, more menacing, mountains. As I ventured beyond the safe confines of the Gaelic-speaking areas, I found accept-ability and animosity towards my native language in almost equal measure. It was my joy to study and teach the language and its culture, and my great sorrow to encounter tokenism, trivialisation and sometimes sheer disparagement. The Scotland that so often growled at England, and expressed the pain of being a repressed nation, could show its internal animosities in fine style, and give surprisingly little place to its own indigenous treasures.

As I have struggled to present the just claims of Gaelic to a Scottish Executive in the post-devolution Scotland of the early 2000s, the tensions and contra-dictions of Scottish institutions, particularly with regard to Scottish subjects, have given me pause for thought. This is a nation struggling to be free, but it is also one that is still shackled to imperial concepts, and ruled by a mandarin class, shielded not in castles of douce Balmorality but in plate-glass offices in remote Edinburgh. This is a nation which wants to claim its Gaelicness when the couthy clarion call of national identity has to be sounded abroad, but it is only too happy to disavow its Gaelic roots if they need practical, and particularly financial, attention at home. The language is then perceived as a relic for the museum, and not a voice for the street or the croft – something to be anchored as far away as possible from cost and inconvenience, something whose day is done.

Perhaps it all came together in a peculiarly perplexing way on that December evening in Long Beach, California. The *Queen Mary* has Scotland built into her plates. She represents so many of Scotland's aches and aspirations: the grand and gracious imperial design; the belaboured workforce with uncertain futures; the erstwhile hard managers with souls like iron; the Scottish letters of brass; the enduring memorial shimmering in the setting sun. She was the great liner that almost never was, as men lay idle in the great Depression and she languished on the stocks. Then, one day in 1936, her sleek bows pierced the Atlantic waves at thirty knots, and she sailed the Atlantic on a thousand voyages until 1967. For once, I recognised the true achievement of those Clyde shipbuilders who could make rivets sing, beat hammers into harmonies, and bend steel into gloriously musical curves on a truly massive scale. Those were the men who turned torture into triumph and made Scotland great. Yet, as the evening lights of Long Beach began to pierce the sky, it occurred to me that the *Mary*, now without engines, dead and silent, and moored thousands of miles from home, might be a more fitting symbol of being Scottish than my romantic yearnings wanted to admit.

# Steven Osborne

*Steven Osborne is one of Britain's leading classical pianists with a career that has taken him to Japan, North America and throughout Europe. He studied at St Mary's Music School, Edinburgh, and is a frequent performer at the Edinburgh International Festival.*

This is really difficult. I think I'd rather write about how many angels can fit on a pinhead (fifty-nine I reckon).

I have to start with the fact that I *feel* deeply Scottish. Perhaps as the son of two Scots, brought up in West Lothian, this is inevitable simply because of childhood associations. For years after going to music college in Manchester, every time I came home my knees would almost buckle with the ecstasy of hearing the first broad Scottish accent to cross my path (if only that train guard knew how much joy he gave … ). Similarly the landscapes, the familiar understatement of the people, and even the appalling TV adverts are a source of pleasure and comfort.

However, I don't know if this is enough. I am actually *proud* to be Scottish, and there is a certain fierceness to this feeling, almost as if I would be willing to fight for some cause. It surprises me to realise this as I've lived happily in England for thirteen years with only occasional bouts of homesickness, and I can identify very little which would feed this patriotism. I don't have any interest in the political questions regarding Scottish sovereignty; my knowledge of Scottish history is scant, to say the least; I don't even spend much time around Scots. Did this pride somehow grow out of the easy anti-English banter that I've known all my life? Even one of the men I admire most, on hearing I'd recently bought a house in my home town, wrote to congratulate me on 'moving back to a proper country'. Yet I can't really believe that I nurture some hidden resentment of English oppression. When Paul Gascoigne scored that incredible goal against Scotland in Euro 2000, I found myself cheering. I still think it's the best goal I've ever seen.

So why then should I be proud of my country, a simple accident of birth? The things I admire about Scotland (the character of the people and the beauty of the land) cannot be enough to explain it, for why then do the weather and the infernal midges not redress the balance in any way? No, it has to be more than a question of like or dislike – it's a more fundamental part of my personality, something as basic to me as my gender or shoe size. Beyond this, however, I am stumped. Perhaps it's simply a natural law that one's physical roots imbue all of life with some distinctive flavour, but I can't pretend to understand it. Rather, my Scottishness is to me part of the mysterious (and wonderful) experience of finding beauty in life and the world.

I move back to West Lothian this coming Sunday. Maybe living in Scotland again will help me understand all this more fully. But when it comes down to it I don't really care: there are more important things to think about, like what colour I'm going to paint my bedroom.

# Anna Paterson

*After assorted degrees in medicine and medical sciences from Sweden and the UK, Dr Anna Paterson has spent most of her professional life as a medical academic in England, the Netherlands and Scotland. Her book* Scotland's Landscape: Endangered Icon *(Polygon at Edinburgh, 2002) is a study of landscape, identity and Green policy in Scotland.*

I'm an immigrant in Scotland and know I always will be, even though I fulfil all the operational definitions of national identity that a Scottish version of the current UK Home Secretary might have dreamt up. Actually, I grew up in a small Northern European country famed for its glorious natural assets of mountain- and seascapes, with a core population of ingenious, brave, hardworking and honest people, turned dour and overly canny by their folk memory of poverty, soldiering and emigration, who are nowadays more than a little concerned about the way their native languages are being displaced by English and the original inhabitants disoriented by wave after wave of immigrants from all kinds of unlikely places.

That should define my country of origin, shouldn't it? Not so, of course. There must be at least half a dozen nations, including Scotland, who could recognise themselves pretty well exactly from that potted description. Being aware of this meant that trawling my fund of observations for 'what feeling/ being Scottish must be like (specifically)' has tended to get me nowhere. History is the crucial ingredient in a sense of regional identity. That is true of folk history, meaning to know of and care for traditional customs and beliefs and also, more generally, of harbouring passionately detailed ideas about the historical role of your corner of the world. On this count, the Scottish score amazingly high. But then, history is … history. Also, it can become the way collective madness lies. National historical mania is a sadly familiar state, in which absurd attempts are made to fiddle the data and ancient grudges are allowed to distort present policy.

I came to believe that love of the land is the only safe way of sustaining a comfortable and non-exclusive sense of belonging. Loving the land need not be a function of personal ownership – though it helps – or of straightforward variables like 'beauty' or 'grandeur' or 'charm' – though a high quotient of such qualities help too. Above all, that love must rest on some degree of freedom for individuals to shape their environment over many generations and without too much central co-ordination. Until relatively recently, local people and their immediate over-lords have shaped landscapes and cityscapes across the whole span of regional history. There, all around us, is the home we have made for ourselves. It also holds up a mirror, showing us who we are now and what we care for. There is no hope for regional identity when the reflected image is indistinguishable from every-where else, smoothed over and tidied to fit some lowest common denominator of 'good taste' – nor is it enough just to anxiously preserve all that past evidence of people living and working as something called 'heritage'.

It is still important that this kind of rootedness in a place is kept apart from the usual markers of 'identity'. To illustrate the point, here are two quotes about Northern European nature, one from Scotland and one from Sweden. First, from one of Hugh MacDiarmid's beguiling poems:

[ … ] above the tree-line, where the track is the bed of an amethystine burn
in a bare world of shining quartz and purple heather
is the Scotland that is one of the sights of the earth
and once seen can never be forgotten.

Next, a naive but equally heartfelt – surely? – few lines

Under a yellow sun in bright blue sky
my white Swedish snowlands lie.
Dark fir forests against the snow stand
Here I shall die, in my native land.
The land of the midnight sun.

Beware! As it happens, the next verse begins: 'Far too many refugees stream/ in to kill our Swedish dream'. The quote is from a neo-Nazi 'pop-song' with the title 'Now the Storm-troops are marching'.

Instead of merging fondness for native land- and cityscapes, however subtly, with an overall satisfaction with the excellence of the region's people, culture, history and so on, the environment must be seen as an end in itself. The importance of locality and of a sense of place has informed some of the best 'Green' thinking, though the reminder to 'Think Global' is as essential as it is unsettling. We have to live in a world of incessant and unstoppable human migration, where tolerance is at a premium. But wherever we come from and whatever our other convictions about goodness and propriety, we can join forces to care for the landscapes and buildings, trades and patterns of cultivation of our region. And beyond lies nature with its demands that our concern should be extended to the non-human inhabitants of the land, from the trees and birds in an inner-city courtyard to the wild creatures and plants of the hill. We are all parts of the same living entity, after all.

# Donald Paterson

*Donald Paterson was brought up in Tain and currently lives in Elgin. He works as a teacher of English in Aberlour. He has had poetry and fiction printed in various Scottish publications and is working on a novel.*

## Mountains and a Train

I have a picture; which I've had framed – it's on the wall in my study. It's called *Auchnashellach*, and it shows craggy, imposing Scottish mountains, rocky verticals and distant slantings; swirled in white romantic clouds. A river springs from the middle distance, and cascades to the front of the drawing, where it pours, foaming, into my room. The rocks in the foreground are nearly black, gloomy with an imposing darkness, only a rag of rough grass clinging to the cold slopes.

The picture is a hand-tinted drawing that once formed part of a publication (possibly a magazine of some sort) – if you look closely you can see the lines of print showing through the lighter parts, such as the sky just above the most distant hills. It dates from the mid-nineteenth century, I think, and it gives just about as fake a picture of the Scottish Highlands as you might ever want to see. All that is missing is the Highland cow in the foreground, tended by a noble peasant in a kilt.

But the painting escapes condemnation because of one little detail that renders it odd. Across the centre of the paper runs a railway line, appearing and disappearing among the mass of stone, running over the torrent on an apparently decaying stone bridge. A train, made tiny by the cliffs, runs along the track, from right to left, and the last carriage is just leaving the bridge. The engine, hauling a vanishing miasma of steam behind it, is already hidden behind the outcrop on the left of the picture.

It is this train that keeps me looking at the picture. Certainly the mountains are born of a nineteenth-century imagination that has little to do with reality, but then the train seems a genuine detail. Who is travelling on it? Where is it going? Why has the artist (S. Read, if my interpretation of the signature is correct) bothered to include it? The train allows the painting to transcend its romantic-period origin to become, to me, a kind of comment on Scotland.

Does the train contain sensation-seeking city dwellers travelling to the Highlands for a fearful taste of the sublime? Or are the passengers going the other way, representatives of that long-lasting exodus that leads from a scraped living on a peaty hillside to a tenement slum with grey washing stretched between windows?

These movements still go on, as they have been going on for 200 years. Folk were leaving the Highlands long before, and long after, the depredations of the Highland Clearances. The perpendicular rain of dark cities still urges people to the open space of the hills; and the wide dream of solitude.

So I like to think of the train impossibly, carrying both sets of passengers, simultaneously. It travels right to left across the picture, and I would like that direction to be both towards the city with its safe civilisation and industrial noise, and also towards the north, a land of barrenness and the sounds of deer in the autumn.

My parents gave me this picture some time in the nineties as a birthday present. They were Glaswegians who moved north, who never stopped thinking of their native city. They felt that we would have a gentler upbringing in the back-water of Ross-shire than in the urban cascade, but they never tired of going home, to watch the tenements fall, the cranes begin to stand silent, the surging streets turn to pedestrianisation. I don't know what the picture meant to them, and I don't know even where they bought it, north or south.

My father, a socialist, believed in Scotland. He belonged to the city of Mackintosh, MacDiarmid and Morgan, of whom he never tired. He died before Thatcher was thrown out and before Scotland got its own kind of parliament. I suspect the picture, to him, said something essential about our country back then, in the mid-nineties, the cities in decline, the countryside tight in the chill grasp of the privileged few. My mother, still living in the Highlands, feels the warmth of rural consideration wrapping round her, a cover as she ages.

Being Scottish? What better metaphor than this representation of a country from 150 years ago? The journey itself is a metaphor, a shuttling back and forth between two vistas of our land, trying to decide which one is true. Perhaps the picture appeals to me because I recognise in it something from within myself, an unrootedness that comes from living in a country of people always on the move, always intently staring into the distance, always wanting to look over the last horizon to see if we can get a glimpse of our home.

# Lindsay Paterson

*Lindsay Paterson is Professor of Educational Policy at Edinburgh University. He has academic interests in the sociology of education, in Scottish politics and in Scottish culture.*

Being Scottish includes believing that the state can help individual citizens to flourish. From that flows much that is good in Scotland today, but also some things that are problematic.

There are two main aspects of the belief. The first concerns redistribution of opportunity and resources. Scotland has a long history of holding that individual opportunity ought to be distributed fairly. The most obvious example is in education. For over a century, the main issue facing educational policy makers has been how to enable people's talents to be expressed fully, not only as a means of personal fulfilment, but also to ensure that the nation as a whole could draw on all the capacities of its members.

The same could be said for the provision of public welfare, notably in the National Health Service. The social origins of ill health have been a recurrent concern in this debate, from the investigations in the 1930s that led to the NHS's formation to a recent report by the Chief Medical Officer. There has also been a belief in Scotland that the state has a role in promoting economic development. Between the 1930s and the 1970s that took the form of regional development activity, especially the provision of grants to attract inward investment. Since then, it has paid more attention to building up infrastructure in support of enterprise, for instance through training or transport.

The point here is not to evaluate the outcomes of all this activity; it is simply to note the broad feeling in Scotland that creating a just society entails a public concern for just distribution. That, then, is the second aspect of Scottish social thought – the firm belief in public provision. Government is regarded as legitimate because it is believed to be the only means by which a socially just community could be built.

Some of this left-of-centre culture grew most recently from the experience of the eighteen years between 1979 and 1997 when Scotland was governed by a Conservative Party it had not voted for. But it also goes back further. It was expressed in the consensus around the welfare state, which was established in the 1940s and 1950s. And that cross-party sense of the necessity of governmental action is due ultimately to much older theological principles. The Presbyterian ideal of a godly commonwealth dominated Scottish social policy at least until the late nineteenth century; in the Labour Party especially, that strand was then joined by Catholic social ideas in the 1920s and 1930s.

Much of this approach has been expressed as a commitment to community. But the very strength of ideas of community in Scotland accounts for some further aspects of this dominant way of thinking, aspects which complicate any description of it as straightforward social democracy. Although public action is favoured, political action is – paradoxically – treated with suspicion. That stems from the centuries of union where politics seemed to belong to the remote forum of Westminster. It appeared that a consensus about social policy could be established without having to indulge in the messiness of partisanship. Social justice could be inaugurated by committees of dour experts. Until Margaret Thatcher came along and tried to disabuse the Scottish professional classes of this assumption, politics seemed distinctly unattractive. Even today, part of the problem faced by the Scottish Parliament is establishing a sense of the value of politics.

That, further, relates to the one kind of politics that did operate in the old Scotland: a form of unobtrusive nationalism that involved having to present a united face to London in order to extract resources for the social welfare on which Scots agreed. This non-partisan nationalism became the means by which the Scottish Parliament was achieved, but it makes normal political dialogue seem awkward. This is why there is still a sense that political debate about social problems is vaguely disreputable – that these things are still best settled by committees of experts, rather than by elected (and inevitably partisan) politicians. This old distrust of politics is now being reinforced by a wider cynicism about politics across the Western world, and by the vicious hostility to the Scottish Parliament of the Scottish right-wing press.

The resulting networks of professional governance and community allegiance seem impenetrable to outsiders, or to dissidents. It is as tough being a Conservative in Scotland these days as it was not being a Presbyterian Liberal in the middle of the nineteenth century. By and large, incomers are eventually welcomed in Scotland, but only on Scotland's terms. Assimilation is encouraged, continuing cultural distinctiveness treated with suspicion.

So being Scottish is a form of strong communitarianism. The challenge for the nation over the next several decades is to liberalise this, while not losing the principles of social solidarity on which it rests.

# Norman Pender

*Norman Pender was born in 1948 in Bridlington, Yorkshire. His mother's family hails from Berwickshire and his father's from Hawick. The family moved to Hawick when Norman was three and he has remained there since. He was employed in the hosiery, transport, building and agricultural trades as well as spending a period as a slaughterhouse manager and a sales rep. for Boots. He has also had various careers in self-employment, as a scrap dealer, car salesman, taxi proprietor, riding school owner and property developer. Norman is best known for his love of sport. He played rugby for Hawick, the South and Scotland and raced pigeons for many years. He enjoys horse riding, hunting and the Common Ridings. He is currently a Scottish Liberal Democrat councillor for the Scottish Borders.*

Having dual qualifications – born in Bridlington, Yorkshire, by a Scottish father (Hawick) out of an English-registered mother (who was by Ewart x Kerrs of Berwickshire) – I wonder at being asked to contribute to this book. I was due to come into the world at the Knoll maternity home in Duns, Berwickshire, but while my mother was making a Christmas visit to her sister in Bridlington, she found herself stuck there because of one of the worst winters in living memory (1947/8). Whoops, I've given away my age. When challenged on the subject of my birthplace I usually respond by saying, 'If I was born in China ah widnae be Chinese, would I?' Having pulled on a Scottish shirt and played against the 'Auld Enemy' I suppose I have declared my allegiance, but often reflect on my decision not to play for Yorkshire and England.

Scotland, I think, is like a child that has been physically abused by its parent (England) for centuries, from the Highland Clearances until recent times, when it has taken from us the royalties from our natural wealth, mainly oil, coal, gas, electricity and now water. This money should have been invested in Scotland for the benefit of the Scottish people instead of being taken to Westminster. A situation that may have been somewhat rectified of late.

The Scottish people, an adventurous, inventive hard-working race, have planted their Pict/Celtic seeds all over the world, just as have the Irish and Welsh. These I feel were good genes to share. Albeit it was not always through choice that many of our ancestors left these shores as willing immigrants but it must have been meant to be, in the greater scheme of things. American President Theodore Roosevelt said of the Scots 'they became the vanguard of our civilisation'. One can list with pride great Scots who are a recorded in history: John Logie Baird, Alexander Graham Bell, Robert Louis Stevenson, Robert Burns, William Wallace and Robert the Bruce. To this endless list of world-famous scholars, writers, poets, leaders, discoverers and inventors, one can add the names of present-day sportsmen and women.

It is easy to be bitter but we must remember that the Scots for a large part have themselves to blame. The Scots when weary of peace fight among themselves, clan against clan. This is still the case today when one looks at the politicians and Scottish sporting bodies. The psyche of the Scots has been damaged over the centuries by acts of treachery and duplicity, by bribes of promises of lands, wealth and power, which have set Scot against Scot. The Romans could not defeat us because there were no English kings in their wake to bribe Scottish lairds with gold and lands to betray their own fellow Scots.

Having said all this, I recall the sermon by Jesus in the Bible about the twigs. One twig on its own is easily broken but a group bound together is strong and hard to break. Nothing unites people more than a common enemy. Devolution, yes, control our own autonomy, yes, but to leave the United Kingdom to become independent is another consideration.

Whether one considers in football terms or rugby terms, which would be the stronger team playing in a World Cup, a Scottish, Welsh, English, Irish or *British team*? Therein lies the answer to many questions. Whether I would expand on this analogy when considering entering Europe is another matter. If we do go in as part of Britain then we will lose even more control of our country's autonomy. If we go in as an independent Scotland then that would be an entirely different scenario. Our fellow Celts in Eire seem to be doing reasonably well, so I would urge Scots to 'watch that Euro space'. (At the time of writing, the euro has just been launched—will it go up or down?) I sometimes think that Britain is like a big battleship anchored off Europe, and if we did not join Europe then the Americans and the Far East may invest heavily in the United Kingdom to launch a commercial onslaught into Europe. Who knows – a theory that will probably never be tested?

Although at times we Lowland Scots feel as though we are on the wrong side of the great Scottish north/south divide and we often cast an enviable eye northwards towards the blossoming centre belt, I can't help feeling that we have the best of it. For we have a beautiful sparsely populated scenic Scottish borderland with historical customs and traditions dating back for centuries, which gives us a unique pride and sense of place. Pilgrims and tourists alike are now assured safe passage through our lands these days as there is no bag of gold paid by English kings to wreck havoc on their enemies.

Whenever I am asked my nationality I feel like saying, 'I am a Hawick man first, a Borderer second and a Scotsman third,' but to keep it short I usually say overall, with great pride, 'I am Scottish.'

# Hugh Pennington

*Hugh Pennington is Professor of Bacteriology at Aberdeen University. He qualified in medicine in London and worked there and in Madison, Wisconsin and Glasgow on viruses including smallpox and hepatitis B. He currently works on tracking bacterial infections using molecular methods. He chaired an inquiry for the government into the 1996 Central Scotland E.coli O157 outbreak. He is a member of the Food Standards Agency Scottish Food Advisory Committee, and is a Fellow of the Royal Society of Edinburgh and of the Academy of Medical Sciences.*

I am only a Scot by domicile. A Lancashire accent says where I was brought up. Nevertheless, I claim that more than half my life living and working in Glasgow and Aberdeen confers at least a quaich of Caledonian credibility. For thirty years I have been proud to be a member of universities in those cities where in the last five centuries great things were done by academics like Thomas Reid, Alexander Bain, and George Thomson. Who? They are people whose contributions have put them in the global hall of fame for all time coming. Reid invented Scottish Common Sense Philosophy. Bain was a founding father of psychology. And Thomson got the Nobel Prize for showing that electrons could behave like waves as well as particles. That we don't celebrate them properly as famous Scots is scandalous. Self-deprecation is our forte. We work hard on it to fuel our lack of self-confidence. The Americans and the French have many outstanding intellectual and scientific achievements to their credit. So do we. But unlike them we keep quiet. This wouldn't be so bad if Scottish universities were in a mess. But they are not. They are efficient, economical and effective.

To add insult to injury recent times have been very rough. For more than half my time at Aberdeen the university was in crisis. It was spending beyond its means. Cut was piled upon cut and reform upon reform. It was rescued. But it hurt. In an attempt to save itself a student orchestra from the music department played outside the Senate room during the crucial meeting. But it was closed, along with the physics department, where Thomson did his brilliant work. The worst time I had as medical school dean was fighting off a lunatic plan to make it into a kind of NHS training camp in which things like original thought and intellectual development would have been sacrificed to the production of cheap medical robots.

Much of this turmoil was due to government policies made in London. But in Aberdeen there was a peculiarly intense inflexibility of purpose. Even though the financial crisis was acute, I have no doubt that Scottishness played its part. Henry Thomas Buckle in his *History of Civilisation in England* (which is untrue to its title because it devotes lots more space to Scotland) claims that Scots always work deductively from first principles, whereas the English are driven pragmatically by facts and circumstances. There wasn't much pragmatism in Aberdeen in the 1980s.

Buckle's analysis is facile, but has a kernel of truth. Contrast the Kirk's disruptions with the Church of England's co-existing happy clappy bishops and incense-burning celibates. The classical academic case is Professor William Robertson Smith who between 1877 and 1881 was tried twice for heresy by the Free Church because of his articles on the Bible in the *Encyclopaedia Britannica* and sacked from his chair at its Aberdeen College. He was warmly received by Christ's College Cambridge, whose history describes him as 'one of the very ablest men ever in this Society' and by Cambridge University as Professor of Arabic. As an atheist I don't grieve to see that Smiths' College at the top end of Union Street is now a restaurant called 'Babylon'. Maybe a hidden hand rights injustices after all.

So being a Scottish academic is no bed of roses. But our universities have never been ivory towers. Aberdeen and Glasgow are *Arbeitsuniversitäten*. And they have stuck to the civilising mission laid down by their fifteenth-century founders as well as keeping local roots well nourished. My greatest academical pleasure is attending graduations and seeing all sorts and kinds of people, local and incomers, being dunted with big smiles on their faces as they go furth to run the country.

Other rewards of being Scottish are those of living in a small country where size-induced parochialism is tempered by powerful rival city states and influential landward loyalties. Another pleasure is going to London, where we are envied because we run our own affairs and, sometimes, feared because we run theirs, too. Just as well. There is a downside. I used to stay in Cumbernauld and will never forget the horizontal sleet and the Carbrain bus stop decorated with the words 'I nearly died here waiting for a bus to Airdrie.'

But living in the north-east is good. The best money decision I ever took was to cash in a life-insurance policy to buy a fisherman's but and ben near Banff. The architectual fitness of purpose of Moray Firth seatowns, how they meet the ocean and the weather, and the way my Whitehills neighbours care not a jot about where you come from but keenly judge you by what you do symbolise Scottishness for me.

# Robina Qureshi

*Robina Qureshi was born and brought up in Glasgow to Pakistani immigrants. Through her work for a Scottish charity, she is actively involved in challenging institutionalised racism and the government's policy towards refugees. She has contributed several articles about racism for newspapers and social policy journals. In 1995, she received the Ujima Pookar Award for 'outstanding contribution to the black community'. In 2001 she played an acting role in* Gas Attack *(directed by Kenny Glenaan), a film about what could happen if a chemical weapons attack (in this case Anthrax) were launched on a major UK city.*

I was born here and spent my childhood in Pollokshields, where there was – still is – a large Pakistani and Indian community. Within the community, I felt like this was my home, where I belonged – well, as much as it was possible to feel at home given the other reminders that we were really outsiders. Around the age of eight, I remember walking home from school and seeing lots of copies of the same fly-poster on the wall, saying 'yesterday they came for the Jews, today they come for the Asians, tomorrow they will come for you'. It was written in big red letters by the 'socialist worker'. I thought they must be nice people.

The National Front was on the news a lot, angry white men with shaven heads shouting about 'too many immigrants' and us being a drain on society, having too many children and smelling of curry. My mum and dad were at the shop and it was just us seven girls at home. My older sister said, 'We can't go out anywhere'; we were scared. 'Why do they want us to leave the country?' I asked. 'Because they say there's too many immigrants.' Sure enough, looking out of the window of our tenement, there were in fact quite a few of us. My parents did their very best to protect us and my mother would get into a rising panic on several occasions and tell us 'Just remember this isn't your country; one day they're going to throw us out and send us back home. So don't get too comfortable here. We're Pakistanis.' It used to scare me, that.

Away from the reality, I read a lot of Enid Blyton books and was convinced that was how all white people lived. I mean, we lived next door to white people but we never actually mixed unless it was to play with their kids outside – we never got much closer. There was this one summer, I would go to the Pollokshields library every day and read at least one Famous Five book a day. I wanted to be like them and drink ginger beer, even though I hated ginger beer. Anything other than to be loathed for being Asian.

I don't blame myself or feel ashamed for thinking that as a child because I see it now as a reflection of how society looked down on our communities, denigrating our culture then and even today. Nothing has changed, every day racism continues on the streets, in our faces and insidiously behind our backs. The refrains I heard in childhood – 'Go back home, Paki', 'Go back to where you belong' – still remain and manage to cut me. I know the anger I feel at how our communities have been rejected and disenfranchised and labelled as inferior to this society, and at being given stupid justifications for injustices by very stupid people claiming to be intelligent and more superior. What a veneer. At least admit your racism. I don't any longer want to be accepted by a society that pays lip-service to equality and liberty.

Against that context it is difficult to feel Scottish. In fact, I don't really feel Scottish unless I go abroad, but then I say 'I am from Scotland', not 'I'm Scottish.' No way, not unless it is to annoy the hell out of someone who is determined that I don't come from here. Scotland is not my home in that sense of the word; I only really felt that when I went to Pakistan for three weeks at the age of eighteen. During the flight, I felt nothing about 'going home' but as soon as the plane landed and hit Pakistani soil, something happened in my heart, I had arrived somewhere very special, with which I had a real and indisputable connection.

I now accept that this society rejects us but doesn't want to admit its complicity. Things have not really changed and nowhere is this more evident than with the way refugee communities are being treated, being segregated into housing that absolutely no one else wants to live in, facing epidemic levels of racist attacks and then being criminalised by society. Don't be surprised when in a few years' time the children of these communities express their outrage at this society's treatment of them. I don't like being fitted into other people's history. The history of Scotland is a whitewashed one that forgets the sponging off poorer countries that Scotland did during its colonialist era. As for this oath of allegiance they are talking about for new 'immigrants' – what a disgrace. An oath of allegiance to a deeply racist society?

One of my first memories was when the headmistress called me into her room and told me I was a good girl and I was from India. I said, 'No, I am from Pakistan' and she said no I wasn't and I should repeat after her 'I am from India.' Twenty years later, I remember the first day of my wee boy's school, and the headmistress asking Ibrahim rather sternly 'And what is your name?' He replied, for the first time ever pronouncing his name 'Abraham' instead of 'Ibrahim'. Still pisses me off, that.

# Selma Rahman

*Selma Rahman was born in Edinburgh, married and lived in Karachi and Dhaka, Bangladesh. There she ran her own nursery school and edited and published a Keya/English language woman's magazine. She has four grown sons, no cats … but had her house fung shuied about two years ago. She is currently Director of the Fife Racial Equality Council.*

Well, here's a to-do. I'm being asked my view on Scottish Identity Today, and being Scottish. Now there's a turn up for the books!

I remember playing on the pavements in Edinburgh as a child in the 1950s and being called a 'wee toe-rag'.

I remember leaving Edinburgh tearfully en route for Liverpool, 1960, to catch a ship to take me to Pakistan for the first time ever. On that train, during what I thought was an intelligent conversation with a fellow passenger (I was twelve, my father was in his fifties, my mother had just died; the passenger was alive but of indeterminable age) the fellow passenger turned to my father and said, 'She's got a very broad accent, hasn't she?'

I also remember having trouble getting anyone to understand me further east of Gib. To this day, people tell me I tend    to    speak    very        slowly.

I found it easier to talk quickly and learn other languages: Karachi, and Urdu, then Dhaka (following on from my arranged marriage) and Bengali.

So that is part of my being Scottish. My beginnings, my roots, my personal voyages (can I skip that part, please? I got very sick in the ship as it crossed the Bay of Biscay), my arranged marriage, my four sons, and my return to Scotland. There was a lot in between that has inevitably shaped me, a revolution that saw the birth of Bangladesh, military coups, losing my home, having to flee, having to start all over again … and being 'successful' eventually. But isn't that a microscopic view of

Scotland? People coming, people going, changes in government, governance and democracy; the manipulation of democracy … in the name of the people; fragile security linked to fragile economics … and the ever striving to be 'better', to be 'successful'.

Irrespective of what and how I feel about being Scottish, and anyone who ever 'hears' me is in no doubt about where I come from, two things set me apart that mean I can be judged on those two things: first is my name … it identifies me as being Muslim, and of Pakistani origin, and the second is my colour. And those two things influence how others feel about me being here and being Scottish. Their feelings, views, the occasional aggro (for aggro read 'racism') thus impact on how I feel about being Scottish.

Scotland for too long viewed itself as the 'victim' and collectively has denied its past, its roots, its exploitative history as part and parcel of the British Empire. But hey, as they say – or near enough – 'that's in the past now, and in the past now, it must remain' (Corries … respect!). But it has contributed to a crisis in identity, even if submerged under the trauma post the Unions of the Crown and then parliaments.

But if that was post then, what of post now, and post devolution?

Will social strategy, social inclusion, equality agendas and political rhetoric translate into social action? Will we all be contributing into and taking from a vibrant, eclectic Scotland?

Will the politically changing face of Scotland impact on the physically changing faces in Scotland? Will it be vice versa?

Will it be change brought about through accountability, or the unaccount-ability of fear?

The fear of change, the fear of outsiders, incomers and any other derogatory term the bigots hide behind.

(Will Scotland ever win the World Cup? Women, Curling, Gold, victory … respect! Passion, hope tears, dreams … as ever.)

So, that's me, the wee toe-rag, the wee keillie, the mother, the worker, the Scot.

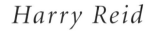

# *Harry Reid*

*Harry Reid worked in Scottish journalism for over thirty years, latterly as Editor of* The Herald *(1997–2000). He has just completed a commissioned book on the state and prospects of the Church of Scotland. He is Visiting Fellow at the Faculty of Divinity, Edinburgh University, and an honorary doctor of Edinburgh and Glasgow Universities.*

I was born in Glasgow and brought up in Aberdeen in the 1950s. Everyone I knew was Scottish. I first became conscious that there was a difference, that other people were not necessarily Scottish, when I started reading.

I was a voracious reader, and whether it was Richmal Crompton or Enid Blyton or the Biggles books or Eric Leyland (a particular favourite) I was aware that this fictive world was *not Scottish*. Slowly I learned about the English, how they were different, and the difference defined my Scottishness. When, later, I became a fan of John Buchan this process was accentuated. In his most popular if not his best book, *The Thirty-Nine Steps*, the hero Hannay eventually arrives in Berkshire to make contact with Sir Walter Bullivant, the mandarin who represents order and the forces of good. Having concluded his desperate adventures on the exposed uplands of Galloway, Hannay meets Sir Walter by the River Kennet.

'After Scotland the air smelt heavy and flat, but infinitely sweet … ' Here the subconscious deference of Buchan, a Scotsman on the make, is surely speaking. I also read again and again that marvellous passage early on in Grassic Gibbon's *Sunset Song* when Chris Guthrie reflects on her parents and their Scottishness: 'and then you were back to the English words so sharp and clean and true, for a while, for a while, till they slid so smooth from your throat you knew they could never say anything that was worth the saying at all'. And a tiny bit of me still believes that to be true.

Then I really learned about the English by mingling with them for the only four years that I have lived outside Scotland. I spent three years at Oxford University, studying history, and then a year at Newcastle upon Tyne learning to be a journalist. I made English friends. I learned more about our two countries. Years later I was commissioned to write a book, outlining a Scotsman's view of England, which was published in 1992. If I had to sum it up I'd say the burden was that England's greatest years are behind it while Scotland's might just be ahead. If this suggests a tentative disposition to Scottish nationalism, I plead guilty. I have certainly worked journalistically for a Scottish Parliament; on *The Scotsman* in the 1970s, and on *The Herald* in the 1990s. I now hope that this parliament will act as a stepping stone to independence.

But I admire the English enormously. They have given Scotland so much. The greatest Scot, John Knox, was a consistent Anglophile. The Scottish Reformation, arguably the pivotal event in our history, was secured when a tyro English queen, bravely and against the counsel of her senior advisors, sent both her army and navy north to help the Scots drive out the occupying French. When Scotland does contend for its independence, I hope that move will be predicated on a positive and pragmatic view of relations with England. Apart from anything else, as I have suggested, the English help us to define ourselves.

As I grow older my love of Scotland increases, day by day. I sometimes think that my marriage has survived, on the whole well, over twenty years and more because my wife Julia and I share an intense love of Scotland that transcends any glib patriotism. Yet I detest the cultural distortion of our country (for which Walter Scott, supremely, must be blamed). I don't like tartan or Burns. I think we choose the wrong heroes. I'm a literary man and I think Galt is better than Scott, MacDiarmid better than Burns, Violet Jacob better than Stevenson.

As a nation we seem woefully ignorant of our complex and action-packed history, despite the splendid work of popularising scholars like Chris Smout and Tom Devine. In particular there is ignorance of the defining sixteenth century.

I have lived and worked in three of our four great cities; I remain, to my shame, somewhat ignorant of Dundee (apart from Dens Park and Tannadice). I love tramping our hills in the summer. These days I am less keen on the busy Munros, but I know of several places within sixty miles of our capital where I guarantee that you can walk for twelve hours without meeting or seeing another soul. Scotland is a staggeringly, heartbreakingly beautiful country and I just wish more young Scots would explore it instead of constantly rushing abroad.

The good things about Scotland: our smeddum, resilience, literary excellence, dryness (not in the literal sense), inventiveness, industry, incredible landscape and our whisky. Our negatives: a tendency to sentimentality, particularly about our past; ignorance of our country and its history; excessive suspicion of big ideas and projects; an occasional meanness of spirit; and our midges.

We are better as individuals than we are at working together. The list of titanic, world-changing individuals we have produced is extraordinarily impressive.

Living and working in Scotland ain't easy; it was never meant to be a facile country. We like to cut folk down to size, sometimes too aggressively. Whatever we are, we are not smooth or bland (beware of Scottish smoothies, rare and dangerous creatures). But this is a land of paradoxes and although there is an essential grimness about Scotland there is also a reductive demotic honesty about our nation that is ultimately life-enhancing. And I hope we can argue in heaven.

# Susan Rice

*Susan Rice, a Chartered Banker, became Chief Executive of Lloyds TSB Scotland in August 2000, the first woman to head a UK clearing bank. Susan chairs the Committee of Scottish Clearing Bankers and the Edinburgh International Book Festival and is a member of the Boards of Scottish Business in the Community, the SCDI and The New Charity Bank. She provides leadership and guidance to the private, public and voluntary sectors on the issues of financial exclusion in the UK. Previously Susan was Managing Director, Personal Banking, at Bank of Scotland and, prior to this, Senior Vice President and Division Head of National Westminster Bancorp. Born and brought up in the United States, she lives with her husband and three children in Aberdeen, where she is a Burgess of Guild of the City. She was recently elected a Fellow of the Royal Society of Edinburgh.*

People I meet through work often ask me, 'Where are you from?' My immediate response is 'Aberdeen'. Invariably, I get a quizzical look and another question 'Where are you really from?' and I realise they have heard my accent and know that it isn't Scottish. Yet I live here permanently. I work in Edinburgh. My children attend school in Aberdeen, which is my family base. My husband is a Scot. For me, Scotland's home.

There's an interest here in things American – in how we do business, in the American optimistic, 'can-do' approach to life. Scots are open to what they perceive as different. This openness, along with an inherent civility and courtesy among most Scots, makes way for an incomer.

I have never lived in a place where there was such widespread fascination with the economy, infrastructure and services, with what's wrong and what could be right. These are topics that recur in the press, on the tongues of people in government, in business, in the local shop. There is an extraordinary engagement with the country and where it might be going. Everyone has a view, often self-critical and often meliorated by a pervasive, wry sense of humour. Everyone is informed or thinks he or she is. What's marvelous about this is that everyone cares so much.

The country is a bit like a teenager. Anything can be wrong with it today but there is infinite hope and promise for tomorrow. It's as if there is a great prize and people are desperate to reach it. However, if there is a collective desire for Scotland to thrive and become more important, there is not always a collective belief that this can happen, or agreement about how to get there. Put this alongside the continuous historical and intellectual thread that survives so well. I don't know of any other place which supports so many learned lectures attended not just by academics but by people from business and the professions. The Royal Society of Edinburgh links directly back to David Hume and Adam Smith.

Scots created saving banks, the overdraft, the Western economy, indeed much of what we consider modern. Its people are trained at universities far older than America, such as Aberdeen, where my husband is Principal. Perhaps it's the currency of the past which, consciously or unconsciously, supports a belief in Scotland today.

This is not to say that all is rosy. Health statistics are anything but. The divide between rich and poor is marked, though not as much as in my own country. The infrastructure, particularly transport, badly needs investment. Scots still talk about their schools as providing a superior education to other countries. It's not clear that this is any longer the case. But so long as people believe it, the situation won't change.

Yet things do change. Twenty-five years ago, people throughout Scotland were not so inclined to display the visible badges of their country. Today, hardly a wedding or a sixth-year school dance happens without a plethora of kilts. But the kilt is a surface emblem. Underlying that display is a burgeoning self-confidence.

I frequently speak on Scotland, its economy, its cultural base or its social issues. I find myself astonished at how often I use the pronoun 'we'. Being Scottish isn't about where I was born or about parentage. Nor is it about Highlanders or tartan or whisky. It's about engagement with the country and what it might become.

Indeed, for me being Scottish is actually about becoming Scottish. On having very good news recently about the annual performance of my business, I used the word 'chuffed' for the first time. That's actually how I feel when I think about becoming Scottish.

Becoming fully focused on Scotland's current condition, its people, its physical assets, and what the future holds. I find myself at the centre of some things here – running a major business, sponsoring cultural events, being known by more people than I know, advising government, bringing up children, who are now Scottish, working on behalf of the socially disadvantaged. I have become linked to Scotland, to its discourse and its reach for a bright future.

Furthermore, there's another aspect of being Scottish, separate from profess-ional or domestic life. It is feeling humbled by its magnificent landscape. Ever since my first visit here, I've had the sense that the land is closer to the sky than anywhere else I've been. It's a beautiful land, in its micro-spaces, for instance the rock-pools along the coast of Harris, and in its mega-places, such as the Cairn-gorms. It's a landscape that at once challenges and embraces us. Its hills were here long before we came, and will be here long after we leave. It puts us all in our places.

# Kat Roberts

*Kat Roberts was born in England twenty-five years ago but has lived in Scotland all her life (apart from the first couple of weeks, obviously). She lives in Edinburgh and is currently researching a Ph.D. in Hindu Pilgrimage. Kat has a cat. And a husband.*

First of all, a confession: I was born in England. There is plenty of Scottish blood in my veins though, passed from my mother's side. And I would defy anyone to tell me I'm not Scottish. My father's a Geordie and they're nearly Scots, aren't they? (If that last cattle raid had finished a few miles further south, they might've been!) As if to make up for my English birth I was brought to live in Scotland when only weeks old, and have thus absorbed that wonderful, if somewhat intangible, state of being Scottish. It's all I have ever known. (Apart from a few brief months as a seven-year-old when I wanted to be English because I thought their flag was prettier than ours. It's okay; I got over it.)

Being Scottish isn't that easy to define; it might seem so initially, but think about it. There are many obvious and stereotypical examples which could be given here – the stirring sound of the pipes, the pride at seeing the Saltire, the prickle on the back of your neck when you sing at a rugby match. But they are a small and really an unimportant part of how it feels to be Scottish. Those things do not differentiate us from any other nationality. Every nation uses different symbols but they still evoke the same feelings in their people. This tells us nothing of what it is to be Scottish. Is it anything in particular to be Scottish?

Although I believe the Scots have a clear sense of identity, I do not believe it has that great an impact on most Scottish lives. Being Scottish is certainly not the primary influence in my life. For example I have found this very difficult to write as I have never thought about what being Scottish means to me before. I have never had occasion to. I suppose the closest I have got is on my last research trip to India. I was asked what my nationality was and had to think hard about how to answer. I wanted to say 'Scottish' but was aware that in a remote village 16,000 feet up in the Himalayas it cannot be assumed that that means anything. I didn't really want to say 'British' as in India I had visions of those around me tutting at my imperial ancestry. So I said I was from Scotland and explained where that was and was met with approving cries of 'Oh, many mountains, like ours.' I then had to confess that in comparison we had very small hills but, yes, Scotland is renowned for its mountains. 'Oh, your biggest mountain is only 4,300 feet. That is very funny!'

And we can laugh at ourselves too. Just look at the popularity of *Rab C. Nesbitt* and *Chewin' the Fat*. Both see the less than enviable side of Scottishness and have cleverly made that something to entertain us with. Hopefully not everyone will believe this is all there is to our country! Of course we love to poke fun at our dear neighbours too. We know how ridiculous Morris dancers are (but think men in kilts with pointy toes doing Highland dancing is fine!). However, this teasing can get a bit out of hand. I have long been a student at Edinburgh University and the rivalry between the English and Scottish contingents, while often good-natured, can be so vicious, it is shaming. Or just so unfathomable, such as a girl I knew when I was an undergraduate who simply refused to even attempt any kind of friendship or relationship with any student who dared to be from England, purely on the grounds that they were English.

I hope that this kind of inferiority complex masquerading as haughty superiority is disappearing now that we have our own parliament of which we are rightly proud. But I also hope that it is not to be replaced with a belief that we can cut ourselves off from the rest of our country. We must now stop dwelling on the past (although our heritage must not be forgotten) and look towards our place in the future. We are a nation, yes, but a nation within a nation, and although I am proud to be Scottish that does not diminish the pride I feel in being part of a nation within a United Kingdom.

# Kenneth Roy

*Kenneth Roy is Director, Institute of Contemporary Scotland, Editor of* The Scottish Review *and Publisher of* Who's Who in Scotland.

On the day of my childhood that I remember most vividly, we formed an orderly queue outside Greenhill Primary School and walked to the village hall, a green hut packed with uniformed and awestruck children, Within a few hours, we were exposed to the two great cultural influences of the 1950s: the deity known as royalty and the magical box in the corner. I was seven years old on the day the Queen was crowned. I didn't think of myself as belonging to any nation, but I realise now that I was brought up British.

We weren't taught contemporary Scottish history at Greenhill Primary or, later, at Denny High. The name Hugh MacDiarmid meant nothing to us; the reasons for the depopulation of the Highlands were never explained; no one told us how the dark and dangerous city of Glasgow came to be so poor. Because our education lacked any immediate context, we were ignorant about the background to our own lives. We existed in a state of un-Scottishness. It must have been an official conspiracy, yet no one complained.

Was this indifference peculiar to the Falkirk district? I think not. Editing the journalism of Alastair Hetherington, I came across this devastating account of the 1951 general election campaign north of the border: 'Scottish issues, as such, are unimportant. 'Dead as a dodo' was one Conservative comment in Lanarkshire, and a Labour speaker in Dunbartonshire said: 'Scottish questions? We don't get any.' They are, nevertheless, being raised at some meetings, to the obvious boredom of audiences.' In those days, the Tory in our constituency (West Stirlingshire) called himself a unionist. He invariably polled strongly.

The failure to recognise Scotland as any sort of entity went beyond politics; the vigorous working-class culture I knew as a child expressed itself on a broader canvas. I think of my father, moving his toy actors about a cardboard stage in preparation for the winter season of plays in Bonnybridge Public Hall. He had a sentimental fondness for J. M. Barrie but a greater intellectual regard for Pirandello, and Joe Corrie, the only Scottish writer he produced regularly, in Corrie's dramatisation of the plight of coal-miners, which spoke to the cause of international brotherhood, though in a domestic setting.

The institution I joined in my twenties, and which shaped the first part of my working life, was quintessentially British and, naturally enough, London called the shots. At first I accepted implicitly that the metropolitan masters of BBC Scotland knew best. I was finally shocked out of complacency when the Controller in Glasgow – the same Alastair Hetherington a quarter of a century later – was fired for demanding greater independence over budgets and programmes. Such a brutal exercise of a remote, centralised power compelled me to look at Scotland in a new way. I became a reluctant convert to devolution.

Although the idea of 'being British' now seems faintly repellent, even ridiculous, the alternative most obviously and aggressively on offer – Scottish patriotism for its own sake – is no less so. The parliament in Edinburgh, for all its shortcomings and absurdities, would be worth nurturing if it turned out to be the mere political manifestation of a more general cultural movement. Insofar as there is any evidence of such a movement, it has been in the wrong direction, expressing itself in the depravity of Irvine Welsh's fiction and the celluloid triumphalism of *Braveheart*. If this is 'being Scottish', count me out.

Sadly, there is nothing brave at the heart of Scotland. Almost one in three of our children lives in poverty, a whole generation is in danger of being lost to drugs, and the spirit of the native entrepreneur has been bottled and exported, leaving us with a branch factory economy vulnerable to corporate whim. Anti-English sentiment erupts even among the educated classes and we have recently made the shocking discovery that the famously tolerant Scots, who had the audacity to sings 'A Man's A Man for A' That' at the opening of the Scottish Parliament, are as racially intolerant as the next bigot.

What did we expect of that parliament? In practical ways: too much. Its powers are severely circumscribed and stop well short of any ability to ameliorate the economic condition of the people. This we should have known. But its existence should be changing us in subtler ways. I am with the actor Andrew Cruickshank, who longed for a 'gentle and civilised nationalism' which is secure enough to put thinker, inventors and artists at its core. We did it once before, and it was called the Enlightenment. We need a new Enlightenment, with the vital condition that this one should be open and accessible to all. Then, and only then, will I derive any satisfaction from being Scottish. It's a long way off.

# Trevor Royle

*Trevor Royle is an Associate Editor of the* Sunday Herald *and the author of numerous books on the history of war and Empire. He is also Vice Chairman of the Airborne Initiative, which offers young offenders an alternative to custodial sentencing.*

**Shades of Grey**

A few years ago a senior army figure asked whys it had seemed necessary for the Welsh Guards to ask an Englishman living in Scotland to write their latest regimental history. Somewhat bemused by the question, a Welsh Guards officer retorted that the author concerned, Trevor Royle, just happened to live in Scotland. Nothing more, nothing less. He was of course both right and wrong; facts are never clear-cut when race and nationality are called into question. Not a drop of Scottish blood runs in my veins – my father's family hails from Cheshire and the Welsh marches, my mother's is solidly southern English leavened by long years in India – but as an individual who has spent the better part of his life in Scotland (quantitatively and qualitatively) I cannot think of myself as being anything other than a Scot. In any case, as I am a product of the country's education system I am at least a writer of Scots formation, the memorable phrase coined by Muriel Spark to describe her own uneasy relationship with Scotland and her sense of perpetual exile from it.

Half a century ago, when I came to Scotland as a young boy that would have been a dangerous claim. Even in a solidly unionist Scotland there was a dichotomous attitude about the southern neighbour which stopped short of xenophobia but still simmered unpleasantly below the surface. On a sunny day people would remark with an air of self-congratulation that it was raining in England, a classmate showed no embarrassment in claiming that the air seemed fresher once the train had crossed the bridge at Berwick, and I remember being at the receiving end of a bashing for no other reason than my accent annoyed my attacker.

Would that happen today? I doubt it. For all that there is an edge in sporting fixtures with English teams, that is sport and not the real world. In any case a person's nationality is the least important of their characteristics and at the beginning of the twenty-first century Scotland seems much more parti-coloured, vibrant, grown-up and open to challenges than it ever was before. Devolution has helped to lance the boil by removing political resentment, the influence of a globalised popular culture has opened minds and other parts of Britain have changed too, not least England and its half-baked stereotypes. Who would have thought that estuary English would be a common denominator, uniting people from different social and racial backgrounds? Nevertheless (another of Spark's principles), for all that Scotland is more at ease with itself, compared to other parts of Britain and Europe, it is still a predominantly white country. True, there is a vibrant presence from the Indian subcontinent and from Hong Kong. Their contribution to Scottish life has been substantial – many of the outstanding entrepreneurs and innovators come from their communities – but a suspicion remains that Scotland is not always such a happy home-from-home. The new century began with Kurdish refugees being attacked after they had been rehoused in Sighthill in Glasgow. One man was killed and the violence revealed a deep-seated resentment which was fired as much by economic jealousy – the refugees were thought to be gaining benefits denied to longer-standing residents – as by simple racial prejudice. It was not untypical, similar incidents were reported in England, but in Scotland, a country whose birthrate has dropped and whose population is becoming increasingly older, it seems insane not to welcome a policy of active immigration. We should be encouraging people from other parts of the world to settle in Scotland and to bring with them their different skills and different cultural strengths. After all the process has hardly harmed the United States of America – and not just historically. There are few cultural or historical links between India and the USA yet the computer technology revolution in the latter has been pushed forward immeasurably by bright young sparks from Bangalore and Hyderabad. Forget jokes about the climate but what benefited northern California would not look out of place in Glenrothes or Livingstone.

Yet it would be wrong to end on a pessimistic note. In recent times the army is no longer the nation in uniform, its links to the civilian community weakened by growing professionalism and the end of conscription, but it is still capable of showing the way forward. The Royal Scots is the oldest line infantry regiment in the British army, yet far from being a bastion of white privilege its ranks now include Gurkha riflemen and Fijian soldiers who stayed on after performing at the Edinburgh Military Tattoo. They had no difficulty in fitting in and, what is more, the Fijians helped the regiment to win the army rugby championships. If ever there was an incentive, that might be it.

# Michael Russell

*Michael Russell is an SNP Member of the Scottish Parliament for the South of Scotland. Currently Shadow Minister for Children and Education, he also speaks for the SNP on Gaelic and on Culture. He was Chief Executive of the Party from 1994 to 1999 and is a writer and television producer.*

Two snapshots from the occasional travels of a member of the Scottish Parliament:

In February 2000 I was sitting in the main committee room of the Indian Parliament in New Delhi on the opening day of a small Commonwealth Parliamentary Association conference behind a saltire and a nameplate saying 'Scotland' much to the astonishment of the UK Parliament delegation and the British High Commissioner.

In November 2001 I was standing with three other members of the Scottish Parliament in the Speakers Gallery of the Quebec National Assembly, receiving a standing ovation from the members of that Assembly before they started their daily Prime Minister's Question Time.

Being Scottish used to mean being politically invisible to the rest of the world: today, Scotland and its Parliament are the equivalent of the new kid on the block, a source of endless interest if the number of overseas politicians visiting Edinburgh since 1999 is anything to go by. And not just visiting: the number of full-time Consuls and Consuls General permanently based in Scotland has more than doubled in the last five years, though the first – the American Consul – took up residence here over 200 years ago.

For a nationalist this is exciting stuff: tangible signs of progress in getting Scotland out into the world in its own right. For other countries it is also exciting – a new parliament means new ways of doing things and new ideas that can be copied elsewhere. Even Westminster pronounces itself 'impressed' with family-friendly hours and wants to give up meeting all night. Despite the growing pains, we have at last discovered what some of us knew all along – we are not the only country in the world that is quite unable to govern itself.

A nation hobbled with an inability to speak for itself and no voice at all in the wider world will become an introverted nation, gorging itself on substitutes like football, whisky and shortbread. For a time that was our fate – we became a parody of ourselves, with a 'Here's tae us'! Wha's like us?' narrow minded, insular bumptiousness taking the place of that relaxed, easy-going self-confidence that is the hallmark of those with nothing to hide.

Now we have the chance to be at peace with ourselves – to start to live a little, without worrying that others will see through the tartanry to the hollow, unachieved centre. We can start to make a reality of our desire to have a home fit to live in, not constantly cover up the fact that we haven't even started building it.

What a burden that lifts from each one of us. We can accept and even celebrate our diverse culture and our mongrel nation – in every aspect of those portmanteau words – without the angst that comes from trying to catch and hold the shadow in the cave that is 'national identity'. We no longer have to measure ourselves against some false template of Scottishness, defined by either academics or xenophobes (or defined for us by those that hardly know us) and always at one remove from the real, delightfully chaotic, world.

What a personal burden I feel it has lifted from me, a middle-aged, Bromley-born, Gaelic-learning, Episcopalian educated at a grant-aided school, without a west of Scotland accent, who has never been to a Rangers–Celtic football match, who only rarely drinks whisky, who doesn't know how to dance the Highland Fling, and who listens out of preference to late nineteenth-century English music in an old farmhouse in Argyll. And one who counts among his family a brother born in Libya, a sister-in-law born in India and a nephew born in Ireland, but also a wife born on the island of North Uist, and a son born in Lanark.

Being Scottish can be as simple as wanting to be in Scotland, wanting to add to the mix and learn something from it. It can be an accident of birth or geography. It can speak in many different tongues and its feet can tap to many different tunes. It can be a desire merely to see all those who share this small corner of the planet do better than they have done. For me, it is inextricably intertwined with finding a way to live on independent terms in this country with those who live independently in every other country: being neither better nor worse, but just a little bit different in background, in influences and in perspective.

What it no longer means is worrying about it all. The puberty of Being Scottish is over.

# Suhayl Saadi

*Suhayl Saadi is an award-winning writer who has been awarded a Scottish Arts Council Writer's Bursary. His book* The Burning Mirror *(Polygon, 2001) has been short-listed for the Saltire First Book Prize. His novel,* Kings of the Dark House *is due out in 2002.*

When I gaze at old portrait photographs, I wonder at the lives within. In photographs of myself, it is always autumn. It may be the chemical process, which turns all things, ultimately, to sepia. Or perhaps it's an essence of some sort, imbibed from the atmosphere which swirls over this white, northern island. Scotland holds autumn within itself, a bleeding stallion, a silver tree, birds battling on the hill. A Masonic spire. With my pen, I draw refrains from the sighs of the dead and trumpet them as tales of the new Alba. My long, hirpling fall is a supra-mythic Scottishness which I cannot explain. Neither tribal or territorial, it is an Albannach shroud which emerges liminally through fiction. I mistrust walls, stridency and final definitions, since the lumpen application of any one philo-sophy leads to animalistic exclusion and averts our gaze from the stars. I embrace subtlety, the striving for excellence and all things polyglot, musical and oceanic. I have affinities with the Graeco-Egyptian tenements of the Green City and the pinnacles and junk-shops of Odin's town; I yet may find Horus, perching amidst the spinning weather-vanes of the Canongate. I dive into the mammoth lochs up north with their deep, grey worship of the sky and I, too, long for bedrock and ziggurats. I roll with Lothian song-speech and granite Mounth precision. Even Knox transubstantiates on the Day of the Dead. I dance in the blue-black energy of Glasgow rock and in the flat nakedness of the Clyde river, which springs, not from the Ballencleuch Law but from Lough Dergand, which, late at night, turns jokes and bottles with the salmon. Through paradox does beauty manifest, and the vacuum of Empire fill with the emptiness of gnosis.

I celluloid my forehead and hastily scribble: SCOTTISH. But that is inadequate, so I add: English, British, Pakistani, Indian, Afghan, Sadozai, Asian, European, Black(-ish), Minority Ethnic, Male, Non-resident, twenty-first century person, fifteenth century being, Glaswegian, Middle-class, Writer, Seeker, Lover, Physician, Agha Jaan, Son, English-speaking, Music-loving, Left-leaning … until I run out of space and time and ink. Scottishness becomes a metaphor through which I perceive other things. The ends of twigs catch in the stream.

Massed kilts 'n' cocaine ceilidhs unsettle me, though I love the Zen thrum of Gaelic song. I once bought a Clan Sinclair (Hunting) tie because of its mystical Levantine links and a MacPherson (Dress) one because it looked good. I have never felt any identification with the psycho-mechanics of Scottish football; this has nothing to do with the Sufi game, rather, I feel excluded by flag-waving and terrified by teams, mobs, tribes, which seem inherently unthinking and poten-tially fascistic. I connect with Ludhiana, Lahore and Herat, but not in the ken of the old gin Raj. I want to hear the tap-tapping of sepia fingertips at business board-table and parliamentary bench, I long to seed Ibrox turf and to ink the pages of long rags. Indigenisation, a physical, economic and spiritual dynamic, is a multi-dimensional, trans-mythic concept which requires, on all sides, a seeking after love, a need to be. We all negotiate our psychic relationships with land, icon and totem.

Something in me will remain beyond the pale of the photograph. I am outside the Outsider. I am the murdered Arab on the beach, the Mudejar sound-sculptor who alights upon the mudflats of Greenock. Tide by tide, I am sinking into this land. I stare at the sun through a veil of golden leaves. The Scotland within the photograph, within me, seeps into the pages of winter libraries, where a silent, dark galaxy of words pullulates beneath vellum: town plans, city mothers, glass houses, blown leaves, the souls of large trees, the sea, the grinning lunatic of Glasgow Green, puraana zindagi, pichla janum, the drifting, larken voice of my apron'd mother as she sings by the window in Urdu, with the Beatles playing in the sky; and all the while, ordinary people scream at me to wash the dirt from my face, the blackness. I, screaming at myself.

All this tidal ebb and flow is a creative tension. Things wash up on the beach; some sink back into the ocean. Rolling in perfect darkness on the seabed is a sealed jar. In the jar, where everything is light, there is a very old, singing djinn. The songs are strange, alchemical silver, and can be heard only by dead prophets. I am that jar, and the quietest, most subliminal song of all is called, *Nad Albannach Honay Kay Nateh.*

## Glossary

*Agha Jaan*   affectionate term for 'father'
*Mudejar*   Spanish Muslims living in Spanish Christian lands; the forms of art created thereof
*Nad Albannach Honay Kay Nateh*   Being Scottish (Gaelic-Urdu)
*pichla janum*   previous life
*puraana zindagi*   old life

# Alex Salmond

*Alex Salmond has been an active member of the SNP since 1987. He became Leader of the party in 1990 and remained so for ten years. At present he is Leader of the SNP Westminster Parliamentary Group.*

Here is the paradox.

In speech, in local culture and in national tradition Scotland is a less distinctive place than it was say half a century ago.

However, in terms of declared Scottish identity it is far more Scottish. Indeed, on the latest attitude survey feelings of Scottishness have risen rapidly to an all-time high, all but eclipsing feelings of Britishness.

Scottish identity is now the dominant underpinning of a separate Scottish political system. Not so long ago I was offering this view to a conference in London and Douglas Alexander, a real guru of New Labour, opined that I was under-estimating the importance of class politics in the achievement of Scottish self-government. I replied that class politics did have a role but that I thought it was something of a news story to hear a New Labour Minister drawing attention to it! The most powerful force in Scottish politics is the ever-strengthening feelings of Scottish identity.

However, the question is why is it not itself underpinned by an increasingly distinctive Scottish popular culture in the way that the Scottish cultural renaissance, or perhaps the folk-music revival, influenced the first rise of nationalism in modern Scotland in the 1960s.

A clue to resolving this paradox might come from a blether I was having the other day with Sandy Stronach, Director of the Doric Festival in Buchan – Doric being the Aberdeenshire usage of Scots. Given that Robert Burns' father came from the Mearns, the cadence of Doric probably had a powerful influence on the national poet.

Sandy was busy bemoaning not so much the loss of language (and certainly not of accent) from one of the heartlands of Scots but much more the loss of idiom. This can lead to more than a degree of confusion. For example, 'Friday next' in the north-east would mean a week on Friday as it would in Germany of the low countries or half eight would mean half past seven. Gradually that usage is dying out under the influence of television and uniformity but not before Ministers frequently turn up for funerals in the wrong week and people arrive for meetings an hour late!

However, interest in the Doric Festival is exceptionally strong, participation in fiddle music, bagpipes and Scottish country dancing remains part of the fabric of the north-east of Scotland, while schools have moved from a position of hostility to Scots usage to benign encouragement.

Sandy's theory, and perhaps fear, is that the popular culture and language is in danger of becoming something of a curiosity for enthusiastic study rather than something natural to the people. However, the fear of losing tradition was sparking off a determined attempt to save it.

Relating this to politics is interesting as well. In the first half of the twentieth century east Aberdeenshire and Banffshire, when the distinctive language and culture of this corner were in the unchallenged ascendancy, were unrepentingly unionist constituencies – never dependably Conservative but always unionist. Now the north-east of Scotland is the heartland of political nationalism.

There is something in all of this, which chimes with my own experience as a lad in Linlithgow growing up in the 1960s. I was taught little or no Scottish history at schools – perhaps a smidgeon at primary level, while Scots was reserved for third-degree Burns every January.

I was, however, instructed in the Scottish oral tradition, literally from my grandfather's knee, and I have little doubt that this was the strongest influence in my life in determining my attitude to nationality and identity. In retrospect I know that most of the incredible tales told to me by my Granda were via Walter Scott or Blind Harry but were always salted with local colour. In Linlithgow, where much of Scottish history was made and unmade, this task was far from impossible.

He showed me, for example, the ground where he said Edward I had camped before the Battle of Falkirk; he showed me the window from where the Regent Moray was shot dead in the High Street. He even told me the names of Bruce's men who retook Linlithgow castle for the Scottish cause by jamming a hay cart under the portcullis. Since my Granda claimed that that well-known Lithgae family and bakers the Oliphants were involved, this caused some degree of confusion in my young mind as I imagined the lads in the bake house dusting the flour off their overalls before storming the gates of the palace!

At any rate because this history was unofficial, almost subversive, it made it irresistible. Years later I found myself at St Andrews University complaining loudly about the difficulty in pursuing studies in Scottish history as anything other than an option in British (i.e. English) constitutional history.

I succeeded finally in weaving it into my degree but have often pondered on two things. First, it should be said that my Granda's *Braveheart* version of Scots history may have been vulnerable in the occasional point of detail but it did get the sweep of things about right, and second, I don't know if I would have been as attracted to studying it if it hadn't been made so damned difficult. If, as now, I could have completed a degree course in Scottish history without any bother then I don't know if I would have been half as keen. I was (and am) thrawn in such matters and I suspect most Scots are.

And so there we have it. The conclusion of these reflections is that Scottish identity is on the rise not because of cultural distinctiveness but, partly at least, because Scots cultural distinctiveness is under pressure.

Behind the force field of modern life, global communications and uniformity, perhaps people regard identity, nationality, distinctiveness as matters of increasing importance – things to be cherished as opposed to be taken for granted.

# T. C. Smout

*Christopher Smout CBE is the Historiographer Royal in Scotland. An Englishman, he was born in Birmingham in 1933, and has lived in Scotland since 1959. He is Professor Emeritus of Scottish History at St Andrews University, a Fellow of the British Academy and of the Royal Society of Edinburgh.*

I am English. My wife Anne-Marie is Danish, and we have lived in Scotland since 1959. I have never had a job outside Scotland. Our children were born in Edinburgh and went to school there, but both went to university in York. Penny regards herself as Scottish and has always worked here. Andrew probably regards himself as English, and has worked mostly in England. At last he could stand it no longer, and now he also works in Scotland. My grandchildren, born in Yorkshire, are sure they are English but go to school in Crail. So we are a comfortably muddled family.

Does it matter in my profession as a historian of Scotland that I am English? As long as I stick to finding out what was aboard boats sailing from Könisberg to Leith in 1602, or discovering the price of candles in Glasgow in 1744, or calculating the illegitimacy rate in Banff in 1861, it does not matter a little bit. But when I offer a historical opinion on the benefits of the Union in the eighteenth century, or the character of the Scottish Enlightenment, or the nature of education in the nineteenth and twentieth centuries, questions can be asked, literally, about where I am coming from. And this can be true of judgement on lesser questions of culture and habituation. As my predecessor as Historiographer Royal once said to me (very courteously), what can I know about the quality of past life in a two-roomed house if I and my forbears never lived in one?

All that is fair. Questions should constantly be asked of historians about where they are coming from – what has their national identity, regional identity, class, gender, income, emotional history, religion and experience done to their judgement? Above all, they should ask this of themselves, all the time, as part of their in-service training to achieve balance and accuracy in their research and writing. My theoretical stance, a colleague tells me, is that of a 'reconstituted empirical positivist'. I think this means that I am old fashioned enough to believe that one story in history may be judged superior to another if it accords with the available evidence. In making my judgement, it may be clouded by all kinds of personal ignorance and myopia which it is as much my job to overcome as it is the job of a Buddhist monk to attain Nirvana, and just as hard. Being English may indeed be a cause of some myopia. So may being Scottish, of course. Some people certainly suspect me (and accuse me) of being insensitive to Gaels because I am not a Highlander, or of ignoring Scottish progress before 1707 because I am not a Scot. I deny both charges, but then I would, wouldn't I?

I am told that there are almost as many English-born in Scotland now as there were Irish-born in Scotland at the height of the Victorian migrations. Twenty-first-century Scots, then, are much less racist, or perhaps more unwary, than their nineteenth-century congeners, for I and my countrymen have been given an easy ride. Nobody breaks the windows of my house or bangs a drum outside my office. When Scottish Watch came to Anstruther ten years ago, they got short shrift: their audience told them that Fifers were a decent folk who welcome strangers. For all this I am very grateful. I do not assume for a minute that this entitles me to wear a kilt or propose a toast to the haggis. It does, however, enable me cautiously, introspectively and very happily to pursue my trade of trying to understand the endlessly absorbing story of the Scottish people in the past. Other people may do it differently or better, but they let an Englishman get on with it, without even the helpful interest of a Research Institute.

But there is much more to identity that just nationality. Amartya Sen, in his wonderful British Academy lecture in 2000, 'Other People', pointed out the plurality of all our identities:

> A person can be a Nigerian, an Ibo, a British citizen, a US resident, a woman, a philosopher, a vegetarian, a Christian, a painter, and a great believer in aliens who ride on UFOs – each of these groups giving a particular identity which may be invoked in particular contexts.

So with myself. I am an Englishman, a Fifer, a Scottish citizen, a Briton, a man, a historian, an environmentalist, a Christian of a kind, a bird-watcher and a great believer in the virtues of organic food and gin and tonic. Being English has no precedence in my mind over being a Scottish citizen, but neither of those have, in day-to-day life, precedence over the ones towards the end of the list. Life is far too much fun to be spent in one stuffy club.

# Bill Speirs

*Bill Speirs is General Secretary of the Scottish Trades Union Congress (STUC).*

In contemplating this contribution I realised that I've never given a lot of thought to my being Scottish, and what that means – despite having been involved for years in the campaigns to secure a Scottish parliament, in solidarity work on behalf of the national rights of peoples such as the Palestinians, and in a range of anti-racist activity which deals, *inter alia,* with complex issues of identity.

The explanation lies, I think, in my having spent most of my working life with the STUC – an independent Scottish organisation within a multinational trade union movement – and my never having had a home more than twenty miles from my Dumbarton birthplace. I also have knowledge of the history of both sides of my family going back several generations in Renfrewshire, Argyll and Skye.

Anyway, enough of this indulgent self-absorption: what does being Scottish mean in the Scotland of today?

In the political field, the arrival of the Scottish Parliament has meant a real change in the dynamics of politics. I found it astonishing how quickly everyone switched attention from London to Edinburgh, much to the discomfiture of Westminster MPs representing Scottish seats – and how quickly media attention is becoming introspective, narrow and hostile. The latter is connected, I believe, to the extent to which we no longer have a Scottish media in terms of ownership, and external ownership of key operators, combined with priority being given to the financial bottom line, will always be a problem for small nations.

Which brings me to the economy. Ah, thinks the reader, we're about to get a

Celtic trade union lament for lost factories and mills, shipyards and mines. Well, mebbes, aye, mebbes, naw, as our great footballing genius Kenny Dalglish would say.

Scotland *has* lost out massively in these industries, and we're the worse off for it with ruined lives, damaged communities and a dangerously narrowed economic base. It wasn't inevitable, either. Take a look at the Netherlands or Spain and you'll see flourishing shipyards; wander into Germany and you'll find coal mines and car factories. The belief of successive UK governments that Scotland's industries were of the sunrise variety has cost us dear. But … working in a coal mine was never a pleasure. We still have some successful manufacturing industries – and the whisky industry remains a mainstay of employment and national identity.

Perhaps the biggest employment challenge to Scotland, though – not least for the trade unions – is the question of public attitudes to jobs that have traditionally been undervalued in terms of money and esteem, such as carers, shop workers, cleaners, tourist industry staff, keyboard operators, telephonists. This, of course, is directly connected to their having been traditionally seen as women's jobs. We have to get others to accept that such work should be judged on its merits. An interesting aspect of such 'service' jobs is that many of them are not transferable out of Scotland: not many people would fly to Korea to save one pound on a haircut, for example.

Okay, but what could sum up the state of 'being Scottish' today? Despite the uncertainties referred to above in regard to how the devolution process is going forward, I see and feel signs that Scots are becoming more confident. I'll refer to just two.

First, the STUC, and the Scottish trade union movement more generally, is increasingly comfortable in dealings with our counterparts elsewhere in Britain and Ireland. We meet regularly with the TUC Councils in the north of England to discuss how we can co-operate in promoting cross-border economic development, and how the STUC can assist them in promoting English devolution. We also now have in place – at the instigation of the STUC – a process of regular meetings of the STUC, British TUC, Wales TUC and the Irish Congress of Trade Unions (when the first meeting took place in June 2000, it was the first time the four organisations had met jointly).

Second, going back to football. I have been astonished at how little controversy there has been in Scotland about the suggestion that Rangers and Celtic might join the English Premier League. I cannot believe that if this proposal had been floated during the Thatcher years, or even more recently, it would have been received as calmly as it has. Instead, there would have been cries of treason, and some real anger, especially among those who see the rivalries of the 'Old Firm' as one of the worst aspects of Scottish life. It may be a measure of growing confidence by Scots in our identity that we can view this proposal with such equanimity.

On the other hand, maybe it's a recognition across the nation that it would increase St Mirren's chances of winning the championship, which would be universally welcomed, except in Greenock.

# David Steel

*David Steel was born in Scotland in 1938. He was elected to Parliament for Roxburgh, Selkirk and Peebles at a by-election in 1965, was Leader of the Liberal Party from 1976 to 1988 and co-founder of the Liberal Democrats in 1988. In May 1999 he was overwhelmingly appointed as the Scottish Parliament's first Presiding Officer.*

What does 'being Scottish' mean to me? To take one perspective, let me consider what it means when I am not in Scotland, because being Scottish has a strong resonance in the wider world. Let me begin with that part of it with which I have the strongest connections: Africa.

In Malawi, whose head of state President Muluzi came to the Scottish Parliament in its first year, and where I have been a regular visitor, I am identified as a Scot, as being a compatriot of David Livingstone. In other parts of Africa the name of Mungo Park – born in the Yarrow valley, close to my home – will sing louder, and throughout the continent there is the benign army of Scottish missionaries, engineers, doctors, teachers, agriculturalists and silviculturalists, whose legacy is held in honour and affection. My family was a part of that tradition and it is part of my identity as a Scot.

Elsewhere, throughout the Commonwealth and, indeed, the United States of America, being 'a Scot' means a connection with the development of these nations from the pioneers on the land and in industry to the political leaders and the framers of constitutions. So, being a Scot is to share in the citizenship of the world.

Nearer home, in mainland Europe, the links are no less strong. 'Fier comme un Écossais' says the French proverb, and the boast of nationality in the land of our ancient ally brings an answering chime of affection and recognition.

Go to the great Russian cities of Moscow and St Petersburg and you're there as the fellow countryman of Robert Burns. It's not just a superficial, nodding acquaintance that the Russians have with Burns – his works were translated in the early twentieth century by the poet Masyrak, whom I met on a student visit in 1960. They caught the mood of the time, and have endured better than communism. But that's not all the Russians will appreciate your Scottishness for – one of their own greatest poets, Lermontov, claimed descent from the semi-mythical figure of Thomas the Rhymer.

But what about here, in Scotland? What has formed my consciousness as a Scot?

At a time when it is unfashionable to acknowledge or rejoice in anything that is middle class or traditional, I am comfortable with the influences that have come to me via the great bulwarks of Scottish identity throughout the last three centuries. In the absence of a parliament, the Scottish education system, the legal system, and the Kirk were guardians of a separate tradition within the United Kingdom. These institutions were all a part of my upbringing, especially the latter.

I grew up a son of the manse, and the Church of Scotland is still an important part of my life. Our particular form of worship is where I feel at home: the great metric psalms, the classic hymns and the emphasis on preaching. At the General Assembly, the sound of unaccompanied singing rising to the roof is one that makes the hairs rise on the back of my neck, and which is unmistakably, and uniquely, a Scottish sound. (I cannot warm to the modern, thin-worded and thin-tuned efforts.) I take pride, too, in the democratic way our national Church is governed, and in the clashes that it has had over the centuries with the state, from Mary of Guise to Margaret Thatcher.

Within Scotland, too, there needs to be a sense of regional or civic belonging. But a manse upbringing often means a peripatetic one, where you do not fully put down roots in any part of Scotland – especially when, as in my case, those roots were for four years transplanted to Africa. It was therefore not until I came to the Borders that I found a particular part of the nation where I felt fully at home. Since then, being Scottish has also meant being a part of this unique corner of our nation, so full of history and tradition, whose inhabitants still have, in the words of John Buchan, 'realism coloured by poetry, a stalwart independence sweetened by courtesy, and a shrewd kindly wisdom'. I have lived here for nearly forty years now, and serving such constituents was always a fulfilment and a joy.

Since 1999 there has been a new element in my sense of Scottishness, with the restoration of the Parliament and the incredible privilege of being a part of that new chapter in our history. It has been harder than anyone of us expected; and our Parliament has been under attack and siege no less than other bulwarks have been in different ways throughout the centuries. All of us who serve it need to call on positive Scottish characteristics for its defence.

Perhaps my sense of Being Scottish is a romantic and idealised one, but I would rather be accused of that than of cynicism.

# Stewart Sutherland

*Lord Sutherland of Houndwood, Principal and Vice-Chancellor of the University of Edinburgh (1992–2002), was educated at Robert Gordon's College, the University of Aberdeen and Corpus Christi College, Cambridge. He is author of several books on the subjects of philosophy and religion.*

David Hume warned us in the eighteenth century. We could be embarking on a wild goose chase. Whenever he was tempted to a piece of personal introspection in search of himself, his personal identity, he never quite found this quintessential self. He found instead a series of impressions or perceptions – 'of heat or of cold, light or shade, love or hatred, pain or pleasure'. In a mixture of exasperation and warning he wrote,

> I can never catch myself at any time without [such] a perception, and never can observe any thing but the perception.

He compared the mind to a kind of theatre in which ideas and impressions come on and off stage, make their appearance and pass away. Indeed, he even suggested that my self, or my identity (Scottish or any other ilk) is no more than 'a bundle of impressions'.

Of course, Hume was one kind of Scot – prepared to be argumentative and sceptical – though never, I believe, sinking to the level of the cursed alter ego, an iconoclast. But his scepticism might license the non-PC question of what all this preoccupation with 'Scottish identity today' really signifies. In fact that is perhaps one answer to the question of what it means to be Scottish today – to want to navel gaze about one's Scottishness, both wallowing in it and simultaneously punishing oneself for that indulgence. That way, however, lies Calvinistic crabbedness, which becomes spiritually lethal when mixed with the Aberdeen granite that lies at the core of any Aberdeen loon.

Salvation from that lies in Hume – to reflect personally on Scottish identity today is to do no more and no less than to assemble and reflect upon the various impressions or perceptions of which one is currently aware.

Where am I? Right now, sitting in my study. What impressions fill the theatre of my mind?

Immediately before me, an image of Hume created by the great portrait medallion maker, Tassie. 'Tassie fecit', the almost invisible Latin signature tells us. But of course, I remember, much of the work of the two Tassies resides in the great Hermitage Museum in St Petersburg – a reminder of the zeal of Catherine the Great to surround herself with and to create her Capital City from the finest talents in all Europe. This was a minor, but not the only Scottish contribution to the megalomania and achievement of absolute patronage.

The associative rush of ideas is now upon me and I do not know whether to follow the cue to Malcolm Bradbury's wickedly funny last novel *To The Hermitage*, which dissects both Catherine's intellectual dalliance with Diderot, and also the absurdities of a modern academic pilgrimage in search of evidence of this; or to follow my eye to the bust of Thomas Jefferson, whose intellect, culture and vision owed so much to Europe and to this small corner hanging on to the north-west of it.

Both of these are impressions which point me outside Scotland if I am to begin to think seriously of what Scotland is and might be. These, I suppose, are the impressions and memories which began to fill the theatre of my mind, rather than those of Ally's Tartan Army on their fruitless way to and from Argentina or the knowing sentimentality of another Burns' Supper.

But the scenes in the theatre change again, for the sun breaks through and flashes off the fire grate and draws my eye through the window, reminding me of the austere beauty of the place – the hills and farms of Berwickshire, of the raiding parties of the past, but equally of the farmers of today who have survived the rigours of Foot and Mouth Disease, descendants of the neighbours of the same David Hume.

There is a sense in which the land is a repository of the past in which we all have our roots, and which reminds us that there is less change than we sometimes imagine. Equally, the land which produced Hume from Ninewells or Adam Smith or Andrew Carnegie from Fife or William Robertson from East Lothian might still produce today those who will change the way the world is. If it does not then we will become insular. However, one thing is for sure, those who change the world today will not be gents in wigs writing eighteenth-century books. But they will share with them a hunger for engagement with the ideas which are changing the world outside Scotland as well as those which feature in the Readers' Letters of the *Auchtermuchty Gazette.*

The impressions are now inhabiting every nook and cranny of the stage of the mind, but two come centre stage, jostling each other for primary place. One is the re-hash of a well-known line to suit the topic:

They know not Scotland who only Scotland know.

The other is the reminder that the three-piece suite in front of me was inherited from my mother, who inherited it from her elder sister, Aunt Bell. There is no other justification for it being here. If I were less Scottish I might have thrown it out by now.

# John Swinney

*John Swinney is the Leader of the Scottish National Party and Member of the Scottish Parliament for North Tayside.*

On the wall of my study at home in Perthshire is a framed cover of *The Independent* newspaper's magazine of 9 December 1989. The caption on the cover is 'It's Spring Again' and the photograph is of a mass of people, mostly very cold I imagine, waving the Czechoslovakian flag in Wenceslas Square in Prague. This huge crowd of ordinary people emerged to celebrate the demise of the communist regime and the rebirth of their democracy.

I often look at that picture and think of a very different rebirth of democracy: the Old Town of Edinburgh on the 1 July 1999.

Children from schools in every corner of our country marched through Edinburgh. Parliamentarians emerged from our historic Parliament House to face the bright sunshine of the parade to our temporary home on the Mound. And, most importantly of all, we came out to the people who had made this day possible – some of the hundreds of thousands of Scots who voted for our new parliament.

As I looked around that crowd I saw constituents – a number of them originating from England – from the great counties of Perthshire and Angus, which I have the privilege to represent, friends from the Asian community in Glasgow, people who have lived all their days in Scotland and dreamed of winning a parliament – a whole cross-section of people who had come together to celebrate the birth of Scottish democracy. And that essentially is what Being Scottish is all about to me. It is about living in a country where the people who have chosen to live here decide what happens here. It means an end to blaming others for our troubles and a start to making our own way in the world. On 1 July 1999 that's exactly how it felt.

But on other days, sadly, it doesn't feel like that.

One recent day brought that home to me. At the height of the storm over the presence of asylum seekers in Glasgow, I paid a very private visit to Sighthill. I met asylum seekers recently settled in the area and I met residents who had lived there for decades. They had no problems living side by side. Their differences of language or background or nationality did not matter to them. What mattered to them was what they had in common. They had poverty in common, and poor housing, and few opportunities, and an anger that nobody was listening to them. And it didn't matter if they had been in Sighthill for ten days or ten years, they felt the same.

But 1 July 1999 didn't change their lives. The changes they depended on could not be delivered by our parliament in Edinburgh or by a sense that the people who have chosen to live here decide what happens here. No, they depended on decisions at Westminster. And that's why 1 July 1999 wasn't enough for me, because it didn't give real life to what Being Scottish means to me. It didn't make it possible for everyone who chooses to live here to decide what happens here.

If we want to live by that sense of Being Scottish we must have the ability to speak out, and, more importantly, act on the issues that concern us. And that means on every issue. On the war in Afghanistan. On the plight of asylum seekers. And on the obscenity of nuclear weapons, which are not welcome in Scotland but are housed here anyway.

So my sense of Being Scottish has been invigorated by the establishment of our first democratic parliament. But for that to be more than just a sense, for it to live and breathe to the full, the people who choose to live here must decide what happens here.

When I look at that dramatic picture of liberation in Czechoslovakia on the wall of my study, I think back to what Scotland was like on 9 December 1989. A Scottish parliament was then a far distant hope – or perhaps even a fantasy. However, today, it is here and our country has changed.

The creation of that parliament makes clear to me that we are just a few thoughts away from making my dream of Being Scottish a living reality.

# Alan Taylor

*Alan Taylor is Associate Editor of the* Sunday Herald. *Formerly, he was Deputy Editor of* The Scotsman, *previous to which he was a librarian. With his wife Irene, he is co-editor of* The Assassin's Cloak *(Canongate, 2002), an anthology of diarists.*

'Have you ever considered living anywhere else?' a colleague asked me not so long ago. It was one of those dank, dreich days that is an Edinburgh speciality, headlights on mid-afternoon, the sort of day I rather like but which sends some folk shivering to the travel agent in search of a cheap deal in the sun. I admitted that occasionally, whimsically, I have considered living elsewhere, New York perhaps, or southern Europe. In my mind's eye I had an image of terracotta roofs in Tuscany. 'Not London, then?' replied my colleague.

London used to loom large in my life. In my teens, in the 1960s, it was a swinging place, or so we were led to believe. I spent a year there, vegetating while flower power withered. London seemed full of hard-drinking Scots who viewed drugs with the disdain they used to reserve for school dinners but who knew a man who knew another man who could get them the latest edition of the *Sunday Post*.

For some, London was the promised land; for many others, it was a bolt-hole. Almost every Scot I met seemed to be on the run: from style-cramping families, unambitious, suffocating friends, small town attitudes, dispiriting weather, pits and bings and mills and insurance offices. In London, they could disappear, dump their baggage and be who they wanted to be. Or so they, we, naively thought.

But then exiles are curious, tortured creatures. Edinburgh, wrote Muriel Spark, the doyenne of exiles, 'bred within me the conditions of exiledom'. She left, she said, because it was 'a place where I could not hope to be understood'. A few lines later she adds: 'Nevertheless, it is the place where I was first understood.' For her, exile ceased to be a fate, and became a calling.

Had I stayed in London I suspect it would have been my fate, like all those itinerant Scots around the globe who hanker constantly after things they'd been desperate to abandon, from Oor Wullie to haggis suppers. We are, it seems, constantly in conflict with the notion of Scottishness, afraid to embrace it too wholeheartedly lest we be accused of chauvinism or sentimentality or hubris. No wonder Scots are not natural enthusiasts. How such a cautious nation has achieved so much never fails to amaze me.

A lot can be explained by reference to size and that super-charged word 'wee'. Size matters, and in Scotland the size of the population and the opportunities that have existed for it have had far-reaching and long-lasting consequences. For many folk facing grim prospects there was no alternative but to go, and over the decades the diaspora, from Andrew Carnegie to Gordon Brown, has spread the Presbyterian gospel of thrift and hard graft around the globe. I dare say it has been generally good for Scotland's international reputation, and inspiring for many who stayed at home, but it is also responsible for the growth of the debilitating myth, invariably broadcast by ex-pats, that those Scots who remained behind were second-rate. This is partly the reason why some Scots are so wary of the success of celebrities like Billy Connolly, the Harry Lauder *de nos jours*.

The truth is that we like to have it both ways. We want the right to celebrate and criticise our heroes in equal measure. To a Scot there is no greater sin than getting above yourself. There is virtue in this point of view but too much time is wasted policing it. But it is evidence, too, of parochialism and envy, which in a wee country, in which everyone knows everyone else's business, is enervating. Devolution, it seems to me, is part of a process which will place London and the world beyond into fresh perspective. The worry is that Scots will turn in on themselves. The excitement lies in the uncertainty, which is what I think being Scottish means, for the moment at least, being here.

# Brian Taylor

*Brian Taylor is Political Editor for BBC Scotland. Born in Dundee in 1955, he was educated there and at St Andrews University. He began his journalistic career in Aberdeen before a spell at Westminster. Brian has contributed to several publications and is the author of* The Scottish Parliament *(Polygon at Edinburgh, 1999). He is married with two sons.*

It's a skoosh, a dawdle, a piece o' cake. Nae bather at a', as my fellow Dundonians would say. It is simply *so* easy these days, being Scottish.

Time was things were rather different. Being Scottish was hard labour, a 24/7 challenge. You could tell a Scot by the jutted chin, the defiant stare and the slightly menacing walk. It was the wearisome burden of all that history, you see. The battles we won, the battles we should have won. The combat, the treachery, England, the Reformation, the Covenant, the Union, the Disruption, the struggle, the struggle.

Even the classic Scottish toast was like a declaration of war: 'Here's tae us! Wha's like us? Damn few, and they're a' deid!' Along with this bombast, we presented a second face to the more discerning. Those who could penetrate the bravado would find a nation collectively anxious, craven, self-effacing, feart. This was Orwellian Doublethink, made real. Jekyll and Hyde, stretched across a nation. The Caledonian antisyzygy of MacDiarmid.

As we yelled 'Wha's like us,' we also whimpered: 'Wha would want to be?' As we strutted and stamped, we cringed inwardly. As we defied the world, we trembled.

Scotland was wee and insignificant, we told ourselves. Yet we detested our own internal conclusion. It demeaned us, dragged us down. So we compensated with grandiose boasting. Here's tae us, indeed.

This phenomenon, of course, hasn't entirely disappeared. We are still blessed with five-foot-nothing Bravehearts, podgy, pasty-faced, prematurely balding –

ready to take on the world, or at least England, the minute the pub closes. And yet something has changed. Being Scottish is now, somehow, a more gentle matter. Less a challenge to combat, more a quiet statement of fact. No more: 'I'm Scottish, right, want to make something of it?' Now it's: 'I'm Scottish. Not English. Not Belgian. Scottish. But it's no big deal.'

Look at the Tartan Army, the Scottish football team's travelling support. Once, theirs was the marauding road, pillaging, plundering, snapping cross-bars, digging turf. Now, they're a peripatetic kilted pantomime, hugging police officers and winning friends. They seem, like others in Scotland, to have relaxed into a new, more assured identity. They no longer need to scream their nationality – as if it were a sickly child, fearful and petulant. Similarly, others. Within Scotland, if not yet further afield, there is a stress-free acceptance of Scottish identity. There is a welcome and sustained interest in the totems of that identity – the literature, the music, the folk culture.

People will dance themselves silly to an Eightsome Reel because they enjoy the experience. Not as a cultural statement. At contemporary ceilidhs, formal High-land dress as often as not gives way to kilt, T-shirt and boots. Writers and rock bands source their work in Scotland because they like the place. Not as some limply defiant gesture, aimed at London. Equally, such artists maintain a broad, international agenda while living and working in Scotland. No return to the kailyard. No more the hideous self-parody of tartan trews and strained accents.

Part of the problem in the past was a lack of definition. It was never clear what Being Scottish meant. Were we a region, a nation, North Britain, a collection of counties, a colony, a state of mind? What? This dithering over identity reflected our own lack of self-confidence and the lingering effect of ancient efforts, in Scotland and from London, to subsume Scottish identity within the wider British state. For myself, I always found this issue tiresome. I agreed with the conclusion in the *Claim of Right for Scotland* which said: 'Much ink is wasted on the question of whether the Scots are a nation. Of course they are.'

I believe further that the issue of identity is distinct from arguments about political structure. For example, one can be patriotically Scottish without endors-ing independence. We remain a nation, regardless of how devolution develops, regardless of whether we become a state. Personally, my core identity is Scottish. A keenly developed sense of the absurd protects me from most of the excesses of patriotism. However, my proclaimed national identity bursts forth frequently. At social gatherings, it is only by dint of physical persuasion that I can be prevented from crooning some Scots ballad, perhaps 'The Road and the Miles to Dundee', hand clutched firmly to ear like a sixties' folk revivalist.

This is my version of Scotland: forebears who moved from rural and maritime Angus to industrial Dundee; a native acquaintance with Scots language and song; a Scottish education; a passionate interest in Scottish literature, particularly the shamefully neglected Sir Walter Scott; an amateur interest in Scotland's history.

I am well aware that is by no means the whole Scotland. There are Gaelic-Scots and Irish-Scots and Asian-Scots. Like most nations, we are a splendidly chaotic mix. Being Scottish is not a question of language or ethnic origin or any other single factor. It is a question of choice. We have become comfortably Scottish.

# Gregor Townsend

*Gregor Townsend was born in Edinburgh in 1973 and was educated at Galashiels Academy, then Edinburgh University, where he gained an MA (hons) in Politics, and Aston University, from which he graduated in 1999 with an MBA. He has played rugby for Scotland 64 times, captaining them twice, and played two Test matches for the British Lions in South Africa in 1997. He has played club rugby for Gala (1990–5), Northampton (1995–8), Brive, France (1998–2000). He currently plays for Castres, France.*

National identities are difficult concepts to define. No doubt we would all prefer to belong to a nation that we think is unique and different. Thus, there is inevitably much subjectivity in how we determine our national identity. Being Scottish must be considered as more than a question of nationality or place of birth. It is an expression of who we think we are or, in other words, a state of mind.

Personally, it is knowing things about my country, its people, its history and culture that non-Scots do not know. It is also about being able to have pride in what Scotland has achieved with its limited size and resources.

For me, being Scottish is knowing Oor Willie's best pals are Fat Bob, Soapy Souter and Wee Eck; it is celebrating the fact that Scotland is the only country in the world where Coke is not the best-selling soft drink (Irn Bru: phenomenon or urban myth?); it is satisfying a craving for deep-fried pizza from time to time; and being able to sing all three verses of 'Flower of Scotland'.

Our national consciousness, or mindset, is unquestionably filled with paradox. On the one hand we can be viewed as dour pragmatists through our Presbyterian past and our inclement weather but underneath there is much colour, warmth and no little inventiveness. This might be somewhat due to the fact that our national costume is basically a colourful skirt, which means we could never take ourselves too seriously. How can one be dour in a kilt?

Having been fortunate enough to have represented Scotland in a sporting context, I am sometimes asked what it's like to wear the Scottish jersey in front of 60,000 of my countrymen. What I feel is an immense pride and determination not to let my nation down. This sentiment is no doubt similar to sportsmen and women across the globe who have played for their respective countries. There is, though, a special something that I've been aware of that can be recognised as Scottish pride: a reassuring feeling that my team-mates will be trying that wee bit harder than their opponents, as all of Scotland expects a little to go a very long way.

The French have a phrase – *Fier comme un Écossais* – which was initially used to describe how proudly the Scots fought in times of war. Today's battles are often sporting, and Scottish sides have not lost their ability to fight until the last minute. My sporting heroes performed with passion and always seemed to give everything they had for the Scottish cause. Whether it was Liz McColgan, Kenny Dalglish, Roy Laidlaw, Jim Watt or even Jocky Wilson, they were all tenacious, stubborn and determined.

Perhaps these pugnacious qualities are Scottish attributes, just like another trait we have latterly been known for in sporting circles – that of being a nation of gallant losers. Subsequently the tag of underdog has unfortunately become part of our sporting identity and has also arguably been woven in to the fabric of being Scottish.

I believe that this is one symptom of our undying sense of inferiority. An inferiority that manifests itself through our national obsession of being anti-English in order to proclaim that we are different. Perhaps we have not been confident enough to establish our identity without continual reference to our much larger southern neighbours, as in the past being Scottish has occasionally meant not being like the English, or just not liking the English.

Furthermore, although we have a reasonably inclusive and tolerant culture, we are at times small-minded when it comes to fellow Scots who leave their country. In a sporting context Alan Hansen and Gary McAllister, among others, have both been at the receiving end of negative criticism from the Scottish media and supporters alike, mainly as a result of choosing to ply their trade in England. Also, would Billy Connolly have had as much negative reaction to his thoughts on the political future of Scotland if he was still a resident of Glasgow? France, a country with fierce national pride and no little self-confidence, celebrates the fact that its footballers, chefs and actors have found success overseas.

It is evident that a crisis of confidence has made us reluctant to express our national identity. Our Celtic cousins, the Irish, whose cultural identity is not too far removed from our own, have had no such anxieties and their 'cultural' package has travelled around the world much more freely than our own. The success of Riverdance, Irish pubs and St Patrick's Day may be marketing triumphs, but they say as much about Irish culture as they do about our own. In the past there has undoubtedly been an aversion to proclaim to the world who we are. However, it seems to be the case that our collective confidence has been growing steadily of late and is now at such a level that this trend may be reversed once and for all.

While many commentators point to the fact that the 1997 referendum result on devolution was a watershed in establishing our identity, I feel the process had already started some twenty years earlier. Let's remember that for eighteen years after 1979, a referendum was never offered to the Scots. Anyway, political institutions seldom have the impact on individuals or communities that they claim. Our collective confidence has been flourishing since the 1970s. I believe this development to be as important to our identity as Sir Walter Scott's much criticised portrayal of the uniqueness of our land and its people in the early nineteenth century.

The examples are abundant. Our own national anthem, created in the 1970s by the Corries, is now sung with pride and recognised throughout the world. With more than half of Scotland's 400 museums having opened since the late 1970s there has also been a tremendous growth in the fascination with our own history. Moreover, *Braveheart* has broadcast our nation's history to a global audience. Visually, too, we have been more inclined to display our identity. I would wager that my father's generation seldom, if ever, thought it appropriate to wear a kilt – now they are everywhere. Finally a building in Edinburgh (if it is ever finished) will embody our national advancement in bricks and mortar.

We must be one of the few countries in the world where multiple identities are a comfortable fit. Although it seems that being Scottish has latterly become more important to us than being British or European, we still interchange as it pleases us. Scotland is different but similar in many ways to the rest of the United Kingdom, equating to both a separateness and an equality we share in our common political union. As the French would say – *Vive la différence!*

# Kirsty Walker

*Kirsty Walker is a travel journalist, interpretive consultant and copywriter based in Edinburgh. She has written and researched all kinds of things from the glory days of the Isle of Bute to glass crystal, pineapples, lichens and water treatment. Her degree was in Art History and her interests include fire festivals, follies and hedonism.*

## Accent

*Where ye fae?*
Near Glasgow.
*Aye? Whereabouts?*
*Near Loch Lomond.*
*Aye, but you're no Scottish. Where are ye fae before tha?*
*Um, I've, um, I grew up there … but I've moved around a lot.*
*Aye right, you're posh then.*

That's the way it went at Scottish raves in the early 1990s – condemned as posh – and that's the way it has always been. It's not comfortable being middle class in Scotland and it's certainly not cool. My mum is English and my dad's from Glasgow, but he went to a private school so it doesn't count. I spoke the language of my parents rather than my peers, stupid in hindsight, but it hardly seemed like a choice at the time. Cries of 'snob' followed me round the village school and thence to the comprehensive. Even my e-ed up fellow ravers, full of goodwill, but not quite enough to overlook my voice, excluded me by my accent. Tired of apologising, I decided it was easier to say I was English. Oddly, I then gained some respect. The conversation would run thus:

*Where ye fae?*
*London.*

*Aye, right, you're a long way fae hame, then? Waa are the eccies like doon there?*
*Waa clubs d'ye go to? Waa d'ye think of Scottish raves?*

Scottish raves were the best. The Scots took to raving like midges to English flesh. Although I was perceived as Scottish, rather than merely posh at southern raves, I missed the tangible excitement which was quintessentially Scottish. Hedonism had never been more hardcore and you could always spot a Scot at an English rave, the one more out of it and more into it than anyone else.

It's depressing to feel guilty for not being Scottish enough especially when I have so many national traits, from passion to pessimism. Living for a spell in the USA, I felt untrammelled and unjudged and my confidence grew in the rich soil of positive thinking. It felt good to be Scottish and no-one condemned me for having the wrong accent. They didn't know. They just thought Scotland was brilliant and therefore so was I – even if I had to explain that it wasn't an island. Were they thinking of Ireland?

The frustrating thing is, they're right, not about our island status unless you go back several million years, about Scotland – it's wonderful. I have travelled a lot, but for me there is nowhere closer to paradise than a sunny day on the west coast. Take last May for instance – one of the best days of my life. Me and my boyfriend (English) hired a boat and explored some islands off the coast of Argyll. The sea was a bottomless blue, seals followed the boat popping shy heads out of watery worlds, Ben Cruachan, still capped with snow, stood prouder than Mount Fuji, and countless seabirds cawed, cried and cooed as we glided through the delightful maze of Scotland's coastline. We landed on an island with a rambling Victorian ruin of a house, its castellations cutting the skyline. Abandoned ten years ago (the tale was wittily disclosed in the pub later) we found old diaries, toys, unopened letters and even a rusted grand piano. As gloaming turned to night we returned to the mainland, our wee boat laden with trophies from a past decidedly posh.

Then the following week, I had the other kind of Scottish day. I was prospecting for work, it was raining and my car broke down. Waiting for rescue, I stared at the grey scenery. It was bleak, barren and inconceivable that sunshine would ever visit there again. The AA man shook his head at the car and seemed to gloat at the money it would cost to put right. In America I would have been told that things could be worse, and, even if that were a lie, my spirits would have lifted a little. By the time we reached the nearest town, the AA man had moaned about everything from the English woman who had opened up a café selling 'cus-cus' to the price of petrol and the tourists that 'couldnae drive'. I found myself sinking into his negativity, each fresh moan pulling me further into the abyss. I went to a Scottish-run café, where the food had had the flavour sucked out of it. (Perhaps the exorbitant prices reflected the cost of the machine which does this.) Then in the bank, I waited as surly, uninterested staff ignored the growing queue of customers, in a way which I can only compare with Poland.

The way I feel about Scotland and being Scottish is as complex, bittersweet and varied as the coastline and weather in the west. I often wish I could dump the baggage of my birth and come to Scotland as a foreigner. I expect that's why I want to emigrate.

# Jim Wallace

*Born in 1954 in Annan, Jim Wallace was educated at Annan Academy, Downing College, Cambridge, and the University of Edinburgh. After practising as an advocate at the Scottish Bar, he was elected as MP for Orkney and Shetland in 1983, holding the seat until 2001. At Westminster he served as Liberal/Liberal Democrat spokesman on Fishing, Energy, Transport, Defence and Scotland and was the first Liberal Democrat Chief Whip. He was elected Leader of the Scottish Liberal Democrats in 1992, a position he still holds. After playing a leading role in the setting up of the Scottish Parliament, he was elected MSP for Orkney in 1999 and led his party into the partnership Scottish Executive, where he sits in the Scottish Cabinet as Deputy First Minister and Justice Minister.*

I was born in Annan, on the shores of the Solway, less than ten miles by road from England and probably less than three miles as the crow flies. Yet, I am unquestionably Scottish.

I am the product of a Scottish primary and secondary education. I was brought up in the Church of Scotland, and probably display more than a fair share of the Presbyterian sense of duty – and the notion that if every silver lining doesn't quite have a cloud, every good night out must have a hangover. My bank account is with a Scottish bank. I have practised Scots law.

At school I was aghast when my teacher thought that Robert Burns would struggle to make the second XI of British poets. I enjoyed other prejudices common to Scottish schoolboys, albeit I attended the secondary school closest to the border – we revered Wallace and Bruce (the Wars of Independence featured on the curriculum for consecutive years between primary and secondary – or so it seemed). We had a sneaking regard for William the Conqueror, who put one over on the English at Hastings, but most definitely did not conquer Scotland. And in sport, we shared the humiliation of the 9–3 defeat at Wembley, only to share the delight when, at the same venue in 1967, Jim Baxter and Dennis Law humiliated the English World Champions.

As a boy, growing up in Annan, I should surely have failed the Norman Tebbit cricket test. Scotland didn't have a cricket team which registered in the conscious-ness, so Australia, and the West Indies, provided appropriate heroes – especially when they were playing England.

Freighted with such prejudices, I left home to make my way in the world – first at an English university and for most of the last two decades as the parliamentary representative of a constituency which sometimes sees Edinburgh as remote as London. Indeed, on my first visit to Orkney as a potential prospective candidate, I referred to the land mass south of the Pentland First as 'the mainland'. I was quickly put right, I was on 'the mainland', Thurso and points south were in Scotland.

So how do I characterise my Scottishness today? I still consider myself a Scot, but I have never had any difficulty in also thinking of myself as British or European. And I have a strong affinity with those of my constituents who would identify themselves as Orcadian. Each has a distinctive and worthy heritage to which I'm proud to lay some claim.

Frankly, to express my Scottishness, I don't need the trappings of a nation state. I feel no less Scottish, just because I can't visit a Scottish embassy when abroad or join the Scottish armed forces. I do not try to oppose the case for independence on a 'can't be done economically' basis, but rather because I think that it is an unnecessary step. Too often I've found nationalists more preoccupied with getting a seat at the top table than with working out what they'd want to say, if they ever got there.

Far from being a nationalist, I feel that a sense of internationalism gives expression to my Scottish identity. I am conscious of the extensive trading links with Europe that our ancestors developed. My legal forebears trained at places such as Utrecht and Leyden, and whatever shortcomings there were with colonial rule, many Scots contributed positively to the development of nations now part of an extensive Commonwealth.

My confidence in my identity as a Scot very much reflects my confidence in the Scotland of the twenty-first century. Over many generations, Scots men and women have shown themselves capable of being world leaders in science, engineering, health, commerce, enterprise and administration. Too often, however, their expertise and talents have flourished furth of Scotland. I believe that one of the challenges of our new constitutional settlement is to encourage these talents to bloom in Scotland. There are signs of hope. Our universities perform disproportionately well in terms of research and academic excellence. For example, we are at the leading edge for biotechnology.

We need, therefore, to rediscover at home a sense of risk and enterprise. Too often success has been sneered at. People and ideas are set up, only to be knocked down. This needn't be part of our national character. After all, the development of education in Scotland was very much shaped and encouraged by the family's desire to see some of their children succeed. It is not the successful who should be sniped at, but the cynics and the whiners who would talk down Scotland and Scottish success, and those for whom glorious defeat is an acceptable second best.

But success must go hand in hand with another traditional Scottish trait – a commitment to the common weal. It is significant, I believe, that many of our ancient burghs had (and some still have) a 'common good fund'. For me in 2002, being Scottish means a proper coming together of individual achievement and community contribution – mindful that the community extends beyond the kailyard to the wider Scotland, and to the wider world.

# Charles Warren

*Charles Warren holds degrees from the universities of Oxford (MA) and Edinburgh (MSc, Ph.D.) and has been a lecturer in geography at the University of St Andrews since 1995. He has published widely in the fields of environmental management and glaciology, and is author of* Managing Scotland's Environment *(Edinburgh University Press, 2002).*

## Landscapes of Scottishness

'The bonnie, bonnie banks', 'your wee bit Hill and Glen', 'over the sea to Skye'. Landscape has been integral to perceptions of Scottishness for generations. No account of Scotland takes place against a topographically neutral backdrop. This is witnessed as much by Glenmorangie's much advertised 'glen of tranquillity' as by the yearnings of exiled victims of the Clearances, famously expressed in the 'Canadian Boat Song':

> From the lone sheiling of the misty island
> Mountains divide us, and waste of seas –
> Yet still the blood is strong, the heart is Highland,
> And we in dreams behold the Hebrides.[1]

Land has always been – and remains – a defining issue for the people of Scotland, whether in politics, rural development or the arts. The 'land question' has been a perennial running sore, but landscape has also inspired creativity as diverse as the eighteenth-century Gaelic poetry of Duncan Ban Macintyre and the rock music of Runrig – the band's very name conjuring croft-rich images.

For me, Highland landscapes form the rocky backdrop for some of my earliest and happiest childhood memories – family holidays spent mucking about in rivers and building bracken houses in birchwoods. Scotland was a playground, and not only for me but for the grown-ups around me. Raised in the south of England, the prism through which I used to view the Highlands (because Scotland *was* the Highlands) was the romantic-historic view of Scotland as a sportsman's playground, an idealised vision developed and cherished by generations of Englishmen since Victorian times. It is a perception nicely captured in the poem, 'At Euston (by one who is not going)'.[2]

> Stranger with the pile of luggage proudly labelled for Portree
> How I wish this night of August I were you and you were me ...
> You will pass my golden roadway of the days of long ago;
> Will you realise the magic of the names I used to know:
> Clachnaharry, Achnashellach, Achnasheen and Duirinish?
> Every moor alive with coveys, every pool aboil with fish ...
> Think of cloud on Bheinn na Cailleach, jagged Cuillins soaring high,
> Scent of peat and all the glamour of the misty Isle of Skye!

This viewpoint contrasts starkly with the 'Canadian Boat Song' – landscape as playground versus landscape as homeland. Growing up, I uncritically adopted the former. Like so many before me, I was bewitched by the uplands in all their moods – squall-scoured lochs raked by sunbeams, ice-crusted crags, and mountains emerging from mists. Far from wearing off, this spell seems only to strengthen its hold. Coming to live north of the border, however, proved to be something of an eye-opener. Not that I have lost any of my delight in the ever-changing light of the country which has become my home. On the contrary, living, and working, here has allowed me to explore far more of the extraordinarily rich diversity of nature that is packed into the crenellated map of Scotland. The unique qualities of the land are foremost among the reasons why there's nowhere else on earth I'd rather live (with the possible exception of New Zealand's South Island – but that would partly be because of its Scottishness!).

That said, moving here confronted me abruptly with the many other competing narratives woven around the Scottish environment, most of them sharply critical of the 'sportsman's playground' version. One of these, summoning up the undead ghosts of the Clearances, sees the countryside as a depopulated homeland. In the haunting words of Hugh MacLennan, 'in a deserted Highland glen you feel that everyone who ever mattered is dead and gone'. Piles of stones and hummocks under the heather are all that remain of banished communities, and there are those who passionately advocate a 'species reintroduction programme' focusing on *Homo sapiens*. Another narrative highlights natural resources – rural produce, energy, minerals, nature conservation. Still another perpetuates the wilderness myth – the unspoiled, pristine land idea. That this version survives at all is remarkable, given the persuasive picture painted by Fraser Darling (and many since) portraying Scotland as an environmentally devastated terrain, drained of its biodiversity by extinctions, deforestation and overgrazing by deer and sheep (Darling's 'hooved locusts'). People have lived here for 9,000 years, so little if any of 'natural Scotland' remains pristine.

But it does not follow from this long history of modification that, just because we are handling 'damaged goods', we can throw caution to the winds and do what we please with our environment. On the contrary, like a cracked Ming vase, our precious natural heritage deserves special care, and every effort at restoration. Encouragingly, the Scottish Parliament has embraced this view. Its legislative plans (not least the beginnings of land reform) are generating intense debates, the very passion of which demonstrates just how much people care about the land. Building consensus can prove well nigh impossible because all the competing narratives jostle for space on the moral high ground. But in the hills – the real high ground – all this social and political jostling drops astern, eclipsed by wildness. For me, it is the imposing, perspective-restoring natural grandeur of the land-scape that is quintessential Scotland.

## Notes

1  Anonymous, but sometimes attributed to D. M. Moir.

2  By A. M. Harbord.

# Mike Watson

*Mike Watson is the Member of the Scottish Parliament for Glasgow Cathcart and is Minister for Tourism, Culture and Sport. From 1989 until 1997 he was the Member of Parliament for Glasgow Central and in 1997 he was made a life peer, as Lord Watson of Invergowrie.*

### What it Means to be Scottish

It seems my sense of Scottishness has developed throughout my life, each passing decade producing a key event which helped refine its definition.

### The Wallace Monument, 1958, aged 8

My parents had moved to Invergowrie, a village on the outskirts of Dundee, when I was barely a year old. That was a time when cars were a rarity, when bus or train were the only means of travel for most people, making Scotland appear much larger and much more mysterious than it now does.

So it was important that the job which my father took in Dundee carried with it more than just promotion. It included the provision of a motor car, a black Austin 8 which took three hours in good weather to chug the road and the miles (all eighty-five of them) to Dundee. No dual carriageways then, and no bypasses, either. Each and every town had to be negotiated, as the larger competing traffic proceeded ponderously, with an uncompromising 'they shall not pass' mentality.

Each journey back west to my grandparents was its own adventure, though I can't be absolutely sure when I first noticed the grey pointy building perched – precariously it seemed, especially on windy days – atop a hill as we approached Stirling. I suppose I must have been about eight years old when I inquired, 'What's that, Mum?' She was a teacher and, to me, an endless source of knowledge. Throughout my childhood I don't ever recall her being stumped by one of my questions. Certainly not that one, and from her initial response flowed many more as I learned about William Wallace: his rout of King Edward I at Stirling Bridge in 1297; the King's revenge three months later; and Wallace's later capture and subsequent execution in London.

For the first time in my life I developed not just an awareness of being Scottish, but a pride in it. An awareness that we were a small country, much smaller than our neighbour, which had at various times in history brought us under its control. And that Wallace had fought against it, willing to give his life for his country. It was a powerful influence on a young boy and it formed the first attempt at shaping my perception of nationality.

### Wembley Weekend, April 1967, aged 17

It was only my second visit to England; football was by then my overriding passion and I played for Invergowrie Boys' Club under-eighteen team. We set off by bus to join the then the biennial invasion by 50,000 Scots to the hallowed ground where our ancestors had witnessed the 5–1 victory in 1928 by the team which became immortalised as the Wembley Wizards.

At the end of the match I was on cloud nine. The reason was simple – Scotland were the world champions! The rationale was simple: England had won the World Cup the previous year, and had since remained unbeaten. Scotland had travelled to Wembley and, marshalled by the majestic Jim Baxter, won 3–2. Applying the logic of boxing to football, having beaten the world champions – and in their own backyard – that obviously made *us* the world champions.

And did we celebrate. The singing was as loud as it was relentless. Wha's like us? Gie few and they're a' daid! In sporting parlance, we had driven a thousand stakes through the heart of the English enemy as surely as William Wallace had done 670 years earlier. Playing a match in Watford the following day, flushed with 'our' success, swaggering, ready to repeat the dose. Had Scotland been beaten we would have been surly, resentful, wanting revenge. Not so the Hertfordshire lads whom we were to meet. They were friendly, welcomed us to their ground, and complimented us on Scotland's victory the previous day: that really astounded us and, with hindsight, it was probably designed to do so because they got their revenge, even though they almost certainly did not regard it as such.

After the match we were given a meal before our journey back north and I recall, for the first time, evaluating the English. It was clear to me that, though they spoke with funny accents, they were really just the same as we were. I also recall that this was a view not shared by most of my team-mates, who were dismissive and seemed to me unnecessarily antagonistic to our hosts.

For the first time I began to challenge my own perception of my nationality – what I had by the age of seventeen already come to regard as the certainty that the English had to be done down in order for us Scots to regain some of the honour lost over centuries of subjugation. It just didn't seem to make sense, and from that point on I was muted when the ritual rubbishing of England and all things English reared its (increasingly ugly) head.

## Devolution Referendum, March 1979, aged 29

In common with many students of the 1960s and 1970s, university was for me a highly-charged political experience. I emerged as a confirmed Marxist, though the politics of nationalism barely registered on my radar.

In the summer of 1974 I departed to Derbyshire for my first job. I did so without a thought that I was leaving my country, rather that I was merely moving to a different part of it. Over the following five years the view of Scotland from 250 miles away became quite different to that which I had experienced from within. It became ever more apparent to me that the English *were* different, at least in terms of outlook (less English than British), attitude (more parochial; no conception of religious differences) and habits (less reliant on municipal housing; much more cautious about alcohol). But in my mind these differences did not amount to a negative notion of English compared to Scottish people. I had no sense of superiority, I was simply conscious of the fact that there were many traits which illustrated the differences.

This was highlighted by the fact that, at that time, it was virtually impossible to obtain news of what was happening in Scotland, political, sporting or otherwise. I found this intensely frustrating and used to have my parents send Scottish newspapers to me each week, just so I could keep abreast of events. Perhaps the most important of these was the passage through Westminster of the legislation to provide for the devolution referendum. And I was intensely angered with the unnatural and unnecessary obstacle placed in the way of Scotland having its own assembly by the requirement for 40 per cent of those entitled to vote recording a 'yes' vote.

Despite not having a vote myself, this prompted me to travel to Scotland at weekends to urge my fellow Scots to do just that. The excitement of the campaign as much as the narrow failure to clear the bogus hurdle made me decide I must return to Scotland. Months later I did, believing that I must play a role in over-turning the vote the next time the referendum was run. It never occurred to me that it would entail a wait of almost eighteen years.

### The Introduction of the Poll Tax, 1988, aged 39

The attempt by the Thatcher government to reform the system of local taxation reorganisation was in itself a corruption of democratic values, in that it sought to achieve a reverse redistribution of wealth. To that was added the profound insult to the people of Scotland in that they were chosen as the testing ground for the new system, quickly dubbed the poll tax.

Nothing less than the self-esteem of all Scots was the target of this gratuitous insult, and for my part I felt it strongly. The campaign of opposition became mired in the rights and wrongs of withholding payment of the new tax, but that could not disguise the sense of injustice which it seared across the collective Scottish psyche. Any doubts I may have harboured about developing nationalistic leanings were outweighed by the sense that, as a Scot, my people were being treated as guinea pigs. The imperative was to channel my political energies into ensuring that the Labour Party fully appreciated the need for a broad approach in the drive for what was now more necessary than ever – the delivery of a Scottish parlia-ment. The next year a crucial step down that road was taken with the establish-ment of the Scottish Constitutional Convention.

### The Official Opening of the Scottish Parliament, July 1999, aged 50

I started keeping a diary after being elected to the Scottish Parliament. The entry for 2 July 1999, referring to the previous day's official opening, said: 'What a day, what an occasion. It was not as good as I had hoped it would be – it was much better. I campaigned for twenty-three years for this day and all the effort was more than justified. I feel prouder than ever before to be a Scot.'

It was a day that I wished would never end, and in some ways it was an end in itself. The Parliament's very existence was a powerful statement by the people of Scotland that they wanted their future to be decided in a manner more sensitive to Scotland's needs than was possible from the remote legislature in London.

I regard myself as pretty much a mainstream Scot: proud to be Scottish, but not ashamed to be British. The depth of that Scottishness is, for me, emphasised by the existence of our parliament, yet I regard it as no contradiction to declare that so too is the extent to which I feel British. The latter is strengthened, first, by the fact that the British political system was sufficiently robust and secure to decentralise power and, second, that, by doing so, it retains the confidence of most of those people served by that decentralisation.

After almost 300 years, the abnormality of being a native of the only country in the world with a distinct legal system but no legislature has been ended. Scotland now frames and passes its own laws in a manner worthy of any mature democracy. It became a matter of increasing importance to me that that anomaly should be ended and now it has. My modest part in that process had a major influence in defining my Scottishness and my role as a Member of the Parliament will continue to do so.

# Irvine Welsh

*Irvine Welsh is Scottish of Irish extraction and lives in England. He is the acclaimed author of six books; his most recent is* Glue *(Jonathan Cape, 2001).*

A few years ago I was drinking in a bar in the Upper Haight district of San Francisco with a girl called Corrine. Corrine is a singer/songwriter in a rock 'n' roll band, and like a lot of Americans she is proud of her Scottish roots. Indeed, she constantly refers to herself as 'Scottish'. We were talking about what it meant to be Scottish and I had to confess that perversely she seemed to have a better idea than me, who was born and brought up there. At one point she looked at me quite seriously and asked, 'What's it *really* like to be Scottish?'

I was completely dumfounded. I wanted to say something profound but I didn't have a clue. I pretty lamely tried to explain that the next-door neighbours, the milkman, the bus driver, the other kids at school, all were Scottish. You just took it as given. Even now, when I get off the train from King's Cross, and move out of the could-be-anywhere tourist-land centre of Edinburgh, I can't believe all the white faces I see. The lack of a substantial visible multi-ethnic presence, at least compared to cities in England, is quite visually overwhelming.

Corrine came out with some interesting observations, and I was reflecting that maybe it is the perspective of distance that puts the whole thing into focus. I remembered a Cockney pal of mine once saying, 'You Jocks have got it made. You get to drink and swear and people just expect it. A lot of geezers here would get locked up if they behaved the way you did.'

This was meant as a joke, but it still brought home that Scotland is a ridiculous place, and now that I've travelled the world the strangeness and exoticness of it is more apparent than ever. Back to the bar on Upper Haight, I was still aware of the inadequate nature of my response to Corrine's question. I decided that the best way round it was to tell her a travelling story.

Some time previous to this conversation, I was working with a film production company in London, we were trying to get this ill-fated movie on the go. Next door to their Soho office was an establishment from where prostitutes conducted their operations. Whenever I went down to the office I was discreetly asked by one of the girls, 'You looking for business?'

A week or so later I was over in New York, at a party in the Lower East Side. A friend and I were making our way home through the darkened streets when a corner girl asked us, 'You wanna date?'

A short time after this I was back in Scotland, at another party in Glasgow. We were exiting from a basement flat, tired and extremely emotional, and heading back towards the Great Western Road. It was a freezing-cold winter's night. Crossing over Blythswood Square, I was approached by a girl in a fur coat who opened it up, displaying a skimpy party dress. She looked at me brazenly and bellowed into the night: YE WAHNNNT YIR HOLE, BIG MAN?

That comparative approach to trade by working girls came as close as anything at summing up to me what being Scottish was all about. I've never found a better way to express it, and probably never will. To be honest, I don't think it enlightened Corrine that much, but it certainly pulled things into focus for me.

Soon we'll all be globalised and everywhere, Scotland included, will be pretty much like the blandest parts of Pennsylvania or Belgium or Surrey. Right now, enjoy the dark pubs, the brown sauce on the chips (which are stacked on both shoulders), the black, raucous humour and the eccentric use of the English language.

# Kevin Williamson

*Kevin Williamson is a writer and activist, as well as founder, publisher and disorganiser of Rebel Inc. He lives in Edinburgh with his daughter Marie, where he is currently planning to open a Rebel Inc. cannabis coffee shop that intends to sell at least eight different types of quality weed.*

The two most famous lines from the two most influential Scottish films ever say something about our so-called national character: 'They may take our lives but they'll never take our freedom' and 'It's shite being Scottish … we're the lowest of the low.'

When you hear people talk about national characteristics of any country it's a sure sign that the speaker has a bad dose of verbal diarrhoea. If anything, *Braveheart* and *Trainspotting* nailed the idea that Scotland has some sort of homogenous cultural identity. This country is a lot of things to a lot of people, and not all of them pleasant.

Scotland can be a surreal, grey, beautiful and ugly land with the most wonderfully diverse and motley collection of contradictory, schizophrenic, creative, fucked-up and brilliantly rebellious people anywhere … or north of Hadrian's Wall at least.

I feel nothing but contempt for narrow-minded Barbour-jacketed nationalism, especially of the eighty-minute variety, and I'd rather eat my own toenails than stand next to a bunch of off-duty policemen and solicitors singing 'Flower of Scotland' at Murrayfield while swigging blended whisky from a steel hipflask. But put me on a train with a mental bunch of drunken football fans en route to Hampden and I'll be the one slurring 'Sent Who?' in the chorus of our official/unofficial national anthem.

Being Scottish is not a statement of nationality; it's a state of mind. And one that varies according to the individual in question, who they're with, when they think it, how much dough is in their pockets, and how much they've had to imbibe.

As I write this, on a beautiful afternoon on the seventeenth day of April 2002, with the sun streaming in my window, a view of Arthur's Seat to my left, a nice fat joint to my right, and sheriff's officers hassling me for money I refuse to pay on a point of principle, I feel some contradictory things about this place that I do genuinely love.

These feelings are usually compounded by the drivel in the Scottish press I read religiously every morning. From the guttersnipes of the *Daily Record* to the muzzled pages of *The Scotsman* we're fed a constant stream of anti-independence propaganda instigated by sad little twats pontificating from their London-financed editorial chairs.

I don't feel British that's for sure. I grit my teeth with resentment whenever I'm forced to put the letters U and K into any little box beside the word 'Nationality'. It's a futile gesture, I know, as if it should mean anything, a couple of squiggles on a piece of paper. But being forced to scrawl those two seemingly innocuous letters makes me feel – every fucking time – like a sell-out bastard who is aligning himself with all the historical crimes of English and British imperialism, and Jeesus they amount to an ocean of innocent blood spilt in the name of dominance and greed; as well as aligning myself with the overseas policies of a phoney, gutless, slimy, jerk-off, no-mark like Tony Blair – a man who will justify dropping cluster bombs on women and children in faraway lands if it will get him re-elected and score a few brownie points with his arsehole-in-arms across the Atlantic.

But a puff on the aforementioned joint, combined with the view of Arthur's Seat, brings back memories of the best days of my life, here in one of the most beautiful and exciting cities in the world, and just sitting here, thinking, and watching the clouds drift by, listening in my office to the exquisite love song, 'Susan Identifier', by one of my favourite Scottish bands of all time, Nectarine No. 9, and as if by magic all the suits and bankers and media and the walls of bureaucracy and injustice just melt away …

Is that being Scottish? Or just being any old Joe in any old town, head full of all the usual contradictory crap you accumulate over the years, impotent about the big things, embracing the small, wondering what's going to happen next.

The contradictions are important. It shouldn't come as any great surprise when you consider most Scots are bilingual in a way our dearly-loved next-door neighbours haven't a Scooby about. We speak two languages in our head, subconsciously switching back and fore between the two, from Scots to English and back again, all the bloody time.

One of these languages is practically invisible, even though it is historically older than the dialect of Olde English that has been foisted on us over the years. But those are the tools of freedom we've been given to work with, so we just have to get on with it.

As a socialist I've previously been a bit wary about shouting too much about being Scottish. But, fuck it, I am proud to be Scottish, and I do love this place, and I love living here among my mates. It must be the good weather.

# Ruth Wishart

*Ruth Wishart is a journalist and broadcaster who contributes a weekly column to* The Herald *and presents a current affairs programme for BBC Radio Scotland. She is Chair of the Centre for Contemporary Arts in Glasgow and a Governor of Glasgow School of Art.*

For the most part it's like having blue eyes and a crooked scar from taking a header over the fairy cycle handlebars aged seven when hospital stitching erred on the utilitarian side of aesthetic. For the most part being Scottish is a garment you never shed to examine the fabric, design, or texture. You wear it like the second skin it is. Then there are those odd, unexpected personal encounters or seminal political moments which bring identity into sharper focus. Sometimes they even merge such as the day I went to speak at an event hosted by Scotland's librarians and found a fellow guest at a small round table was to be George Cunningham. Some years before, when an MP in Islington, London, George had devised the 40 per cent rule for the 1979 referendum. In essence it meant that a simple majority of Scots voting for what was then a modest Scottish Assembly would not gain that prize. Instead more than 40 per cent of all those on the electoral register would have to say yes. This had the not unintended result of every non-voter effectively being counted as a no voter. Scotland said yes, but not loudly enough for the London-based Mr Cunningham, and it was to be another twenty years before sufficient momentum was built for a second, successful, bid to give Scotland back its parliament. At the time of that vote I was appalled at the level of apathy, distraught at the result, but, mostly, apoplectic about Mr Cunningham and all his works. And here we were destined to break bread together at the behest of a mutual friend. It would be pleasant to report that I behaved like the socially skilled, mature person my mother always hoped she had raised. Instead I found myself only able to contemplate re-lighting the conversational blue touch paper, or remembering another pressing lunch engagement. I found one. It was quite extraordinary how painful and potent that memory still proved to be and how profoundly it all still mattered. It wasn't so much about bearing a long-term grudge, never the most constructive emotional response to any disappointment. More that George Cunningham was a life-size reminder of what had been so needlessly squandered.

A second such salutary moment concerned another London-based Scot. Charlie Wilson is a first-rate journalist who left his native Glasgow in his teens and plied his trade in various publications north and south of the border until reaching dizzying heights of the Editor's chair at the London *Times*. We had known each other many years, his second wife was a close friend, and his youngest daughter my godchild. I thought I knew him well. But one evening, round his dinner table, we were discussing sporting rivalries in anticipation of an upcoming encounter between Scotland and England. Charlie – immortalised in *Private Eye* magazine as 'Gorbals' Wilson and with an accent linking him unmistakably with his home town – was generally regarded as a senior member of London's Scottish mafia. 'But you must understand,' Charlie told his guests, 'I always feel English in my head.' We all have a Richter scale of shock and I well remember Charlie's throwaway line going well off the end of mine. It wasn't anything to do with a value judgement about whether thinking 'in Scots' or thinking 'in English' was a superior form of intellectual recreation. Just that for me the notion of thinking as if I were English would seem to require a head transplant, or, at best, some form of precision lobotomy.

You can draw differing conclusions from these vignettes. One is that those Scots who flourish on a wider stage than their native land gain a broader per-spective and view their roots through a more sophisticated prism. Another is that those Scots who continue to live and work in the country of their birth or return there to raise their families having gained experience elsewhere are impelled so to do by a gut instinct which defies logical analysis.

Ireland's tigerish economy takes the credit for paving the way for a satisfying level of reverse emigration as it welcomes home talented and energetic sons and daughters. Scotland's new political dawn is still characterised by too substantial a brain drain. But it is not many hours since that dawn broke. Scotland too may yet lure the kind of immigrants it needs to help shape its new destiny. They'll be welcome: whatever racial language they think in.

# Kenyon Wright

*Canon Dr Kenyon Wright CBE is Chair of 'People and Parliament', Convenor of Vision 21 (the Scottish Churches group on Sustainable Development), Chair of Alcohol Focus Scotland, and a Consultant to NHS Tayside Board. He chaired the Scottish Constitutional Convention and was a member of the Consultative Steering Group on the Scottish Parliament.*

*Time and time again it seemed like the end, but the obstinate awkward identity always overcame and survived. The Creator surely never made any-thing so odd, contrary, intriguing and unlikely as the Scot ever to let it fizzle out.   One day the same Scots are going to reach out and take their destiny into their own hands again – and that will be the day!'*

(Nigel Tranter, *The Story of Scotland,* 1987)

That day has come at long last – a good time to look afresh at who we are and where we are going as a people.

All nations have good and bad – and we Scots seem to have both in larger dollops than most.  On one hand, we have contributed to European culture, science, knowledge, literature and philosophy to an extent vastly beyond our size. On the other, we continue to bear the shame of  poverty, homelessness, sectarian-ism and racism.

What is the foundation stone of that 'obstinate awkward identity'?  Professor Lindsay Paterson once wrote that all who come to Scotland soon become aware of a 'world of dense Scottishness',  hard to pin down but impossible to avoid.

In the two years before the election of the Scottish Parliament, the 'People and Parliament' project stimulated some 500 groups and thousands of individuals throughout Scotland – in the main ordinary people – to complete three assertions:

We are a people who ……… (Identity and Values)
By 2020 we would like to see a Scotland in which ……… (Vision and Hopes)
We expect our parliament to work with the people in ways which ………

The answers showed more than a touch of the old Scottish toast: 'Here's tae us! Wha's like us? Damn few, and they're a' deid!'

Here are some of the statements which summarised views on the first assertion, 'We are a people who …'

- put the good of the community before the interests of the individual
- have a strong sense of national identity, while recognising the fears and hopes of an increasingly multicultural, multiracial and multifaith society
- see ourselves as 'canny, tolerant, humorous, honest, educated, civilised, fair, talented, inventive, creative, trustworthy and lovers of freedom and justice' but
- conversely and paradoxically are aware of our many faults and our lack of confidence and self-esteem
- feel disempowered, and often socially excluded and devalued, through poverty, ethnic origin, disability and age
- are disillusioned with politicians and the way they operate, locally and nationally
- believe our nation could be great and influential, not in power or wealth, but in vision and spirit, and could play an important role in Europe and internationally

Somebody once wrote, 'To be English is to have won first prize in the lottery of life.'

I would like to think that to be Scottish is to know that life is not a lottery, but a family in which all can win a prize.

In other words, I believe that Scottish identity, though hard to pin down, is based at its best – often unconsciously and inarticulately – on a gut conviction, nurtured by our history and institutions, about human relationships. The high point at the opening of the Scottish Parliament in 1999, was the singing of Burns' 'A man's a man for a' that', which seemed to 'break the heart' (like the little white rose of Scotland) and left not a dry eye in the hall. Speaking just after it, with uncharacteristic emotion, Donald Dewar said, 'This is about more than our parliament and our laws. This is about who we are, how we carry ourselves. In this quiet moment of history, we might hear some echoes from the past; the shout of the welder in the din of the great Clyde shipyards; the sound of the Enlightenment when Edinburgh and Glasgow were indeed a light held to the intellectual life of Europe; the wild cry of the great pipers; and back to the distant noise of battles in the time of Bruce and Wallace. The past is part of us – part of every one of us – and we respect it, but today there is a new voice in the land – the voice of a democratic parliament – a voice to shape Scotland, a voice for the future.'

That definitive conviction – that we are equal citizens – has social, economic and political consequences. Our identity is not based on  race or ethnicity or language. It belongs to Europe and to the world. It rejects the idolatrous claim of Westminster to absolute power. It just might be capable now of creating that 'new political culture' which would be a light to Europe, and to the United Kingdom, the threat of good example.

# Mel Young

*Mel Young is co-founder of* The Big Issue *in Scotland and President of the International Network of Street Papers (INSP).*

Being Scottish for me is a contradiction. On the one hand I am fiercely proud of being Scottish, on the other it makes me feel wretched, embarrassed and sick.

Gerry died two days ago. There was no fuss, no obituary in the papers. He was a homeless man and after years of neglect his body finally just gave up and he passed away in Glasgow Royal Infirmary. Like many other homeless people there was an inevitability about his death. It came as no surprise but I was upset all the same.

I must have known Gerry for nearly nine years. He was one of the first people to come and sell *The Big Issue* in Scotland, a magazine sold by homeless people on the streets, which I had set up with my friend, Tricia Hughes, in June 1993. We'd seen the magazine working well in London and decided that it would work well in Scotland, where there was increasing poverty and homelessness. We loved the simplicity of it and that by selling a magazine, homeless people themselves became the centre of a solution rather than being the recipient of continued handouts.

The magazine worked from day one and quickly surpassed our wildest dreams. Homeless people queued to become sellers, the Scottish public loved the concept, and sales went through the roof. We had turned homeless statistics into real people, which the general public could see and relate to. We had empowered both the seller and the buyer. We had created a connection between those who were part of Scottish society and those who were excluded.

I've seen the best and worst of Scottish people. There are many examples of outstanding human kindness as well as acts of brutality. Despite years of a market-driven doctrine in Scotland during the Thatcher years, the people still held on to a semblance of the notion of community and a place for everyone in society. To many, like me, the thought of having homelessness in Scotland was as repugnant as it was unnecessary.

People, understanding we had created a vehicle for homeless people to improve their situation, would join in the process. The stories are legendary – presents and cards at Christmas time, a kind word, some advice, a smile, offers of employment and much more – with vendors returning the compliment – presents and cards at Christmas time, opening doors, giving directions, handing in lost property and, of course, those wonderful jokes!

Whilst it would be true to say that Scottish people are the most supportive of street papers in the world, the opposite is also true. Spitting at vendors is common, verbal abuse usual and actual violence more regular than you imagine. Scottish people have even delighted in setting homeless people on fire. Politicians looking for a cheap headline will sometimes blame homeless people for all the ills in Scotland. 'Get rid of these homeless people and more tourists will come,' is their mantra. Some of the most vicious assaults have come from the Scottish press, which regularly has a go at our vendors. They seem to delight in attacking the weakest in society.

These days I travel a lot. The idea of street papers has spread throughout the world and I have an international brief, which involves creating partnerships and helping development. I always introduce myself as a Scot. If someone introduces me as British or English, I always correct them. I am not a nationalist but I am proud of being Scottish and I find being a Scot opens doors for me. Scots have a good reputation abroad and it always something I am trying to build on.

Some years ago, I spoke with an old homeless man in St Petersburg, Russia. When he found out I was from Scotland he was beside himself. He told me how he had read all of Walter Scott's novels, loved them, and wanted to spend time with me talking about Scottish literature. He knew more than I did. Russians have a great sense of themselves not only in history but also in areas like literature and art. As Scots we seem to have lost this. Despite having absolutely nothing, this

Russian homeless man had a genuine richness of soul.

I believe the world is divided into two halves, between those who have and those who do not. There is plenty of evidence which suggests that the gap between the rich and poor grows larger daily. Those who have little are simply excluded from society and this division exists in almost every country in the world. The people who run the street papers throughout the world talk endlessly about finding more effective and practical ways of finding solutions and ending exclusion. Being Scottish just now means we are at the centre of this discussion.

Later this week, many people will attend Gerry's funeral. Despite his homeless situation he was a real Glasgow character – intelligent, verbose, irritating – but ultimately excluded. His situation was a failure of Scottish society. To progress we need to see people like Gerry as assets rather than problems.

Being Scottish is a challenge – a challenge to build on what's already in our collective soul and create a society where everyone can play an active role.

# *Postscript:* Being Irish *and* Being Scottish
# *by Tom Devine*

In 2000 Paddy Logue, the co-editor of this book, published *Being Irish: Personal Reflections on Irish Identity Today* (Oak Tree Press, Dublin). The approach was similar to *Being Scottish*. One hundred contributors tried to define what it meant to be Irish at the start of a new millennium. Comparing the content of the two volumes provides an interesting insight into the debate over national identity in the two countries with some parallels but also several intriguing differences.

Both Scotland and Ireland have experienced unprecedented change over the last few decades. Perhaps, however, the speed and scale of transformation has been even more visible in Ireland. Scotland, after, all had undergone massive industrialisation and urbanisation in the nineteenth century. Structural change was not new. Ireland, on the other hand, outside the area in and around Belfast, remained a broadly rural society, even after the Republic of Ireland emerged from British rule in the twentieth century. In the last decade, however, Ireland has changed more than it had done for most of the previous 100 years. Five factors were basically responsible for this revolution. First, Ireland joined the European Economic Community in 1974. This was followed five years later by the country becoming part of the European Monetary System. Then in 1999 it joined the European single currency. Logue had little doubt about the profound impact of Ireland's journey to the centre of Europe and the weakening of some of the old ties with Britain:

> The process has brought huge economic benefits to Ireland, advanced the pace of social policy legislation and given Ireland a stage on which it displays the talents of its people in all walks of life. Psychologically it has transformed a small introspected, backward-looking, peripheral country overshadowed by Britain into a confident, modern society that looks to Europe and beyond for fresh conquests. (*Being Irish*, p. xvii)

Second, as a result of the European connection together with internal decisions on investment strategy, fiscal policy and social partnership between government and trade unions, Ireland enjoyed remarkable economic growth. The Celtic Tiger, as it became known, was now the fastest growing economy in the Organisation for Economic Co-operatioin and Development (OECD). Among several achievements of note, Ireland became the world's number one exporter of software products in the 1990s. Third, after three decades of conflict Northern Ireland entered a period of relative political stability with the signing of the Good Friday Agreement, its very positive endorsement in two referenda on each side of the border and the creation of a power-sharing devolved government in Belfast. Fourth, the hegemony of the Roman Catholic Church in the Republic of Ireland was shaken by a series of sexual scandals, child-abuse cases and attempts at cover-ups. Though the Church remains a powerful force in Irish society, its earlier domination of Irish life is now in the past. Mass-going, especially among the young, has declined dramatically. Ireland is a more secular country than before. Fifth, the self-confidence produced by the Celtic Tiger phenomenon together with the benefits of the European connection have resulted in what has been termed the 'hibernisation' of cultures outside Ireland. It is cool to be Irish. Irish music, dance, pubs, films and literature seem to be everywhere. As one contributor to *Being Irish* put it:

> The modern signature of the identity is the global awareness of all things Irish. Rather than being swamped by the international explosion of the last few years, the Irish people and culture have gained a stature and recognition in a way that has never been achieved before. There is a knowledge of Irish music, dance, business and sport in all corners of the world that could not have been imagined in the past. (p. 136)

Compared with these successes, Scottish achievements might appear more modest but they are nonetheless significant for all that. In the 1980s, for instance, the nation experienced the painful process of shedding its old dependency on heavy industry. Shipbuilding remains a shadow of its former self while the last deep coal mine in Scotland at Longannet closed in early 2002. The Scottish economy of the 1990s, based on oil, services, tourism, electronics, finance and scientific industries, is as much the product of revolutionary change as the Irish economic miracle of the same decade. The crucial difference is, of course, that Scotland did not match Irish rates of economic growth, although Ireland was starting from a lower base than its Celtic neighbour.

Again the constitutional changes associated with the Northern Ireland Peace Process have their echoes in the devolutionary settlement for Scotland with the opening of the first Scottish Parliament since 1707. Both countries have become involved in the political realignments related to these changes. Scottish and Irish representatives sit on the British–Irish Council, popularly known as the Council of the Isles. The new warmth of these 'East–West' connections is illustrated also by the establishment of an Irish Consulate in Edinburgh, regular meetings between Scottish and Irish ministers, developing scholarly connections through such bodies as the Irish–Scottish Academic Initiative and the joint 'Celtic' bid by the two countries to host the European Nations' Soccer Championship in 2008.

There are parallels also in the area of religion and culture. Like Ireland, Scotland became a more secular society in the later twentieth century, though religious influence in Scotland started to decline at an earlier date. Membership of the churches in Scotland peaked in the 1950s. In 1956, 46 per cent of Scots had a formal church connection. By 1994, the figure had fallen to 27 per cent with the Presbyterian Church of Scotland suffering even greater decline especially during the 'Swinging Sixties'. Similarly, while Scottish culture does not yet have anything like the global impact of the Irish, Scottish music, literature, painting and history have all experienced a vigorous renaissance, especially from the 1980s.

What then do the commentaries in *Being Irish* and *Being Scottish* tell us about the current attitudes in the two nations? Inevitably, there are many similarities. The problems of the early twenty-first century are not likely to be confined within national boundaries. Thus, Irish and Scottish contributors show concern about the modern maladies of drug abuse, social inequality and exclusion, the corrosive effects of a materialistic culture, and issues of racism and multiculturalism, which affect both countries to a greater or lesser extent. Equally predictably, there is plenty of evidence that these two small nations have been able not only to sustain but also to strengthen their sense of themselves despite globalisation and the relentless influence of an internationally homogeneous mass popular culture.

More interesting, however, are some of the clear differences which emerge.

The bubbling confidence and vigour of contemporary Irish society come through in several of the contributions in *Being Irish*. For the editor, the country has a 'new, wild excitement and energy', though he recognises the economic boom also poses an unprecedented social and political challenge of 'managing' the Tiger in order to ensure the emergence of 'a prosperous and inclusive society and not one with a wealthy and selfish core surrounded by poor communities and alienated minorities' (*Being Irish*, p. xvii). Other essayists stress that the old Irish national inferiority complex now belongs to 'a dim and distant past', that Ireland has become a 'flourishing, confident, successful, educated little country', that it is 'an exciting time to be Irish', and that the modern Ireland is 'a bustling land ... that has still managed to treasure most of its traditions' (*Being Irish*, pp. 3, 58, 101, 123, 137, 220). Amid this heady chorus some awkward facts are given less attention. The Celtic Tiger thus far has passed by that one-third of the Irish population who still live below the poverty line. Again, xenophobia provoked by the recent influx of a small number of asylum seekers into Ireland has powerfully challenged the prevailing image of a hospitable and welcoming people. One contributor saw the irony here in articulating his own sense of shame at these responses: the Irish 'should know better because of their own history of poverty, oppression and emigration' (*Being Irish*, pp. 237–8).

A deep pride in Scottish values and achievement also comes through in the essays in this book. The broadcaster Billy Kay in his essay sums up what he sees as some of the defining characteristics of the Scottish people:

> Having made documentary features for over two decades, I have interviewed almost 2,000 people from different walks of life, and I never fail to be impressed by our human kindness in adversity, our rampant egalitarianism, our wild, dark humour, the power of our stories, music and songs, our insatiable thirst for knowledge, our passionately shared desire for sense and worth ower aw the earth tae bear the gree, an aw that. For aw that potential to bear fruit is something definitely worth waiting for.

David McLetchie, MSP, insists that 'Scotland has produced more great men and women per head of population than almost any other country in the world. We have a guid conceit of ourselves and it is well founded.' Norman Pender quotes with enthusiastic approval Theodore Roosevelt's comment that the Scots became 'the vanguard of our civilisation'.

Behind the rhetoric there is of course plenty of historical evidence to support the popular image of the Scot as inventor, thinkers, empire-builder and business pioneer. The problem for several of the essayists in this volume, however, was that this fine record of the past did not match the reality of life in contemporary Scotland. This may be because, as Hugh Pennington suggests, 'self-deprecation is our forte', a national vice which then fuels a lack of self-confidence.

Whatever the reason, the stark difference with the general tone of easy self-assurance in *Being Irish* is very striking. Here is a small sample of such views. The Scottish outlook is 'fatalistic'; 'the Scottish cringe is everywhere'; if Scots make such good politicians and businessmen and women outside Scotland, why not inside it – a question which merely adds to the 'debilitating myth' that the Scots who remained behind were second-rate; 'to a Scot there is no greater sin than getting above yourself'; 'we are backward-looking, misty-eyed and wistful, even. As nostalgia writhes Celtic-mistily around us, tainting us with insubstantial, outdated images.'

But not all contributors to *Being Scottish* indulged in such self-flagellation. Indeed, unlike the Irish volume, widely different views were articulated both on identity and the nature of contemporary Scotland. Richard Holloway, for instance, saw Scotland as 'a vibrant part of a complex and changing European culture' and rejoiced at the new multicultural society emerging in Scotland. Brian Taylor also detected the development of a more assured identity and a welcome new interest in 'the totems of that identity', literature, history, music and the folk scene. For Tom Hunter, the modern Scotland is 'a land of opportunity with an almost unsurpassed heritage, a stunning landscape and a creativity that needs to be unleashed'.

The disparate and often contradictory views expressed by our essayists should not surprise anyone. Scotland is in the throes of a political and cultural transition which is likely to provoke widely different responses and, as every Scot knows, robust argument, the clash of ideas and disputation, often laced with demotic humour, are all essential attributes of being Scottish.